MANAGING
COMMUNITY
GROWTH

MANAGING COMMUNITY GROWTH

Policies, Techniques, and Impacts

Eric Damian Kelly

PRAEGER

Westport, Connecticut
London

Library of Congress Cataloging-in-Publication Data

Kelly, Eric D.
    Managing community growth : policies, techniques, and impacts /
Eric Damian Kelly.
        p. cm.
    Includes bibliographical references and index.
    ISBN 0-275-94495-6 (alk. paper)—ISBN 0-275-94957-5 (pbk.)
        1. City planning—United States.   2. Land use—United States—
    Planning.   3. Cities and towns—United States—Growth.
    4. Urbanization—United States.   5. Urban policy—United States.
    I. Title.
    HT167.K44   1993
    307.1'416'0973—dc20   92-36549

British Library Cataloguing in Publication Data is available.

Library of Congress Catalog Card Number: 92-36549
ISBN: 0-275-94495-6
        0-275-94957-5 (pbk.)

First published in 1993
Paperback edition 1994

Praeger Publishers, 88 Post Road West, Westport, CT 06881
An imprint of Greenwood Publishing Group, Inc.

Printed in the United States of America

The paper used in this book complies with the
Permanent Paper Standard issued by the National
Information Standards Organization (Z39.48-1984).

10 9 8 7 6 5 4 3 2

To my parents and grandparents,
who taught me that good citizens can
and should make their communities
better places to live

Contents

Tables and Figures

Tables

Figures

Acknowledgments

This book is the product of many years of experience and many years of thought. Thus, thanking everyone who deserves it is a virtually impossible task. Even trying is difficult because of the risk of omission. On the other hand, not trying would be most unfortunate.

I owe great thanks to the City of Westminster, Colorado, which permitted me to learn about the practical aspects growth management as a consultant to it very early in my career. City managers Steve Garman and Bill Christopher and City Attorney Jim Stitt were particularly helpful.

Three academic institutions have played important roles in my learning about growth. Bill Lamont, then head of the planning program at the University of Colorado, provided me with my first opportunity to teach. Growth management was the subject of the course I offered as an adjunct faculty member. I subsequently had the pleasure to teach there under a succession of program directors, including Dan Schler, Herb Smith, and Peter Schaeffer. Herb and Peter were particularly helpful to me in a variety of ways.

Dean Thomas Galloway at Iowa State University took at least as big a leap of faith as Bill Lamont once had. Tom hired me as chair of the Department of Community and Regional Planning at Iowa State. There I have not only had the opportunity to continue to teach about growth management and other planning topics but also had the flexibility in my schedule to write this book. My faculty colleagues and my office staff have been very supportive as I have completed this project. Gail Stecker, our department secretary, helped to proofread it. She and Becky Abu-Hawash and Ronda Espeseth have managed the office while I hid at home to finish the manuscript.

The Union Institute provided me with the opportunity to earn a mid-career doctorate, and that is the context in which this project started. My committee members, Nancy Owens, Keith Lovin, Peter Schaeffer, Michele Jacobson, and Lynn Gilbert were most supportive of this endeavor and provided many useful comments from a variety of perspectives. Norman Williams, Jr., Ken Pearlman, Susan Connor, and David Callies also were nice enough to read parts or all of the draft manuscript and to share their comments with me. Obviously the final product is my responsibility, not theirs, but it is a better product for the support of all of them.

Longtime professional colleagues have influenced this work in ways they may or may not recognize. John Rahenkamp and Skip Sachs, along with partner Roger Wells, gave me my first real planning job. I still use techniques and ideas I learned from John and others in the firm. From my own former firm, Kelly & Potter, my partners Anita Miller, Earl Potter, and Gary Raso taught me a great deal and supported me in my land use work. Longtime staff member Karen Hovis also supported my writing and teaching endeavors. In more recent years, my most frequent planning associations have been with Jim Duncan, a practical and public-spirited planner from whom I learn constantly. Many friends at the American Planning Association have influenced my teaching and my writing, but I want to mention particularly Rodney Cobb, Jim Hecimovich, and Frank So, all of whom have frequently exhibited their confidence in my work.

My wife Viana, busy with her own academic endeavors, and our teenagers, Douglas Heeren, Damian Kelly, Valissitie Heeren, and Eliza Kelly, allowed me to hide in my study on weekends to finish this project—even when they suspected that I was really playing a computer game that the teens could play better. I cannot complete the acknowledgments without mentioning the Kelly sheepdogs. Shamrock helped me start this project but was not with us as we completed it. Blarney, who can never replace her but who takes three times as much energy to manage, has done all he could to make me fetch for him (or fetch him) instead of working on it. Despite his best efforts, it is finished.

1

Introduction

Planners in the United States now have more than two decades of experience with growth management programs. During the last two decades, planners, public officials, lawyers, and others have written extensively on the subject; but most of that literature addressed the issue from one of three basic perspectives: "how to do growth management," "how my community did growth management," or "is growth management legal?" What is largely missing from the literature is a careful consideration of whether growth management is indeed a useful tool and, if so, under what circumstances. The purpose of this book is to fill that gap.

GROWTH MANAGEMENT

Growth management is a land use planning tool. The types of growth management programs discussed in this book are those designed to regulate the location, timing, or rate of community growth. Some of those programs directly or indirectly limit the amount of growth that can take place. Others simply control the timing or location of development without attempting to limit the total amount of development or overall population growth. Figure 1.1 compares growth trends in two Colorado communities, Boulder and Westminster. The two are about 20 miles apart. Each adopted a growth management program in the 1970s. Clearly the one in Boulder has had a far greater effect on the growth rate. Those differing effects are entirely consistent with the different intentions of the two communities (Snyder 1982;

Figure 1.1
Growth Trends, Boulder and Westminster, Colorado, 1950–90

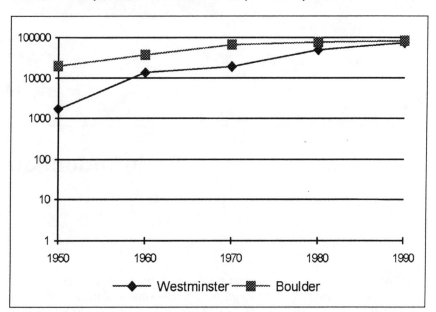

Sources: Bureau of the Census, 1991, *Census of Population and Housing: Summary Population and Housing Characteristics*, Part 7, Tables 15 (county) and 16 (cities); Bureau of the Census, 1981, *Census of the Population: Characteristics of the Population, Chapter A, Number of Inhabitants*, Part 7, Table 5; Bureau of the Census, 1972, *Census of Population, Vol. 1, Characteristics of the Population*, Part 7, Table 10 (includes 1950 and 1960 data).

see descriptions of the programs in Chapters 3 and 4 of this book).

Clearly a number of different public policies may affect the location, time, or rate of community growth—anything from construction of a new highway to a successful (or unsuccessful) economic development program can have such an effect. However, the concern of this book is with programs that are expressly designed to regulate the location, timing, or rate of community growth.

Many citizens, and even some public officials, may believe that most communities play a direct role in determining the location and timing of growth, if not its rate. That belief is wrong. The system of land use controls in the United States is largely reactive. Local governments review proposals from private developers and approve, disapprove, or conditionally approve them. Thus, both the timing and the location of growth are substantially dependent on initiatives from the private sector. For a variety of reasons discussed in this book, ranging from somewhat intangible "quality of life" issues to the need to plan highway and other infrastructure investment, local governments have a significant stake in the location and timing of growth. A small but significant number of local and state governments have addressed that need by adopting growth management programs.

This book not only traces the history and background of those programs and reviews them but also tries to provide a context from which a particular community can answer these questions:

- Does growth management work?
- Is it appropriate for our community and the particular problems that we are trying to address?
- Is one type of growth management program more appropriate than another for our community?
- Will it have undesirable (or desirable) side effects?

A NOTE ON THE USE OF TERMS

Cities, towns, townships, villages, boroughs, counties, and parishes make land use decisions in various parts of the country. Throughout this book, the term *community* refers to whatever form of local government may interest the reader. In some parts of the book, the distinction between cities and other forms of incorporated municipalities, on the one hand, and the unincorporated areas of counties, on the other, is important; in those sections, the terms *municipality* and *county* refer to those entities.

The structure of these local governments varies, but some group of elected officials makes policy decisions for each of them. That body may be a commission, a board of commissioners, a board of supervisors, a council, or a board of freeholders. The principal distinction important to this book is that such a body exercises the legislative authority of the local government (some may also have administrative duties, which is not important here). The body with such legislative authority is called the *governing body* throughout this book.

The early zoning enabling act, still in effect in most states, created the concept of a "zoning commission" as the adviser to the governing body on zoning matters (Advisory Committee on Zoning 1926). Under a separate model law, more frequently modified by the states but still widely adopted, local governments were authorized to create a "planning commission" with broad planning responsibilities and with primary authority for subdivision control. That act also provided that the local government adopting the controls could assign such duties to a zoning commission, making it a "planning and zoning commission," the name still found in many jurisdictions (Advisory Committee on City Planning and Zoning 1928). Thus, the term *planning commission* is used throughout this book to refer to the local body with primary responsibility for planning and land use issues, regardless of the precise local name of that body; where those duties are divided between two bodies, the affected local government must make its own interpretation of how the comments in this book relate to the respective bodies.

Local laws and rules exist under a variety of names. Most municipalities have the power to adopt "ordinances," which constitute the broadest form of local laws. Some states now give ordinance power to some or all counties. However, a number of other states give counties land use control powers without ordinance authority; in those states, zoning and similar enactments are adopted by counties by *resolution*. Under the early enabling acts, subdivision controls were to be adopted by the planning commission rather than the governing body. Because planning commissions had no authority to adopt laws, the commissions adopted such subdivision controls as subdivision "regulations." Although most (but not all) communities now adopt subdivision controls through the same process as zoning controls, many practitioners still refer to subdivision "regulations." For purposes of this book, these distinctions are insignificant. The term *ordinance* is generally used to refer to local laws, but it is intended to refer to all local controls, regardless of how they are adopted. The terms *regulations* and *controls* are occasionally used interchangeably with *ordinance*, and no distinction is intended.

A number of staff members of a local government are involved in the planning and zoning process. Titles vary widely, but for purposes of this book, the following terms are used: *planning director*, for the staff person who directs the planning efforts of the community; *zoning officer*, for the staff person who directs zoning enforcement and administration; *public works director*, for the staff person who directs that department or division of the local government that controls roads, sewer lines, water lines, and storm-water systems. In reality, two or more of these jobs may be combined, or a job listed here as one may be divided among several individuals with a variety of titles.

A number of private parties have a stake in the system. For purposes of this book, the following terms are used to refer to those players: *landowner* refers to someone who owns raw land but is not a developer; *developer* refers to an entity of any sort that turns raw land into a functional part of a community by installing streets and other public improvements and selling or leasing tracts of land (note that a developer need not necessarily construct buildings); *speculator* refers to a person who buys land with the expectation of a rapid, "unearned" gain resulting from some public action such as granting a rezoning or building a new highway (see generally Chapter 5); *homebuilder* refers to one who builds homes; *neighbor* refers to a person residing near a proposed development or public project.

2

Growth Management in Context

Growth management as a tool in the U.S. system of land use controls evolved in the second quarter of the twentieth century and developed rapidly through the 1970s and 1980s. Although growth management is itself a useful tool in the appropriate context, it is part of a much larger system. A basic understanding of that larger system is essential to an understanding of growth management and its appropriate uses.

AN OVERVIEW OF THE SYSTEM

Growth management is a tool to implement planning. The system of planning for future growth and land use patterns in the United States is enormously complex, particularly in comparison to systems in other nations that have much stronger central planning functions (Davies et al. 1989; Wakeford 1990). This complex system provides a relatively complex context for growth management.

Corporations, families, branches of the military, and local governments are among the many entities that plan. Plans may address social, environmental, physical, fiscal, or other matters. The kind of planning discussed in this book relates to the physical change in communities and regions through development and redevelopment. That activity is generally called "land use planning" (So and Getzels 1988). Although there is a strong physical emphasis in the field, it also includes related social concerns, such as the affordability of housing and its accessibility to those of the community who may not own automobiles.

A democracy is not an ideal environment in which to implement planning. Reasonable minds can and will differ both about what constitutes a desirable future and about what means are best suited to achieve that future. If a community adopts a broadly participatory planning process, the process itself may become paralyzed by conflict, or the resulting plan may look like a potluck plan—with conflicting, inconsistent, and redundant provisions. The representative system of government, in which a smaller but presumably representative group actually makes decisions, facilitates the development of plans but does not ensure that those plans will be truly representative of community interests or that they will be implemented. The topic of planning in a democracy goes beyond the scope of this book, but it is important to remember that this problem contributes to the complexity of the context for growth management. (For additional discussion of this topic, see Callies, Neuffer, and Caliboso 1991; Kelly 1986; for a more general discussion of the issues involved, see Caves 1992.) Regarding the initiative and referendum process described by Caves and lying at the heart of "pure" notions of democratic decision-making, Callies noted, "The kind of public participation that extends to absolute public decision making erodes, if not destroys, the planning process" (1992, p. 142).

Planning and land use control in the United States take place largely at the local government level (a small number of states are also heavily involved in planning, a subject discussed in Chapter 6). The United States contains more than 3,100 counties[1] and 19,000 municipalities[2] (Bureau of the Census 1988, App. B and C). Not all local governments are active in planning. Many municipalities are too small: 70 percent of the total (about 13,000) serve fewer than 2,500 people; another 19 percent (about 3,700) serve more than 2,500 but fewer than 10,000 (Bureau of the Census 1988). Few of the very small local governments are likely to be active in planning, although some certainly are. Virtually all municipalities with populations of more than 25,000—numbering about 1,000—have some sort of land use controls.

Counties participate in the land use control system in some states. In other states counties have little or no land use authority, for two different sets of reasons. Some states, particularly in the New England and Middle Atlantic regions, are entirely divided into municipalities for general government purposes, with township governments providing local government services in rural areas. Specifically, in Massachusetts, New Hampshire, New Jersey, Pennsylvania, Rhode Island, and Wisconsin, every parcel of land in the state falls within either an incorporated municipality or a township (Bureau of the

Census 1987). Although counties in those states have a variety of duties (most typically social service and law enforcement), no land in such states is located outside municipalities and under exclusive county control. In other states, particularly in the West, large areas of land outside municipalities receive substantial government services from counties; however, some of those states have made a policy judgment that counties should not engage in full-scale land use control. Even among local governments with the authority to plan and control land use, a number of counties and many smaller municipalities do not exercise their zoning authority. Even allowing for all those local governments that do not exercise such power, it is safe to estimate that well over 3,000 local governments in the United States are involved in planning decisions, and perhaps as many as 10,000.

Having several thousand local governments involved in planning over the vast land area of the United States may not seem significant. In heavily populated and growing areas, however, virtually all local governments are likely to be involved in their own separate planning and land use decisions. For example, in the Denver metropolitan area, five counties and at least a dozen municipalities make land use decisions. In the Des Moines region, a much smaller metropolitan area, there are two counties directly involved in the primary growth area, two other counties affected by (and affecting) it, and ten municipalities making land use decisions. Within the Portland urban growth boundary, there are portions of three counties and a total of twenty-four cities; in the Chicago region, there are literally dozens of local governments involved in the system. In the New York region, there are similarly dozens of municipalities involved in land use decisions, and those municipalities are located in three different states. In the Washington, D.C., metropolitan area there are a similar number of municipalities, plus several counties, and the combination of those is located in both two states and the District of Columbia, with its own jurisdictional complexity.

Including special districts (such as fire districts and water districts), the 1987 Census of Governments found a total of nearly 32,000 local government entities cluttering the nation's 115 Metropolitan Statistical Areas (Bureau of the Census 1987). Although in one sense the figure is statistically meaningless, simple division indicates an average of nearly 300 local governments in each MSA; even if not meaningful for any particular MSA, that figure is indicative of the complexity of the planning problem. In 1969 the National Committee on Urban Growth Policy referred to this pattern as a "crazy quilt of political jurisdictions" (Canty 1969). It has not improved.

Local governments that have adopted growth management programs have largely been located in exactly such complex metropolitan regions. Each of the local governments in such a region has its own territory, its own concerns, and its own interests. Further complicating the situation is the fact that not even the territories of these local governments are discrete. Those territories may effectively overlap and conflict. Through "extraterritorial jurisdiction" in some states and through the power to annex additional land in most, municipalities often exercise significant authority over lands not within their limits and thus within the primary control of other local governments and possibly within areas of interest to still others.

Although there are "regional planning commissions" in a number of metropolitan regions and in other areas, these are largely ineffectual in land use matters. In a few areas, one or more local governments have entered into agreements to plan jointly for land areas of mutual interest, and such agreements can work well. In virtually every growing metropolitan region, however, many local governments make decisions that do not form part of a logical and comprehensive plan.

Even within a particular local government, there are differing and competing interests. For example, planners may be eager to add more open space to a community, while the parks director, frustrated with recent budget cuts, opposes the addition of any land to the department's maintenance responsibilities. Fiscal and engineering considerations often dominate public works projects. The financial and technical goals driving the process may or may not result in decisions consistent with the more general land use goals of the community. For example, a public agency may choose a highway alignment based on engineering and cost considerations alone; the result of that decision may be to locate a new, growth-attracting roadway in an area where the community really does not want growth. The differences among these interests become manifest in a variety of local plans. Most larger local governments have "capital improvements programs" (CIPs) that are often partly or wholly inconsistent with adopted land use plans. Many local governments have separate plans for such substantive interests as parks, circulation (streets and pedestrian systems), and even wetlands, all of which may or may not be consistent with one another.

The federal government does nothing to make things better and in some ways confuses the situation further. Despite the reductions in federal spending for local government interests, federal capital expenditure on such public works as highways and sewer plants remains a major influence on the timing and location of growth (Urban Systems Research & Engineering Inc. 1976; Hanson 1992;

Transportation Research Board 1991; Newman and Kenworthy 1989; and, generally, Chapter 5).

Except in Hawaii, Florida, Oregon, California, Washington, and Vermont (and now, possibly Georgia), the state role is similar to the federal role — little involvement in planning and a number of decisions on funding public projects that may or may not comport with local plans (see, generally, Chapter 6).

As if the system of land use controls itself were not complicated enough, the task assigned to that system poses enormous difficulties. Through the planning process, a local government attempts to plan for the use of land within its jurisdiction. Most of that land is privately owned, and many landowners have no idea what they will do with their land in the future. Some are happy farming it now and have no plans to do anything else, although one or more of them may cheerfully sell out to a developer within a year or a decade. Other landowners may be holding the land primarily for investment, carefully seeking the best opportunity for sale. Still others may have plans that will never be implemented because of economic or other constraints.

A local government must try to plan for the future of such land, even though its owners, who are more intimately familiar with it, have no plans, impractical plans, impossible plans, or plans that simply may change. Although some local planners would resolve that situation by simply dictating future land uses to private owners, residents of the United States relate closely to land, emotionally as well as financially and legally; and they generally resent perceived intrusions on their ownership rights. Most landowners in this country (and perhaps elsewhere) favor land use controls for their neighbors; few actively favor such controls for their own property. Thus, although most responsible owners recognize the need for some system of controls as a part of creating an orderly society, the political burden of proof generally remains on the local government to demonstrate why a particular restriction is necessary and reasonable. The system itself thus remains, in most cases, largely a reactive one.

To provide some basis for order to this potential chaos, the governmental system in this country has given most local governments certain tools to conduct and implement land use planning. The primary tools are zoning and subdivision controls, concepts developed early in this century in large cities and subsequently adapted to broader use. These tools arose from particular needs in those cities at the time and still best address those needs. Although in some respects, adaptation of zoning and subdivision controls to other needs has been surprisingly effective, large gaps remain. Because growth management programs attempt to fill two prominent gaps in the regulatory system (described later in this chapter), it is important to understand the system to understand the gaps.

EARLY TOOLS

The earliest land use controls in this country are beyond the scope of this book, but it is important to remember that land use planning is not just an invention of the twentieth century. The first planning law in the country was a Spanish document called the *Laws of the Indies*. The laws were a series of pronouncements on urban design issued by the Spanish monarchy beginning early in the sixteenth century. Those design standards, which specified the dimensions of the town square, the orientation of major streets, and even general land use patterns, influenced most early Spanish settlements. The effects of the plans remain clearly visible in the original Spanish settlement areas of San Antonio, Texas; Santa Fe, New Mexico; and St. Augustine, Florida (Reps 1969; de Montequin 1990).

Although lacking the monarch's broad authority, many early urban planners in this country owned or controlled the land they planned to use, thus making their task simpler than that faced by modern planners. The railroad companies, which platted generally rectilinear blocks and lots along the railroad tracks on their grants of land, are prime examples (Reps 1969).

Planning for and managing the patterns of development of contemporary U.S. communities, however, is a far more complex task, involving multiple landowners, divergent interests, and the democratic system of government. Contemporary U.S. land use controls themselves evolved from several different efforts late in the nineteenth century and early in the twentieth.

One was the tenement house movement, which was a powerful influence in leading New York to adopt the nation's first comprehensive zoning ordinance in 1916 (see, generally, Bassett 1936; Babcock 1966; Scott 1969). Responding to concerns about squalid conditions in which families lived in overcrowded rooms without light and air, reformists developed concepts of height limits and setback requirements designed to ensure that most rooms would have direct access to "light and air" (Scott 1969). Height limits on buildings, now included in most zoning ordinances, were litigated in the courts and ultimately upheld in the U.S. Supreme Court before zoning evolved as a more comprehensive regulatory technique.[3]

At the same time, others were concerned about the impact of uses that many would call "nuisances." Particular uses may or may not have met the legal definition of nuisance, but they were either industrial or commercial uses of a kind that clearly had adverse external effects on surrounding uses (see, generally, discussion in Mandelker 1971). John Stuart Mill puzzled over the problem of regulating "beer and spirit-houses" in *On Liberty* in 1859, although he concluded that limiting their number (the kind of approach that zoning or licensing might take today) would be an undue infringement on liberty. Later, dealing with such issues at a practical level, the U.S. Supreme Court upheld the City of Los Angeles in prohibiting the manufacture of bricks in a residential neighborhood.[4] An interesting aspect of this case is the fact that the industry had been in operation before most residents moved into the area. Nevertheless, the high court upheld the city's use of police power in closing it down.

Competition among incompatible land uses involved more than the obvious strife between residents and polluting industries. Retailers in New York were a major force behind the adoption of a zoning ordinance there. They wanted such industrial operations as garment-making banned from shopping areas (Bassett 1936; Babcock 1966).

In short, zoning did not just appear upon the scene suddenly in the second decade of the twentieth century. Rather, it evolved not only from its European roots (Bassett 1936; Babcock 1966; Scott 1969) but from a variety of efforts already under way in the United States to resolve specific land use and development problems.

ZONING

From the combined efforts of the housing reformers, the retailers seeking purity in their commercial areas, and others came the New York City zoning ordinance of 1916 (Bassett 1936). The experience of the committee that drafted that ordinance provided the basis for the Standard Zoning Enabling Act, published by the Department of Commerce in 1924 and in a revised edition in 1926 (Advisory Committee on Zoning 1926, process described in Bassett 1936, the act's principal author, and Babcock 1966). That act provided a model that each of the fifty states adopted and that remains the basis for basic land use controls in more than forty of them. Even those few states that have substantially amended (or, in a half-dozen cases, replaced) the model act, have retained zoning as the basis of land use controls. Thus, the New York City ordinance, which was developed in response to turn-of-the-century big-city problems, became the model for land use control in the entire nation.

Zoning is a very simple concept. It provides for the division of the community into districts, or *zones*, that are most typically called "zoning districts." Within each district, the community provides regulations that address three general sets of issues:

Use. The use of land and buildings generally falls into four general categories: agricultural, industrial (or manufacturing), commercial (or business), and residential. Larger communities may have a number of subcategories of each general category, providing for such special districts as neighborhood business, office, light industrial, warehouse, or downtown.

Intensity. Zoning regulations limit the amount of a particular use that can take place on a designated piece of land. A community may regulate residential density indirectly through the specification of a minimum lot size (for example, a minimum lot size of 9,000 square feet generally allows about four dwelling units per acre, after allowing for streets) or directly, through a limitation on the number of dwelling units per acre. Communities typically express intensity limits in commercial and industrial areas by "floor-area ratio (FAR)," a number specifying the number of square feet of floor area of building permitted for each square foot of land (for example, an FAR of .5 would allow a 5,000-square-foot building on a 10,000-square-foot lot). Height restrictions affect the intensity of use, as well as the bulk, of a building.

Bulk. Bulk regulations address such matters as building setbacks from lot lines or streets (sometimes expressed as requirements to preserve front, rear, and side yards), and maximum building coverage (the amount of land that can be covered by buildings on it). Height regulations also affect building bulk. Although height regulations are perhaps most important as restrictions on intensity in downtowns and other commercial areas, they are important determinants of building size in residential neighborhoods where intensity is established at one or two dwellings per specified lot (Kelly 1988).

The use, intensity, and bulk regulations vary from district to district within a community, although they must be uniform throughout a particular district. As indicated earlier, the major differences among categories of districts depend on use types. Residential subcategories typically differ by the intensities allowed in various districts, whereas commercial and industrial subcategories may differ as to both the lists of permitted uses and the intensities at which such uses may be conducted.

A recurring phenomenon in U.S. zoning law and practice is the primacy of the single-family residence. Early zoning ordinances were based on the concept of a pyramid, the zone at the top being the most restrictive and each zone below it permitting all uses permitted in the zones above it plus some additional ones. A residential zone permitting one-family and two-family residences typically appeared at the top of the pyramid, with industrial or manufacturing zones at the bottom. Later, communities restricted the zone at the top to single-family dwellings. The pyramid has largely disappeared from current practice for a variety of reasons (Kelly 1988), including the fact that in today's litigious and environmentally conscious climate, industries are as eager to avoid incompatible (or complaining) neighbors as residents have always been.

Williams cited three periods of regulation in residential zones. In the very early period, from the adoption of the New York City ordinance in 1916 until the early 1920s, he found that zoning emphasized the provision of light and air to residential units; in a second period, from the 1920s to about 1960, there has been a distinction among residential building types, differentiating single-family houses from duplexes, duplexes from townhouses, and townhouses from apartments; and in the current and third period, the emphasis is on regulating total residential density (Williams and Taylor 1988, p. 856). That was a logical step in the evolution to growth management. Residential density is a better measure of development impact than residential building type because it addresses with reasonable accuracy the number of probable residents. The number of residents, in turn, determines the probable demand on everything from schools to the street system. The substance of Williams's third period thus coincides with the current interest in growth management.

The Zoning Map

The key to zoning is a zoning map, which identifies the boundaries of the various zones or districts in a community. Because the regulations vary by district, the map shows boundaries at which regulations change, becoming relatively more (or less) restrictive. Such a map works well to preserve established areas in their present character, but it does not work well in undeveloped areas; in such areas, it legally institutionalizes public planners' best guesses as to what undecided property owners may want to do with their properties at some point in the future. The politics of zoning—and the resulting litigation—focus heavily on the frequent local decisions to grant (or deny) property owners "rezonings," or map changes. Clearly such changes are necessary, because it is impossible for public planners to predict accurately how each undeveloped piece of property within a community will (or even should) be used in the future. Despite the importance of such changes, those who drafted the original act clearly were not much concerned with changes in it. In a book written a decade after the act was written, the principal author of the act mentioned map amendments only in a brief paragraph on the notices required for such amendment. The book included no discussion whatsoever of the difficulties involved in making the substantive decisions to amend this legal document (Bassett 1936; for a more thorough discussion of this issue, see Kelly 1988).

Although in a general way a zoning map should influence the location of growth, it has relatively little impact, for two reasons: first, it is so frequently changed that it is seldom taken very seriously (see, for example, Clawson 1971); and second, most communities "overzone" by designating excessive areas of land for some uses. The latter phenomenon is a simple function of the fact that in most communities there is far more vacant land than development is likely to consume in the foreseeable future. It must be designated for something; and communities typically designate it for agricultural (a designation that serves essentially as a "holding" zone), residential (a designation generally considered acceptable in most locations), or industrial (a designation that may encourage uses that help the economic base). However, because the zoning map does nothing to set development priorities among the various tracts of land in each category, private sector initiatives still determine which of those tracts will be developed in the near future.

Clearly this problem with zoning springs directly and logically from its roots. The creators of zoning designed it to solve problems of established neighborhoods, not of undeveloped areas. Within an established neighborhood, the problem of determining the correct zone for a particular piece of property is simpler. With a large, undeveloped area, it can be much more complicated.

Despite these problems, zoning remains the dominant form of land use control in the United States. There is no survey indicating how many of the 22,000 general local governments in the United States have zoning, but most larger local governments in all 50 states have adopted it. Houston, the only large American city without zoning, was in the process of developing a zoning ordinance in 1992. Zoning is the most widely used local land use control, the one that evokes the greatest emotion and resulting local political interest, and the one that generates the most litigation—now approaching some 20,000 appellate court cases in roughly seven decades (Babcock 1966; Williams and Taylor 1988). Despite the apparently dominant role of zoning in the system of development control in the United States, it is important to remember that it regulates only three things—use, intensity, and bulk—and that it really does not address the critical issues of the timing and location of growth.

SUBDIVISION CONTROL

Clearly there is more to land development than simply deciding the use or intensity of use of the land. New development requires new streets, parks, sewers, and schools—all of which should form a logical part of a larger system.

Many local governments use subdivision controls to address some of those issues. Although the definition varies slightly from state to state, a typical definition of subdivision is, "all divisions of a tract or parcel of land into two or more lots, building sites, or other divisions."[5]

Scott identified efforts both in Los Angeles and in Cincinnati in 1922–24 as major early efforts at subdivision regulation (1969, pp. 207–208; 230). According to Scott, the Los Angeles effort required that new subdivisions conform to a general gridiron pattern of principal streets; and Cincinnati based its subdivision controls on a state law that permitted cities with adopted long-range plans for streets and parks to regulate subdivisions (1969).

Clearly the focus in those early days was on roads and highways. Land developers create roads in the process of developing their respective properties. If the roads in one development have no relation to the roads in the next development or to the general road system of the community, the result is a maze. Such a maze is not only inconvenient to the public but also capable of creating hazards by limiting access for public safety vehicles.

Although it is not documented in the literature, the early concerns with subdivisions clearly extended beyond planning. Before subdivision regulations, a developer could simply grade in a "road" of whatever width the developer might choose with few, if any, improvements. Eventually, the unimproved road would become a rutted or muddy mess, leading residents to request (or demand) that the government improve it. The local government might then find that the roadway was too narrow or too steep or otherwise not easily suited to improvement, thus requiring the acquisition of additional land. Affected landowners, who were typically also residents and voters, undoubtedly greeted less than warmly any public acquisition of additional land. Further, public officials faced the difficult choice of having to pay for the road improvements either from general revenues or from a special assessment of the property in the neighborhood. Using general revenues to make major repairs in one neighborhood was not likely to be popular among taxpayers in general. On the other hand, property owners in the neighborhood would be likely to protest the special assessment. Public officials who had played no part in creating the problem faced the frustrating practical and political burdens of solving it. Through advance public regulation they could require a developer to develop the roads to reasonable public standards, thus avoiding this unattractive choice later.

Although Yokley (1963, p. 1) cited early subdivision acts (including an 1833 law in Michigan), Freilich and Levi noted that such laws before 1928 simply addressed the issues related to land titles, requiring an orderly process of recording plats with a consistent method of identifying blocks and lots (1975, pp. 1–3). Freilich and Levi identified four periods of subdivision regulation, beginning with the "title" period just described and then entering a period from 1928 through World War II focused on subdivision arrangement and the completion of internal improvements. They identified the post–World War II period as a third phase, during which communities began to look at the adequacy of public facilities and to address the availability of park lands and open space. Their fourth period coincides with the growth management period addressed in this book and focuses on the same issues (1975, pp. 3–6).

Early subdivision regulations focused on road issues, but subdivision regulations have evolved easily to include requirements for many other public improvements. Although early subdivision controls regulated only the layout of streets, modern controls include construction and paving requirements. Modern subdivision regulations also typically require that the developer provide curbs and gutters, sidewalks, internal sewer and water lines, and street lights and street signs. Some local ordinances also include requirements for trees along streets, bus stop benches or kiosks, and other items; but the hard infrastructure items form the core of most subdivision controls (Ducker 1988).

The use of "subdivision" of land as the trigger for the dominant form of development regulation, which is really a quirk of history, leaves modern planners with occasional problems. A large shopping center or apartment complex may be built on a single parcel of land and thus not be a subdivision in the ordinary sense of the word. If such a development is not a subdivision, then how does the community regulate the installation of infrastructure and its coordination with the larger infrastructure system of the community? Communities have developed a variety of solutions to this question (including a strained interpretation by one state legislature that such developments are to be construed as "subdivisions").[6] At the same time that this problem arises, increasingly restrictive "subdivision" control acts can bring within their scope land divisions by farmers and others that have no development intent whatsoever and no real impact on the communities. The Arkansas legislature has taken a more rational approach, revising its subdivision act to regulate "development."[7]

Subdivision regulations have been adapted effectively to contemporary problems. It has not been a significant conceptual or legal leap to go from requiring the improvement of subdivision roads that link up to the community's road network to mandating that developers similarly provide sewer and water lines as part of a larger network. Yet, as the discussion below indicates, the issues of public facilities go far beyond what is built by the subdivider on the site.

HOW GROWTH MANAGEMENT FITS INTO THE SYSTEM

This chapter provides an introduction for growth management. It describes an existing and relatively complex system of planning and land use controls. Many developers and landowners believe that land is already overregulated—without such a thing as growth management. With that system of controls in place, why is growth management necessary? The Montgomery County (Maryland) Planning Board noted in its *First Annual Growth Policy Report* in 1974, that "comprehensive planning, at least in theory, has always sought to manage growth" (1974, p. 6). That same report noted that an effective management policy must address three key parameters of growth: location, timing, and cost. It further noted that the traditional model (zoning and subdivision controls) was "strong on location, but weak on timing and cost" (1974, p. 35).

Zoning was not designed to deal with change. As Chinitz commented,

In contrast to zoning, which is passive and static, growth management is active and dynamic. While zoning defines the desired fully built town, the ultimate equilibrium, growth management seeks to maintain an ongoing equilibrium between development and conservation, between various forms of development and the concurrent provision of infrastructure, between the demands for public services generated by growth and the supply of revenues to finance those demands, and between progress and equity (1990, p. 6).

Most local involvement with zoning occurs through the process of "rezoning," or changing the zoning map. However, the system is not well suited to such changes. Zoning evolved in New York City to preserve and enhance neighborhoods that were already largely built. Because of these historical roots, zoning maps are prepared as though the community is static. It would be more realistic to view a zoning map as simply a snapshot of the community and its zoning at a particular moment, because it will almost certainly change. A static map of an already developed area (as much of New York City was when zoning evolved there) works reasonably well and serves the purpose of providing stability, which is indeed one of the principal purposes of zoning. As Clawson noted, there is also political support of existing residents to maintain the status quo, offsetting the political pressure of those who may want changes in the map. Such support generally does not exist for preservation of what may be entirely arbitrary zoning designations in undeveloped areas (Clawson 1971, p. 7).

A static map of undeveloped areas poses a number of problems. If the undeveloped portion of the city is small and if it is surrounded by land used in only one way, then there may be a particular use that is logical for that tract and there may be little difficulty in ensuring that such use ultimately occurs. However, where there are large undeveloped areas of land within a community, as there are in most communities, two types of problems arise. First, it is very difficult to project exactly what will take place where. A zoning map of undeveloped land may be viewed by some as a mandate, but considering the frequent zoning changes in most communities, it should realistically be treated as a "best guess." Further, whether the map represents a mandate or a guess, the community itself may want to change it in the future. Community plans prepared in the 1960s often included vast areas of vacant land along railroad tracks as future locations for industry. Today, the type of industry sought by most communities occupies smaller parcels and wants highway access, often in locations similar to those sought by retailers. This change of circumstance requires both that communities identify some areas formerly designated for other purposes as suitable for industry and that some other use be designated for the lands formerly designated as industrial.

Through the process of updating their master plans, some communities actually change the zoning of raw land as needs change. However, there are political difficulties in accomplishing that. Landowners typically view any zoning changes not initiated by them as disadvantageous and thus oppose them, sometimes in court. Thus, it is more typical for such changes to take place in response to rezoning petitions from landowners and developers.

All of this means that the zoning map is not a very useful tool for planning such capital improvements as new highways, parks, and schools. Few communities are rich enough to build major roads and trunk sewer and water lines into all their undeveloped areas. Thus, to the extent that a community wants to invest in infrastructure for future needs, public officials would like to know where and when growth will occur. Because the zoning map does not guarantee what development will take place in what location, many communities simply wait to see what will occur before making such improvements. However, the result of that very practical policy is that such improvements are not available before development takes place.

Furthermore, simply providing such facilities where they are most convenient for developers may be beneficial to those developers but be bad public policy. In most communities, it is easier to provide such improvements in some locations than in others. It is easier, for example, to provide road and utility extensions to land directly adjacent to the developed parts of the community than to land located further from the urban center. The substantial costs involved in extending improvements to more remote, or "leapfrog," development were well documented in a study entitled *The Costs of Sprawl* (Real Estate Research Corporation 1974). Although other aspects of the report have been criticized, there is no serious question about the basic premise that it is more expensive to provide services to development that is located farther away (see the discussion and critiques of this report in Chapter 7). For several reasons, however, some sites contiguous to the existing community may be easier to serve than others that are equally close. Possible reasons for that situation include topography (because sewer lines generally flow by gravity to the plant, and it is thus difficult to serve land that is lower than the plant or lower than some point between the site and the plant), elevation (because water pressure is a direct function of elevation, and adequate pressure cannot be provided above some elevation), and the availability of existing improvements (such as trunk sewer lines with substantial excess capacity in some locations but not others).

All this is, in part, a function of time. If the state highway department expects to build a new loop freeway around the northwestern part of a community five years from now, land lying along that route will be far more accessible in five years than it is today. If the community is currently building a new sewage treatment plant expected to open in two years, large areas of land that do not currently have public sewer service will have easy access to it when the plant opens.

Zoning addresses none of these issues. It designates the future use of land, without regard to when, if ever, that will take place. A zone designating land as suitable for single-family homes on quarter-acre lots makes no distinction between land developed for such purposes in 1963 and undeveloped land that may not be easily accessible or practically servicable until well into the next century. What the map does is to permit someone who wishes to do so to develop the land for that purpose (subject to other local regulations). However, zoning not only does not offer the basis for reasonably predicting *when* a particular parcel will develop, it may not even predict accurately *how* the parcel will develop. For the many reasons just outlined, the initial zoning selected for a parcel may be proved by later events to be "wrong" or at least no better than some other use. Even if it is not wrong, it may well change. Clawson noted, "In the developing suburbs . . . zoning has proven largely ineffective. Where land is yet to be developed, land use zones, based upon a general plan or on some other grounds, have generally had little popular support when initially adopted or when changes are proposed. Such zoning may even have had negative results; it may be easier and cheaper to break the existing zoning than to conform to it" (1971, p. 7).

Although subdivision controls deal with public improvements, typical subdivision regulations require only that the developer provide such facilities on the site being developed. Nothing in typical subdivision regulations requires that adequate services leading up to the site be available for the development.

The availability of infrastructure in the larger community to support new development has become of increasing concern since about 1970, which is about the time that local officials in many communities became interested in the timing and location of growth. A 1974 survey of communities involved in some way with growth management found that officials in those communities were far more concerned about development timing than they had been in the previous decade (Brower et al. 1976).

This increased concern came during the period in which Congress adopted the Federal Water Pollution Control Act Amendments of 1972 and the Federal Safe Drinking Water Act. These acts, essentially for the first time, imposed serious penalties on local governments that allowed overloaded systems to deliver inadequately treated sewage to the public waters or inadequately treated drinking water to their residents (Binkley et al. 1975; see a discussion of some of the consequences in Greenberg 1974).

Local officials may have had other concerns. Most communities have piping and pumping capacity to deliver or receive far more water and wastewater, respectively, than they can effectively treat. Thus, the treatment plant capacity is the limiting factor for a community. However, the capacity of a treatment plant is not like the clearly visible capacity of a pipe or a bowl. It is not at all obvious when the plant exceeds its capacity. Treatment plants can allow excess water to flow through; the plant simply discharges the excess or allows the excess flow to dilute total output, so that nothing is treated fully. Thus, before the passage of these new laws, there was little to prevent local officials from allowing plants to exceed their design capacity—by a little or by a lot. Furthermore, many plants installed before the passage of those laws used simpler (and less adequate) treatment techniques than modern plants and thus could be expanded more cost-effectively.

Under the federal scheme for environmental regulation, states, with pressure from the federal government, took an increasing interest in the quality of drinking water delivered to residents of a community and sewage received from them through the local sewage treatment plant. The result of this increased scrutiny was, in some areas, a significant number of moratorium orders, under which federal or state agencies prohibited local governments in particular from connecting additional units to public sewer systems. The broader result was clearly a greater interest of local officials in whether their systems could absorb additional capacity (Tabors, Shapiro, and Rogers 1976, p. 16; also see discussion in Greenberg 1974).

Some of the pressure, of course, came from citizens. Many communities had excess capacities in their roads, parks, and schools in particular, as a result of federal public works projects during the depression and World War II. These excess capacities served the initial spurts of growth in most communities. Although most communities continued to expand their infrastructure systems, many clearly did not expand them as fast as the communities themselves were expanding. Overloading conditions on roads and in school buildings occur gradually and may not at first be of great concern to residents. However, as delays at traffic lights stretch from seconds to minutes and as school hallways become classrooms, the crowding takes it toll on citizen patience. Two well-known growth management programs adopted in the early 1970s—those in Boulder, Colorado, and Livermore, California—were adopted by citizen initiative, reflecting citizen frustration both with problems resulting from the rates of growth in the communities and with apparent government inaction to address the problems (James Duncan Associates and Kelly 1991a).

Public officials adopted growth management programs to address directly these problems of development location and timing. Typical growth management programs, described in more depth later, include

Adequate public facilities standards prohibit development except where adequate (defined) public facilities are available. Such controls may not directly address the issue of the location or timing of growth, but they indirectly regulate both, because in most communities adequate public facilities are not available immediately in all parts of the community.

Phased growth programs regulate the location and timing of new development based on community plans. Although such programs typically regulate growth based in part on the availability of facilities, they may also weigh environmental, economic, and general land use factors in establishing the phasing programs. Further, although adequate public facilities ordinances most frequently address the capacity of roads and of sewer, water, and storm-water systems, phased growth programs often account for plans for schools, libraries, and other noninfrastructure services in determining preferred phasing of growth.

Urban growth boundaries limit the long-term location of growth to land within a designated boundary. Although many communities have short-range boundaries beyond which they are unlikely to encourage or permit expansion, relatively rigid long-term boundaries are not common. Hawaii has used a form of statewide zoning to establish such boundaries around all its cities. The state planning law in Oregon requires that local governments there include long-range urban growth boundaries in their plans and implementation programs. Boulder has created a boundary by purchasing an open-space greenbelt around the city.

Rate-of-growth programs establish specified rates of growth for the communities using them. Although the ability of a community to serve development may be a factor in developing such rates, the controlling factor in such programs is usually a local perception of what is an "acceptable" growth rate. Although phased growth programs are likely to allow more development in some years than in others, because there is simply more capacity to absorb growth at some times than at others, rate-of-growth programs impose a continuing standard on the rate of growth. Typically that standard is a percentage increase in the housing stock, such as those in Boulder and Livermore. Petaluma, California, has used a limit of 500 new dwelling units as the basis for its program for many years, although that number represented a decreasing percentage of the community's housing base.

Regulating the timing and location of growth may seem like simple common sense to a reader today. However, few communities were doing it even by the early 1990s, and when the first such efforts began they ran entirely counter to the trend. In 1969, Krasnowiecki noted

With the exception of a lower New York court, *Josephs* v. *Town Board of Town of Clarkstown* [citation omitted; case discussed in Chapter 3], the courts have taken a skeptical view of the idea that inadequacy of school or other facilities, or the added tax burden of providing adequate facilities, is a legitimate reason for preventing development. . . . Accordingly, the principle that comes out of the cases is that a local government cannot justify delaying or limiting development because certain basic services and improvements are inadequate or unavailable, unless it also establishes a justification for the inadequacy or unavailability of the service (p. 82).

In short, the early efforts at growth management represented a significant change in the practical operation of land use controls and required a significant change in the legal climate for such controls.

Communities implementing growth management programs may adopt them separately from their zoning and subdivision ordinances or combine them as part of a unified development ordinance. One of the frustrations of the development industry is the fact that so many communities have added requirements to an already complex system rather than adopting well-designed and comprehensive programs including all requirements as part of a unified regulatory scheme and integrated process (Bosselman, Feurer, and Siemon 1976). However, as Bosselman suggested, the procedural issue is really somewhat separate from the substantive one; it is possible for a community to implement a comprehensive but also efficient system of land use controls or a less comprehensive one that also happens to be inefficient. The management of approval procedures will be left to other authors and other times.

NOTES

1. Counting Louisiana's parishes, some census divisions in Alaska, two new counties footnoted in the census but not included in the table, and jurisdictions in some states where a city essentially covers the territory equivalent to a county (Virginia accounts for most of these at 41), the actual total is 3,139; excluding the latter reduces the total to 3,094.

2. The actual number in the 1988 report was 19,097.

3. *Welch* v. *Swasey*, 214 U.S. 91 (1909).

4. *Hadacheck* v. *Sebastian*, 239 U.S. 394 (1915).

5. N.C. Genl. Stats. Sect. 160A-376.

6. Colo. Rev. Stats. Sect. 30-28-101(10)(A).

7. Ark. Rev. Stats. Sect. 14-56-417.

3

Early Growth Management Activity

Although growth management became a topic in the literature beginning in the 1970s and the best-known early programs were adopted in the late 1960s and early 1970s, two early efforts should not be ignored.

TWO EARLY PROGRAMS

Burrows cited the little-noted example of Milford, Connecticut, which adopted a growth-phasing ordinance early in the 1950s. Under the Milford program, the community adopted a phasing map, establishing high and low priority areas for subdivisions. The community required that a developer in a low-priority area demonstrate that roads and schools, as well as sewer, water, and storm-water systems, were adequate to serve the proposed development. The community limited the impact of the program on developers by allowing the phased development of even low-priority subdivisions, at the rate of 20 percent of the project per year (Burrows 1978).

Perhaps more significant was the early effort of Clarkstown, New York, because it clearly influenced the efforts of neighboring Ramapo fifteen years later; those efforts in turn were well publicized and clearly influential in sparking the trend toward growth management in a number of communities in the United States. Like Milford,

Clarkstown adopted its ordinance in the mid-1950s. The planning and legal issues were well documented by one of the authors of the original program, Norman Williams, Jr., in his treatise on land planning, although he modestly (and characteristically) did not there take credit for his part in the ordinance (Williams and Taylor 1985, pp. 105–110).

Clarkstown is in Rockland County, New York, just north of the New Jersey state line. In the mid-1950s, for the first time it became easily accessible from the metropolitan area by way of the newly constructed Tappan Zee Bridge across the Hudson River. According to Williams, the intent of the plan was to

concentrate new residential development in the area around New City [the county seat], and along a corridor extending south from New City to the intersection of the two expressways. . . . [A] roughly circular area around New City (together with an extension south towards the interchange) was zoned for immediate suburban development with 15,000-square-foot lots. An outer ring was zoned for one-acre development. . . . However, the most important planning principles were involved in the intermediate district, the second ring. . . . [That] area was zoned in a special district where residential development could proceed as of right at any time on one-acre lots, but the town board was authorized to issue a special permit for development on 15,000-square-foot lots, in any situation where that board could make a series of special findings, including a finding that school facilities would not be overcrowded (Williams and Taylor 1985, pp. 106, 107; two footnotes and some parenthetical material omitted from original).

The only court to consider the Clarkstown program upheld it.[1] In evaluating the program after ten years in operation, Williams concluded:

In the ten years under the ordinance, 1955 to 1965, the predominant development in Clarkstown was in fact concentrated in the area around New City and in the corridor extending south towards the interchange. . . . An analysis of the subdivisions approved in successive two-year periods makes it clear that, speaking generally, the subdivisions approved (particularly in the [intermediate] district) in the earlier years were closer in, nearer the older settlement in New City, and that the location of such subdivisions tended to move farther out as time went on (Williams and Taylor 1985, pp. 108–109).

One interesting aspect of the Clarkstown program is that unlike some later programs it preserved the opportunity for development of lower-cost housing types. Williams noted that "in the original

Clarkstown ordinance, substantial areas of vacant land were zoned for apartments and relatively small-lot single-family development" (1985, p. 106, n. 34).

THE MARYLAND PROPOSAL

One of the most foresighted of the early growth management efforts was never adopted. Dissatisfied with the operation of traditional zoning and subdivision controls in addressing the growth issues in the Washington and Baltimore suburbs, the Maryland general assembly created a "Planning and Zoning Law Study Commission" in the mid-sixties. That commission took a broad look at the problems facing local governments in addressing growth issues and proposed a new program. Included in its final report (Maryland Planning and Zoning Law Study Commission 1969) is a proposed "Model Land Use and Development Planning Code" prepared for the commission by Jan Krasnowiecki, then on the faculty at the University of Pennsylvania Law School.

That code, among other things

- Expressly authorized local governments to regulate the timing and location of growth, based in part on the availability of public services;
- Addressed the problem of funding "off-site" improvements, such as roads and parks that serve multiple subdivisions, and required a "fair allocation" of the costs of such improvements;
- Prohibited the imposition of development costs on developers to such an extent that it would preclude affordable housing;
- Clarified the relationship between the comprehensive plan and zoning decisions; and, among other things,
- Bound developers to plans approved by the community.

Had it been adopted, the proposed code would have placed Maryland nearly two decades ahead of most of the country. Many of the later growth management efforts described in this book involved attempts to grapple with the issues that the Maryland proposal so clearly addressed. Montgomery County, Maryland, (see Chapter 4, under "Comprehensive Programs") has addressed more of those issues than any other local government, and the state of Florida has tackled many of them in its state planning and growth management laws (see Chapter 6). However, no operating growth management program as of 1992 is as comprehensive as the 1969 Maryland proposal. Although the emphasis of this book is on the national experience with programs that have been adopted and implemented, Krasnowiecki's proposal for Maryland was so farsighted that this brief history would be incomplete without it.

THE RAMAPO PROGRAM

The first implementation of a growth management program after the one in Clarkstown did not come for a dozen years. At that time, Ramapo, Clarkstown's immediate neighbor to the west, adopted a program that would become far more famous than the Clarkstown program on which it was clearly modeled.

The Ramapo program was elegantly simple. Like many growth management programs, it was added to a local regulatory structure that already included zoning and subdivision controls. The new program required one more step in the public approval process, a step designed to ensure that some public facilities would be available to serve the development. Public facilities providing a basis for project review under the program included these: sewers, drainage, public park or recreation facility or school site, major public road, and firehouse.

The ordinance allocated points to each category (five each to all but firehouses, which received three) and allocated those points based on how well the proposal met the intent of the requirement. For example, a project for which 100 percent of the necessary drainage capacity was available received 5 points, while a project with only 50 percent of the required capacity received only 1; similarly, a project with direct access to a park or major road received 5 points in that category, while one at a greater distance received correspondingly fewer points. In addition to receiving typical zoning and subdivision approvals, a project had to earn 15 of the 23 points under the growth management ordinance. The owner or prospective developer of land that did not meet the basic criterion had one of two choices: to await the construction of additional public improvements or to construct at her or his own expense sufficient public improvements to bring the point total up to 15.

A key element in the Ramapo program, and an important consideration of New York's highest court in upholding the program,[2] was the fact that the community had adopted an elaborate plan, including an eighteen-year capital facilities program. The plan and the program together called for the complete development of Ramapo over that eighteen-year period. The court expressed grave concern about the potentially exclusionary effects of such a program but seemed satisfied that Ramapo had committed itself to a process of orderly development rather than to one of exclusion.

Note that the Ramapo program did not actually ensure the availability of all necessary services. With enough points in other categories, it was possible for a development to qualify for approval with no fire protection or no drainage capacity whatsoever available to it.

Neither the Ramapo plan nor the program itself worked exactly as intended, and the community repealed the growth management program in 1983 after thirteen years of operation. The problems with the program were well documented in a 1977 study (Hammer, Siler, George). Two of the findings were particularly important. Of the facilities used by the town as the basis for the program, the town of Ramapo controlled only parks, sewage collection (not treatment), drainage, and some roads. Many roads, the proposed regional sewer system, schools, and fire protection were the responsibilities of other entities, meaning that Ramapo's "plans" for construction of such facilities were more like wish lists than plans. The second problem was that the town never really followed the system, awarding unearned points because of a planning problem and approving nearly as many lots that did not meet the standards of the ordinance as it approved because they complied with it. Further, the impact of the program was probably just to reduce Ramapo's share of regional growth, not to change the growth patterns. Like most economic trends, the growth pressures that temporarily overwhelmed Clarkstown, Ramapo, and Rockland County had waned by the 1980s as Figure 3.1 illustrates.

Despite its limitations, the Ramapo program was significant for several reasons. First, it was innovative for its time. Second, as Williams noted, the court decision upholding it was the "first opinion by a major appellate court approving an elaborate timing-of-development scheme" (Williams and Taylor 1985, p. 120). Third, the program was well documented in the literature, in significant part through the efforts of Robert Freilich, a land use attorney involved in its development (see, for example, Freilich and Levi 1975, pp. 5–8; Gleeson et al. 1975; Freilich 1975; see also other articles by other authors in Scott, Brower, and Miner 1975b, pp. 1–120). Fourth, even if it was somewhat derivative of the Clarkstown program, that program never became well enough known to influence widely the practice of planning. This author has found only four references to it in the literature: Fagin 1955; Williams and Taylor 1985; Krasnowiecki 1969; and Burrows 1978, who cited an earlier edition of the Williams work as his source.

THE PETALUMA PROGRAM

The other major growth management program that became well known in the early 1970s was that of Petaluma, California. That

Figure 3.1
Growth Trends in Rockland County, New York, and Two of Its Towns

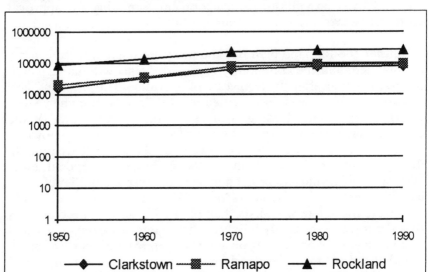

Sources: Bureau of the Census, 1991, *Census of Population and Housing: Summary Population and Housing Characteristics*, Part 34, Table 15; Bureau of the Census, 1982, *Census of the Population: Characteristics of the Population*, Chapter A, *Number of Inhabitants*, Part 34, Table 4; Bureau of the Census, 1972, *Census of Population, Vol. 1, Characteristics of the Population*, Part 6, Table 10 (includes 1960); and Bureau of the Census, 1952, *Census of Population, Volume 1, Number of Inhabitants*, Part 32, Table 6; graph by author.

community's rate-of-growth program was not only well publicized but also the subject of a well known court decision under which it was eventually upheld.

Petaluma, like Ramapo, was far enough from a major city to miss early waves of metropolitan growth. Located in Sonoma County, generally north of San Francisco, the city grew from a population of about 10,000 in 1950 to 25,000 in 1970, after which it endured two years during which its estimated population grew by 5,000 (20 percent) per year. It adopted an initial moratorium and its first "residential development control system" toward the end of that growth spurt (Gleeson et al. 1975; Scott, Brower, and Miner 1975b). As Figure 3.2 shows, the growth rate of Petaluma over the two decades after adoption of its program did not differ markedly either from that of Santa Rosa, a nearby city often compared to Petaluma, or from that of Sonoma County, which contains both cities.

The Petaluma program was simpler and far less interesting than

Figure 3.2
Growth Trends in Petaluma, Santa Rosa, and Sonoma County, California

Sources: Bureau of the Census, 1991, *Census of Population and Housing: Summary Population and Housing Characteristics*, Part 6, Table 16; Bureau of the Census, 1982, *Census of the Population: Characteristics of the Population, Chapter A, Number of Inhabitants*, Part 6, Table 4; and Bureau of the Census, 1972, *Census of Population, Vol. 1, Characteristics of the Population*, Part 6, Table 7 (cities), and 10 (county); graph by author.

the Ramapo program. All it did was establish a limit of 500 new residential dwelling units per year for the community. That limit was suballocated between single-family residences and apartments and between the eastern and western halves of the community. There were a number of exceptions for individually owned lots and other unusual circumstances. On a population base of 35,000 or so, the measure permitted an annual increase of approximately 5 percent in the housing stock. The program remains in effect in 1992, based on an updated plan but still using the original number of 500 dwelling units per year, a number that represented a smaller percentage of a housing base then serving 45,000 people (Petaluma, City of 1987; James Duncan and Associates and Kelly 1991b). Note, however, that in most years applications for new development have not approached the limit established under the program; construction of 500 dwelling units in each year since 1972 would have resulted in a 1990 population substantially greater than 45,000 (see discussion in Chapter 4 and Table 4.1).

Although the Ninth Circuit Court of Appeals and the U.S. Supreme Court ultimately determined to allow the Petaluma program to stand, in part because of procedural problems with a case challenging it, the only court to consider it in depth struck the program down. In a challenge by the homebuilding industry, the U.S. District Court found that Petaluma had "purposefully" limited its public facilities, including a delivery limit requested by the city in a water supply contract under which a water district delivered water to the city. The court found that the city did not have any significant or unresolvable capacity problems but was manipulating public facility capacity to limit growth.[3] In a footnote to its opinion, the appellate court indicated that it would also be likely to uphold the program on substantive legal grounds; however, there is no analysis in its short opinion to support that assertion and no response to the many problems that the lower court found with the program.

Like the court of appeals in the Ramapo case, the federal judge who considered the Petaluma program expressed concern about the potentially exclusionary effects of the Petaluma program; however, unlike the New York court, he concluded that the program was indeed exclusionary, finding, among other things, that the population goal selected by the community was arbitrary and unrelated to regional needs (discussed in Williams and Taylor 1985, pp. 151–159). The Ninth Circuit Court of Appeals reversed the lower court, in part because it found problems with the use of the "right to travel" as the jurisdictional basis for much of the claim. The "right to travel" was a tenuous basis on which a number of early exclusionary zoning cases were brought into federal court. (See a brief but clear discussion of the issue in Gleeson et al. 1975, pp. 70–72 and a more detailed one in Godschalk et al. 1977, pp. 93–104.)

Petaluma's program, although less sophisticated than Ramapo's, had an equal impact on planning practice. It and the Ramapo program were the two featured programs in the second volume of what began as a three-volume *Management & Control of Growth* series published by the Urban Land Institute in 1975 (Scott, Brower, and Miner 1975b, pp. 121–210). Like Ramapo, Petaluma had a professional dedicated to the program who told its story widely. Frank Gray was planning director in the city during important years in the development of the program (see, for example, Gray 1975). Gray and Petaluma's Mayor Helen Putnam were frequent conference speakers in the 1970s. Not coincidentally, Gray subsequently became director of planning in Boulder, Colorado, which modeled its rate-of-growth program on Petaluma's.

The Petaluma program has been a greater success than the Ramapo program in certain respects. Five years after its adoption, Abe found that the program had succeeded in reducing the growth rate of the community and helped mitigate some of the growth-related problems identified by the community, including double sessions in the schools (1977). Williams concluded that in its early years the Petaluma plan had significantly slowed the rate of growth in the community (Williams and Taylor 1985, p. 158). The program remained in effect in 1992, nearly a decade after the repeal of the Ramapo program. Although in the 1980s, the economy and other factors have limited growth pressure in the community to levels below those set by the program, it remains a program of interest to others (see, for example, James Duncan and Associates and Kelly 1991a).

THE EARLY LITERATURE

A significant body of widely available growth management literature published in the early 1970s contributed to the spread of the concept. The Urban Land Institute and the American Society of Planning Officials (now the American Planning Association) both published reports on growth management in the early 1970s. Certainly the publication of these reports in part reflected an already spreading interest in the subject, but the reports also made information about the new techniques available to public officials around the country. Before 1969, there appears to have been only one lonely cry for any sort of growth management: a short article by Henry Fagin, then planning director of the Regional Plan Association in the metropolitan New York region (Fagin 1955).

Thus, to understand the evolution of growth management techniques in the United States, it is important to examine some of the early literature in the field. The American Society of Planning Officials (ASPO) published *Toward a More Effective Land Use Guidance System: A Summary and Analysis of Five Major Reports* in 1969 as part of its Planning Advisory Service series (Heeter 1969). The organization automatically distributes publications in that series to subscribers, thus guaranteeing initial distribution. The organization also sells the PAS reports to others through its direct mail "Planners Bookstore." Although it did not expressly use the term "growth management" and did not refer specifically to evolving growth management efforts in New York, California, and elsewhere, it did provide summaries of five other reports that, at least in part, addressed concerns of planners in urban areas. Those reports, some of which are separately discussed, included:

- a *Model Land Development Code* proposed by the American Law Institute to replace existing zoning and subdivision enabling acts and to provide broader authority for more diverse and comprehensive planning and land use control;

• *Building the American City*, the report of the National Commission on Urban Problems, a commission appointed by President Johnson and commonly identified by the name of its chair, former Senator Paul H. Douglas;

• *Urban and Rural America: Policies for Future Growth*, a 1968 report of the Advisory Commission on Intergovernmental Relations, addressing the complexity of the governmental structure that attempts to manage growth, as well as the urban–rural relationship in a changing economy;

• a 1969 Canadian report entitled *Report of the Task Force on Housing and Urban Development*; and

• a 1967 report actually prepared by ASPO, *New Directions in Connecticut Planning Legislation.*

Each of those reports addressed a number of issues and topics going beyond the scope of the current inquiry, but Heeter's synthesis of the recommendations of the reports for a future land use control system was both interesting and helpful. Among the conclusions he synthesized from the reports were that a future land use control system should involve a dynamic concept of "land-use guidance" rather than a "static, end-state concept," as in zoning; it would involve the creative use of incentives and restraints; it would involve public land acquisition; it would recognize the difference between developed areas and undeveloped ones; it would be controlled by state goals and policies and monitored by a state agency; the use of land use controls for exclusionary purposes would be prohibited (1969, pp. 7, 8). As the descriptions of contemporary local and state programs in the next two chapters suggest, some communities and states have developed programs entirely consistent with Heeter's vision.

Earl Finkler prepared two reports published by the American Society of Planning Officials in the early 1970s, *Nongrowth as a Planning Alternative* (1972) and *Nongrowth: A Review of the Literature* (1973). The titles suggested contemporary concerns with growth, reflected in the publication of two major population growth studies in 1972. One, *The Limits to Growth*, sometimes called "The Club of Rome Report" because of its origins from a group meeting in Rome, explored the implications of exponential world population growth (Meadows et al. 1972). It used a systems approach to explore the carrying capacity of the earth, with particular emphasis on the ability of the environment to absorb pollutants and of the land to produce crops to feed a growing population. The report proposed a model of "global equilibrium" through stabilized world population. The second, a study of population growth in the United States, contained this expression of contemporary thinking:

In the brief history of this nation, we have always assumed that the progress and "the good life" are connected with population growth. In fact, population growth has frequently been regarded as a measure of our progress. If that were ever the case, it is not now. There is hardly any social problem confronting this nation whose solution would be easier if our population were larger. Even now, the dreams of too many Americans are not being realized; others are being fulfilled at too high a cost. Accordingly, this Commission has concluded that our country can no longer afford the uncritical acceptance of the population growth ethic that "more is better." And, beyond that, after two years of concentrated effort, we have concluded that no substantial benefits would result from continued growth in the nation's population (Commission on Population Growth and the American Future 1972).

The U.S. report, often called "the Rockefeller Commission Report" after the commission chairman, John D. Rockefeller III, not only dealt with the side effects of growth but challenged the very premise that "growth is good," or more specifically, that growth brings economic prosperity. The report concluded with seven pages of recommendations, ranging from population research to recommendations that remained appropriate twenty years later—sex education, management of immigration, and availability of abortion and sterilization in government-funded programs.

Finkler's reports provided a local perspective on these national and world concerns about population growth. Drawing on both the Club of Rome Report and the Rockefeller Commission Report, Finkler explored the policy implications of population growth, at the local, as well as world and national, levels. He extended the logic of the Rockefeller Commission argument that "growth is not good" to the local level. In the first report, he identified four "alternative orientations" toward growth:

1. Growth is inevitable.
2. Growth equals progress.
3. Stop all population growth.
4. Growth is a variable to be influenced in pursuit of a desirable quality of life (1972, p. 2).

Finkler urged that planners play a leadership role in establishing local efforts to limit or manage growth:

Nongrowth (in addition to logical, limited, planned, and other forms of growth) should be studied by planners and blended into planning considerations. The topic should be relevant in most communities facing growth, regardless of size or type of jurisdiction. It can be a mistake to deal only with the results of growth, while automatically eliminating growth as a factor in itself (1972, p. 2).

Finkler and David Peterson prepared another work on the subject. *Nongrowth Planning Strategies: The Developing Power of Towns, Cities and Regions* was published by a commercial publisher in 1974. It was more clearly opposed to growth and expressed disappointment at Boulder's failure to fulfill completely Finkler's hopes for it. He lamented, "Ever since I first visited Boulder on nongrowth field research in April 1972, I felt that this might really be the community to send a strong, well-formulated antigrowth message to the nation" (1974, p. 33).

Two other aspects of the book are interesting. First, Boulder was the only community case study included in the book, although Ramapo and Petaluma were probably more famous at the time. Second, in this book, not published by the American Society of Planning Officials (ASPO) which had published his earlier works, Finkler criticized his former associates at ASPO for being slow to include growth management as a topic on national conference programs and in its publications. He also took officials there to task for changing the name of the first such program from one containing the word "nongrowth" to one describing "growth controls" (1974, pp. 62–70).

James Hughes collected a set of essays for the Center for Urban Policy Research, which published them under the title *Growth Controls* (1974). However, despite the title, the focus of the book was on exclusionary suburban zoning and housing opportunity in New Jersey (see the discussion of this topic in Chapter 10). The book presented a balanced view of the issues, discussing the pressures that led to such exclusion as well as the problems resulting from it. However, it added nothing to the real growth management literature.

In 1975, the Urban Land Institute (ULI), with funding from the Department of Housing and Urban Development, published the first three volumes in a series entitled "Management & Control of Growth." They all bore the same title, *Management & Control of Growth: Issues, Techniques, Problems, Trends* (Scott, Brower, and Miner 1975 a, b, and c). The eighteen hundred pages in these initial volumes from ULI provided the first broad and comprehensive look at growth management. The series made that information widely available to planners, local officials, and others interested in the issues. In its introduction, it echoed the concerns of the Club of Rome Report and the Rockefeller Commission Report, as well as Finkler's restating of those concerns at a local level:

The ethic of growth in America is increasingly being challenged; no longer is it being accepted unquestioningly as a premise of progress. Its effects on the quality of life are widely debated, and its management and control are seen by many as essential elements of modern land use policy.

In more and more communities across the country, the costs and benefits of continued growth are emerging as major public issues. There is hesitation over accommodating further development with its attendant consequences of greater numbers of residents and higher densities, economic expansion, rapid consumption of land, and alteration of environment (Scott, Brower, and Miner 1975a, p. 2; footnote omitted).

However, the ULI report also recognized that the issue was complex, with multiple interests affected and multiple points of view. The introduction continued, in the next paragraph, "At the same time, this trend has not been without vigorous opposition; dissent over implications of unwise growth restrictions has been heard from various business interests, property owners, builders, and advocates for the disenfranchised: the poor, minorities, the underemployed, and the aged" (Scott, Brower, and Miner 1975a, p. 2).

Volume 1 of the series examined land policy and environmental policy, presented the national and international debate over population growth, discussed land use controls, and provided an initial look at growth management and one of its possible side effects— exclusion (Scott, Brower, and Miner 1975a). Volume 2 provided in-depth looks at and multiple perspectives on the programs in Ramapo and Petaluma. It examined one of the legal issues raised in some of the cases (the right to travel), provided a brief look at a variety of regulatory techniques for managing growth, discussed the impacts of growth on local government finance, and examined the influence on growth of such policies as interim zoning and utility extension policies (Scott, Brower, and Miner 1975b). Volume 3 examined other regulatory techniques, including transferable development rights, planned unit developments, and efforts to preserve agricultural lands. It also examined the state and federal roles in growth management, as well as the regional implications of such programs. Finally, it provided a broad look at the issues from the perspective of developers (Scott, Brower, and Miner 1975c).

Also in 1975, the American Society of Planning Officials published *Urban Growth Management Systems* (Gleeson et al. 1975). It provided brief descriptions of thirteen operating growth management programs, including those in Boulder, Petaluma, and Ramapo. It also included an introduction to the legal issues involved in growth management and some discussion of the apparent effects of these still-fledgling programs. It included an extensive bibliography, much of it consisting of literature drawn from closely related fields and topics (1975, pp. 115–138).

Is Nongrowth a Local Choice?

The early literature raised this basic question, which has largely disappeared from the growth management dialogue. However, it is worthy of brief consideration here, because it dominated so much of the early literature in the field.

Although Finkler was an advocate of nongrowth, he failed to address the question of how a community can stop growing (1972, 1973; Finkler and Peterson 1974). The examples included in the 1972 report were all examples of managed growth rather than nongrowth. Many current residents of two of Finkler's examples, Los Angeles and Orange counties, California, would probably question whether their communities were even valid examples of managed growth.

A 1975 study entitled *No Growth: Impacts on Metropolitan Areas* studied the effects of nongrowth, but each of the examples was a former boomtown suffering from economic decline and substantial out migration; not one was a community that had consciously decided not to grow (Rust 1975). Whether a community can realistically choose not to grow is a question largely beyond the scope of this book. As a practical matter, despite Finkler's early efforts, few communities have attempted to stop growth entirely through growth management tools. The most publicized such effort, one in Boca Raton, Florida, would have imposed a limit on the number of dwelling units in the city; but the proposed cap was roughly triple the population level at the time it was proposed. Thus, it was, at least over the short run, anything but a nongrowth plan. Although a Florida court struck down the population cap,[4] related zoning limitations remain in effect. (For a short history of the program, see ECO Northwest 1986; for other perspectives on what Boca Raton has done, see also Cobb 1986; York 1986.) St. Petersburg, Florida, briefly considered an actual population cap, but the city council defeated the measure on second reading (25,000 in St. Petersburg 1974). The nature of the proposal, which included a cap that was lower than the current population, and its sponsorship, a council member opposed to growth controls, suggested that it was more a political statement than a serious proposal; however, it garnered four votes of seven on first reading.

The Montgomery County (Maryland) Planning Board addressed the issue of nongrowth directly in its *First Annual Growth Policy Report* in 1974. It stated in part, "In this report, the Board does not recommend a specific limit on the total number of people the County might ultimately house or the number that should be 'admitted' each year. The County is not sovereign; people have a right to move; and we are persuaded that such population 'caps' are both unwise and of dubious constitutionality" (1974, p. 6).

CONCLUSION

Clearly these significant pieces of early literature were both a cause and a symptom of growing interest in growth management. In a 1974 survey of members of the International City Managers Association, 253 communities responded "Yes" to the question, "Has your community adopted policies to limit the growth of its population?" (cited in Dowall 1980). The Urban Land Institute, American Planning Association and other organizations and publishers were in part responding to market demand, but the wide availability of these publications provided information about growth management to more communities. Thus, the experience with growth management from the early 1970s into the 1990s has been quite different from the lonely pioneering effort of Clarkstown in the 1950s.

NOTES

1. In re *Josephs* v. *Town Board of Clarkstown*, 24 Misc.2d 366, 198 N.Y.S.2d 695 (Sup. Ct. Rockland County, 1960).
2. *Golden* v. *Board Planning of Town of Ramapo*, 30 N.Y.2d 359, 334 N.Y.S.2d 138, 285 N.E.2d 291 (1972); *app. dism.*, 409 U.S. 1003 (1972).
3. *Construction Industry of Sonoma County* v. *Petaluma*, 375 F.Supp. 574 (1974); *rev.* 522 F.2d 897 (C.A. 9, 1975), *cert. den.* 424 U.S. 934.
4. *City of Boca Raton* v. *Boca Villas Corp.*, 371 So.2d 154 (Fla. App. 1979).

4

Types of
Contemporary Growth
Management Regulations

This chapter describes contemporary growth management programs in operation. Fifteen years elapsed between the conclusion of events described in the previous chapter and the preparation of this book, but the history of that period is told better by describing the contemporary programs that grew out of it than by presenting a continuing historical narrative. The descriptions provided in this chapter provide the context for the analysis contained in the last part of the book.

PROGRAM TYPES

Four basic types of regulatory growth management programs are in effect today:

- Adequate public facilities requirements
- Growth phasing programs
- Urban growth boundaries
- Rate-of-growth programs

The programs are quite different in philosophy, operation, and effect. Some communities have adopted more comprehensive regulatory structures that include aspects of more than one of these types, but the types themselves are quite distinct.

ADEQUATE PUBLIC FACILITIES REQUIREMENTS

Subdivision regulations, described in Chapter 2, require that public improvements such as roads, drainage facilities, utility lines, and even street lights and signs be provided within the subdivision. Some communities use the subdivision process to require developers to provide fringe facilities, such as a turning lane or traffic light at the entrance to a new development.

However, nothing in a typical set of local subdivision regulations addresses the larger community issues:

- Can the street outside the development, or the street or highway into which it in turn connects, absorb more traffic?
- Does the sewer line in the area have additional capacity, or is there even a sewer line in the area?
- Can the drainage channels downstream from the site handle additional run-off?
- Does the water system have enough raw water, enough flow, and enough pressure to serve the site?
- Do the central sewer and water treatment plants have enough additional capacity to serve this development?

These are all questions to which there are readily ascertainable engineering answers. A sewer line is either full or it is not. Similarly, a water treatment plant or a drainage system has a determinable capacities. The traffic capacity of a road involves some judgment calls, all revolving around the question of how much congestion the public is willing to tolerate at rush hour; however, once that judgment has been made, the determination of whether the road can handle additional traffic within those limits can be objectively answered.

Some communities may also want to ask questions that are somewhat more difficult to answer:

- Can the schools hold additional students?
- Can the police department serve the area?
- Will there be adequate fire protection?
- Can the public library serve the new development?

Although there are cases when the answer to one of these questions is an unequivocal "No," in other cases the judgment is more complex. Driving down another mile or so of streets in a suburban area will probably not greatly tax a busy police department; on the other hand, another hundred miles of streets would; where is the breaking point? Although a school may be "at capacity," it is always possible to squeeze in a few more rows of desks; when does the capacity really become a problem?

Typical subdivision regulations simply do not address these basic community issues. Some might argue that zoning should be tailored to the development capacity of a site as determined by public facility capacities. That argument misses a fundamental point—although most of the zoning map is relatively static, the capacity of public facilities changes constantly as new facilities are built and new development absorbs existing capacity. If the community prepared a zoning map designating permitted uses and intensities based on available capacities in 1989, it was almost certain to be wrong by the time this book was published. Certainly most communities change small parts of the zoning map each year, but most of the map remains basically the same from year to year; public facility capacities change almost daily. Thus, attempting to map the capacities with anything other than a dynamic, automated system, makes little sense; running such a constantly changing map through the rigors of official adoption involved in approving a zoning map, often requiring several weeks in the process, makes none.

Thus, many communities today adopt ordinances requiring that developments not be approved unless adequate public facilities are currently available, or will be available by the time that demand from the new development requires that capacity. For example, Broward County, Florida (Ft. Lauderdale is the county seat) requires that development proposals meet adequate public facility requirements for ten different types of facilities: regional roadway network; road rights-of-way; access to major and collector roads; surface water (storm-water) management; water supply; sewage treatment; solid waste collection and disposal; regional and local parks; school sites and buildings; police and fire protection (James Duncan and Associates and Kelly 1991a; ordinance available in James Duncan and Associates and Kelly 1991b). Vermont's Act 250 (see Chapter 6) contained a similar list. Colorado has long required that counties make findings as to the adequacy of water supply and wastewater treatment arrangements before approving subdivisions.[1] Under the "concurrency" requirements of a 1986 state law, Florida now requires that all local governments adopt standards for the adequacy of a variety of public facilities (see Chapter 6).

Anyone without a great deal of experience in planning matters might reasonably ask how communities have survived without such basic requirements in their local ordinances. The answer is, "Often rather poorly."

If community growth is moderate, excess capacity in existing systems may be adequate to absorb additional growth. Further, local residents may to some extent tolerate increased traffic congestion and crowding in the schools as necessary results of growth. However, in a growing community, eventually some system is likely to fail. The result in such circumstances is typically a building "moratorium," during which the community refuses to issue building permits for new development (see, for example, Greenberg 1974; for a discussion of the legal implications of a moratorium, see Kelly 1984). In Livermore, California, a moratorium was adopted by citizen initiative, resulting from obvious frustration with the impacts of growth. The initiative imposed a moratorium on the issuance of building permits until both double sessions in the school and water rationing were eliminated and sewage treatment was brought into full compliance with applicable regulations (Williams and Taylor 1985, pp. 164–167; LeGates and Nikas 1989, p. 20). The California Supreme Court upheld the program (opinion quoted and analyzed in Williams and Taylor 1985).[2] Livermore subsequently replaced the moratorium with a rate-of-growth program (James Duncan and Associates and Kelly 1991a).

The Livermore case raises an additional issue that should be mentioned briefly, although a detailed analysis of it is beyond the scope of this work. Since the first planning and zoning enabling acts were written in the 1920s, there has been an underlying notion that planning should provide guidelines for zoning and land use decisions, as well as capital investments and other community decisions. Although that notion has at times been lost in practice, the opportunity for planning remains. Local procedures that involve the planning commission in all or most such decisions are designed to enhance that opportunity. When the system fails to the point that the governing body delegates control of the policy issue to the citizens of the community through referendum, the community loses the opportunity for planning. There is no logical way for the voters as a body politic to engage in rational planning (see, for example, Callies, Neuffer, and Caliboso 1991; Curtin and Wood 1989; as well as Callies 1980; Cronin 1980; and other articles in Schnidman and Silverman 1980).

A moratorium is a worst-case result for all parties. Because the moratorium generally takes effect at the building permit stage, it comes after the community has granted development approval. That often occurs at both the zoning and subdivision stage, and sometimes after developers have made significant investments in site improvements. A developer fares better under a program that denies a development proposal early in the process because of a lack of public facilities than under one that allows the development to proceed, with a substantial investment in the project, and then stops it before it reaches the last step before generating sales and a recovery of investment. The problem can be large. For example, when Westminster, Colorado, prepared a detailed study of its development capacities and demands prior to adopting the second phase of a growth management plan in 1978, it found that its governing body and planning commission had approved far more development than the city could serve in the reasonable future. Developments (and parts of developments) approved by the city but not yet containing buildings included 3,630 "permit-ready" platted lots, for which all city requirements had been completed, more than 1,000 additional lots platted but unimproved and thus not "permit-ready," more than 2,000 acres (not lots) of potential residential development in approved active development, and an additional 2,500 acres of potential residential development in approved but currently inactive projects. To place those figures in perspective, the city by that time had enough capacity to serve only 2,600 additional dwelling units (fewer than the number that could be placed on "permit-ready" lots) over the subsequent two- to three-year period (Westminster, City of 1978b, charts 78C(1) through 78C(4) and Report B, p. 13). Westminster's problem was compounded by the fact that it needed the "tap fees" (connection fees imposed on new development, now often called "impact fees") from new development to amortize substantial debt incurred in the early 1970s in order to extend major utility lines into undeveloped and developing areas (Westminster, City of 1978). The Westminster situation in 1977 and 1978 is described in somewhat more detail in Kelly 1982 and in depth in Snyder 1982.

The circumstances of a Westminster or a Livermore clearly reflect a lack of planning that led, in the face of significant demand (which both Livermore and Westminster faced), to a community crisis. With a significant investment held in abeyance perhaps indefinitely, a rational developer may see little choice but to sue. However, public officials in such a community are likely to be little happier with the moratorium than the development community. A community often adopts a moratorium because political pressures on public officials or their duties preclude their allowing continuing overloads on public systems. For example, Westminster needed the revenue from new development to amortize bonded indebtedness on an extensive network of sewer and water lines constructed into developing areas. The city council there adopted an initial brief moratorium and a subsequent growth management program, in spite of that need, because the city lacked the treatment plant capacity and raw water necessary to serve the demand (Westminster, City of 1978; Snyder 1982; Kelly 1982).

Just understanding the problem is not enough; a community needs adequate public facilities standards in its local ordinances. When Chester, Connecticut, denied subdivision approval to a project because the local planning commission found that the road leading to the subdivision was "inadequate to provide safe access and egress to the proposed lots for either residents or emergency vehicles," the Connecticut Supreme Court reversed the town's decision because there was nothing in the subdivision ordinance requiring adequate access to the site and the developer had apparently agreed to meet all the requirements that were in the ordinance.[3]

How do adequate public facilities standards manage growth? There are two answers to that question. First, one of the dominant concerns in rapidly growing communities is the availability of public services; adequate public facilities standards address that concern directly by insuring that new development does not take place unless the facilities are available to support it. Second, an adequate public facilities ordinance directly affects the location of growth by providing additional "incentives" to ensure that growth locates near existing public facilities (see more detailed discussion in Chapter 5).

GROWTH PHASING PROGRAMS

A growth phasing program regulates the location and timing of new development, generally based on the availability, or presumed availability, of public facilities. In principle such a program is thus somewhat like an adequate public facilities program; however, in practice it is quite different.

The Ramapo program described in Chapter 3 is an early example of a growth phasing program. It focused primarily on the timing of growth by allocating points to development based on the availability of public improvements; it was coupled with a plan that called for the installation of necessary public improvements throughout the community over an eighteen-year period (see, generally, Chapter 3 and sources cited there). Clearly the concept of the program was that development would take place generally where public facilities were readily available, enabling developers to earn the "points" necessary under the program, before it took place in areas with few or no public facilities. The timing of development would thus generally follow the timing of public improvements, as described in the plan.

The Clarkstown program, also described in Chapter 3, was a growth phasing program more clearly directed at locational phasing. To quote again from Norman Williams, the intent of the Clarkstown plan was to "concentrate new residential development in the area around New City, and along a corridor extending south from New

City to the intersection of the two expressways" (Williams and Taylor 1985, p. 106).

Although both programs were more effective in ensuring the availability of at least some public facilities than a traditional program, neither guaranteed that all public facilities would be available. Recall, for example, that in Ramapo a total of 23 points signified the immediate availability of all designated public facilities, but the program required only 15 points. It would have been theoretically possible under the Ramapo program to obtain development approval for a project with no road access or with completely inadequate off-site drainage capacity. Such an extreme case might have been unlikely to occur, but it is not at all improbable that, even under such a program, a community may approve a development without the full availability of public facilities.

Growth phasing remains a popular type of growth management program. For example, four of eight programs included in a recent national study of large-scale growth management programs were classified by the authors as "growth phasing" programs (James Duncan and Associates and Kelly 1991a). Those included a comprehensive growth management package in Montgomery County, Maryland, described in more depth below, and the Westminster program, which also includes adequate public facilities requirements. However, it also included current programs in both San Jose and Livermore, California, which are based entirely on the concept of growth phasing.

The Livermore program is largely based on timing. The city adopts a new "Housing Implementation Policy (HIP)" every third year. Key to the HIP is a growth rate established in the policy, based on current public facility capacities, as well as environmental issues and the availability of jobs. Each triennial policy also establishes priorities for the type and location of development that the city desires during the planning period; and staff uses those priorities to rank project applications during that period (see, generally, James Duncan and Associates and Kelly 1991a; and LeGates and Nikas 1989; copy of implementing ordinance included in James Duncan and Associates and Kelly 1991b).

San Jose, California, phases growth in one geographic area of the city, called the "Evergreen Area." Like the growth phasing program in Livermore, the San Jose program was adopted by the city council after an initial moratorium adopted by citizen initiative in 1973. The city staff prepares an "Evergreen Area Monitoring Report" each year, and that report provides the basis for establishing growth guidelines for the following year. The city council then allocates to the Evergreen Area a specified number of new dwelling units, based on the staff analysis of existing and projected road capacity (see, generally, James Duncan and Associates and Kelly 1991a).

As with the Clarkstown and Ramapo programs, there is nothing in the later growth phasing programs in Livermore or San Jose that ensures that actual capacity will be available to serve new development or that the community will permit new development to the extent of available capacity. In these programs, the growth phasing begins with a concept of adequate public facilities that the community translates into a simpler allocation of new dwelling units to be permitted.

Why would a community adopt a growth phasing program, rather than a set of adequate public facilities standards, if both accomplish the same thing? Although it is not possible to document here the thought processes of those who have made all the decisions, there are two probable answers to that question. One possibility is that the growth phasing program may appear simpler than adequate public facilities standards.

First, growth phasing programs are generally simpler for the public and for many developers to understand than adequate public facilities requirements. With an adequate public facilities ordinance, it may not be possible to determine whether any development, or how much development, can take place at a particular location without making a reasonably detailed analysis of each affected public facility. Under a growth phasing program like those in San Jose and Livermore, a citizen or a developer can easily determine that the community will permit 100 more units, 1,000 more units, or no more units, in a particular area during a particular period.

The other, equally valid answer to the question of why a community might choose a growth phasing program over an adequate public facilities one is that growth phasing addresses a different issue. Greenberg cited a survey of citizens in Livermore early in the growth management period in which 74 percent of those surveyed agreed with the statement that "Livermore should grow at a controlled rate, provided services to the residents do not suffer" (1986, p. 321). Note the two parts to that response: (1) protect service levels, and (2) control the rate of growth. Adequate public facilities standards would ensure the adequacy of services, but in a year when systems enjoyed adequate capacities, such controls might not slow the rate of growth. A phased growth system addresses both issues.

The perceived simplicity of the growth phasing programs does not necessarily translate into simplicity in operation. Most growth phasing programs, including all of those described here, are added to the development review process as additional permitting steps. In communities like San Jose, that additional step may be relatively compli-cated (see James Duncan and Associates and Kelly 1991a). Developers and some observers view the proliferation of permitting requirements as a major impediment to the provision of affordable housing (see a number of separate chapters in Bosselman, Feurer, and Siemon 1976; for a 1991 discussion, see Advisory Commission on Regulatory Bar-riers to Affordable Housing 1991). A community can easily integrate adequate public facilities standards into existing development review processes, thus making the operation of such a program often simpler than the operation of a growth phasing program.

There is a political side to all of this. In communities that have experienced a recent crisis, the concern over growth may focus on traffic or on the availability of water. However, a sewage treatment plant that is at 99 percent of capacity or a water system that is near-ing the point of overload are simply not the kinds of things that engender much casual conversation within a community. On the other hand, the perceptions of growth do generate discussion and concern. One of the primary perceptions of growth relates to subur-ban "sprawl." A 1974 publication, *The Costs of Sprawl*, documented these costs in fiscal terms and provided a financial incentive for communities to attempt to limit sprawl, regardless of whether public facilities are generally available (Real Estate Research Corporation 1974). Although not all analysts agree that the economic impacts of sprawl are entirely negative (see, generally, Chapter 7), there are other problems with sprawl. Those include both the consumption of a finite resource and some intangible perceptions about desirable urban form (see Chapter 7).

The fact is that adequate public facilities may be available in a relatively remote location. It is not unusual for a community to extend major public facilities to a remote industrial plant or an airport, thus making those same public facilities available to a strip of intervening land (see general discussion in Chapter 5); some of that land may be relatively remote from the community, and its development may be perceived as contributing to sprawl. A require-ment for adequate public facilities for new development would not preclude the development of such property, but a phased develop-ment scheme might.

Thus, a critical difference between the two types of programs is often the purpose of the program. Those drafting the language for adopting a program may prepare a purpose statement with recita-tions of the limited availability of public facilities. That may be the real purpose of the program, but the city may include such language just because the city attorney believes (probably correctly) that tying the proposal as closely as possible to concepts of the "public health and safety" will improve its defensibility (see, for example, Staff of the U.S. General Accounting Office 1978).

However, the real purpose of a growth phasing program may be to prevent "sprawl" and the changes in urban form and negative perceptions that go with it. In one survey of communities with development timing controls (loosely defined there to include subdivision regulations and capital investment strategies), 78 percent of the respondents mentioned "reduction of urban sprawl" as an objective of the development timing strategy. That purpose tied with "environmental protection" for second place, trailing only "provision of adequate urban services," which was mentioned by 84 percent of the respondents (Brower et al. 1976, p. 109). The prevention of sprawl may be just as valid a goal as the protection of capacity in public facilities, but it is quite a different one.

As the Montgomery County program, described later, demonstrates, it is also possible to combine more than one type of program.

This section has distinguished between growth phasing programs that attempt to phase the location of growth and those like the one in San Jose that control the timing of growth through specific numerical permit limits. Obviously such a distinction is largely significant over the short run; over the long run, the issues are interrelated. The practical question in most cases is when a particular piece of land will be developed. That question contains both the issues of timing and location. Although the Ramapo program, with its eighteen-year plan, was based on timing, some land was immediately available and some was not; thus, at every stage it included location as well as timing controls. Viewed from a community level rather than a neighborhood level, the San Jose growth management program for Evergreen is purely a locational program. That program limits development within one part of the city but does not limit it elsewhere. Viewed at a neighborhood level, considering Evergreen as the neighborhood, it is a timing program which paces development in the area based on the capacity of the road system to handle growth. In short, the issues of timing and location are in one sense separate but in many other ways closely related.

The effect of a growth phasing program on growth is not complex if the community implements the program as planned. As Snyder (1982) noted in commenting on the Westminster requirements for adequate public facilities, "Although the location of development is never predetermined by the City, it is economically advantageous to the developer to locate either contiguous to the city or within the city in the role of an infill development" (p. 248).

Growth patterns and timing may not be entirely predictable with an adequate public facilities program, but they should be reasonably predictable (or at least the maximums should be reasonably predictable) with a growth phasing program.

URBAN GROWTH BOUNDARIES

As the name suggests, an urban growth boundary is a line drawn around a city to define the limits of urban growth. It is a kind of growth phasing program. Some phasing programs, such as the early one in Clarkstown, attempt to phase growth by limiting all growth, or more intense growth, to a particular area of the community at a particular time. The earliest form of growth management in Boulder was a "blue line" around the city, drawn at an elevation (5,750 feet) beyond which water service could not conveniently be offered; it served the incidental, but not unintentional, purpose of limiting growth up the side of the mountains that provide a backdrop for the city (Snyder 1982, pp. 148–150).

An urban growth boundary, as the term is used here, however, is more rigid than a simple phasing program. Boulder later created another form of urban growth boundary through its acquisition of a publicly owned greenbelt that almost completely surrounded the city by 1992 (Boulder, City of 1991; see discussion in Chapter 5). Because the Boulder charter makes it difficult for the city to sell the open space, the boundary is likely to remain stable.

The primary source of most rigid urban growth boundaries is the state. In Hawaii, the state has created a form of statewide zoning under which it designated urban, rural, conservation, and agricultural districts (described in Chapter 6). Although the boundaries have been subject to surprisingly frequent change, they are still far more rigid than any locally drawn lines on a zoning or growth management map have proved to be. Even after the changes, the program has served its purpose by restricting 95 percent of the state's land to agricultural and conservation uses (Callies 1992; see, generally, Chapter 6).

Oregon took another approach in its state law. It required that local governments prepare local plans and implementation strategies that included twenty-year growth boundaries. Thus, since the mid-1970s, communities in Oregon have had urban growth boundaries. The Oregon program is described in more depth in Chapter 6.

Establishing an urban growth boundary requires either a very self-centered attitude for a community or an enormous amount of foresight. Because population growth trends change so much over time, it is difficult to imagine accurately projecting the land area needed for growth over a twenty-year period. Knaap has noted the significant effects of the rigidity of the Portland boundary on the land market (Knaap 1985, see discussion in Chapter 10).

An urban growth boundary establishes a clearer "urban edge" than other forms of growth management. In doing so, it puts a limit to continuous urban sprawl. On the other hand, it seems more likely than other forms of growth management to spur leapfrog, or discontinuous, development beyond the boundary (see Figure 7.1 and the description of such effects from the Boulder program in Chapter 7).

Note that an urban growth boundary addresses urban form but does not directly address the issues of adequacy of public facilities or even the fiscal impacts of growth. Presumably, constraining development within a limited boundary will lead to reduced capital and operating costs, thus minimizing negative fiscal impact on the community, but recent studies do not wholly support that conclusion. Further, urban growth boundaries do not necessarily regulate the timing of growth within that boundary. A phased growth system may suggest a series of concentric boundaries, with growth gradually moving out through them, thus facilitating the gradual expansion of public facilities. The establishment of long-term growth boundaries like those in Boulder and Portland does not provide a basis for planning the orderly expansion of public facilities in the early years, because there is then far more undeveloped land within the boundary than a community can or should serve with major roads and public utilities.

In short, urban growth boundaries address exactly what they appear to address. They limit the long-range boundaries of urban growth and do little else. They can, of course, be used in conjunction with other techniques. However, it is important to remember that these boundaries do not directly address issues such as heavy traffic, overcrowded schools, or overloaded public services that typically lead to the adoption of growth management programs.

RATE-OF-GROWTH PROGRAMS

An adequate public facilities requirement may effectively regulate the rate of growth of a community, based on the actual capacity of of public facilities at any given time. Some growth phasing programs, such as the San Jose program described earlier in this chapter, may translate the availability of public facilities into a maximum permissible growth rate in any given year. However, a few communities regulate the rate of growth directly.

The two primary examples are programs in Petaluma, California, described in Chapter 3, and in Boulder, Colorado, which based its program on the Petaluma program. As described in Chapter 3, Peta-

Table 4.1
Permitted Growth in Petaluma at 500 Dwelling Units per Year Compared to Actual Growth, 1970–90

	1970	1980	1990
Cumulative units allowed by program	N.A.	13,175	18,175
Actual total units	8,175	12,540	16,546
Cumulative difference	N.A.	635	1,729

Sources: Actual number of units from Bureau of the Census, 1991, *Census of Population and Housing: Summary Population and Housing Characteristics,* Part 6, Table 18; Bureau of the Census, 1982, *Summary Characteristics by Governmental Units and Standard Metropolitan Statistical Areas,* Part 6, Table 2; Bureau of the Census, 1972, *City and County Data Book,* Table B-2; other lines computed by author.

luma had experienced constant growth that surged to an annual rate of 10 percent by 1971. In the face of this last spurt of growth, Petaluma adopted the first stage in its growth control program—a moratorium on rezonings, followed by a moratorium on annexations. In August 1972, the city adopted a "Residential Development Control System" that was the predecessor of the "Residential Growth Management Program" that remains in place in 1992.

The Petaluma program is relatively simple. It provides an allocation of 500 new residential units per year, with suballocations between two sides of town and between single-family and multifamily housing. It is noteworthy that, based on the population at the time of the original program's adoption, 500 units represented a maximum annual growth rate of more than 5 percent; by 1991, the effective rate limit was closer to 3.5 percent. That computation is of more academic than practical significance, however, because Petaluma's growth did not approach the maximum permissible rate in the 1980s as Table 4.1 shows. In 1990, the city had 16,546 dwelling units, compared to 12,540 in 1980. Without regard to several exemptions that would have permitted more units, the basic program would have permitted growth to 17,540 dwelling units by 1990.

It is important to recall that in a suit filed by homebuilders the federal district court examined the Petaluma program and found

Table 4.2
Permitted Growth in Boulder at 2 Percent per Annum, Compared to Actual Growth, with Boulder County as Reference, 1970–90

	1970	1980	1990
CITY OF BOULDER			
Actual population	66,870	76,685	83,312
Projected population with 2 percent annual increase (1970 base)	N.A.	81,516	99,366
Projected population with 2 percent annual increase (1980 base)	N.A.	N.A.	93,471
BOULDER COUNTY			
Actual population	131,899	189,625	225,339
Projected population with 2 percent annual increase (1970 base)	N.A.	160,784	195,997
Projected population with 2 percent annual increase (1980 base)	N.A.	N.A.	231,153

Sources: Actual population data from Bureau of the Census, 1991, *Census of Population and Housing: Summary Population and Housing Characteristics,* Part 7, Tables 15 (county) and 16 (city); Bureau of the Census, 1981, *Census of the Population: Characteristics of the Population, Chapter A, Number of Inhabitants,* Part 7, Tables 4 (county) and 5 (city); and Bureau of the Census, 1972, *Census of Population, Vol. 1, Characteristics of the Population,* Table 10; other lines computed by author.

that the city generally had adequate public facilities capacity and that it had "purposefully" limited its water supply. Although the city raised the issue of public facilities in defending its program, clearly the city has never based the limits imposed by the program on the adequacy of public facilities. Even without the detailed analysis by the federal court, one could easily deduce that it is very unlikely that the combination of roads, sewer, water, and schools in a community would be able to absorb exactly 500 new residential units each year for nearly twenty years. Clearly the remaining capacity of such systems is "lumpy," becoming extremely limited at times and then increasing dramatically as a new plant or major trunk line or road is added to the system (see discussion of this concept in Dubbink 1983, pp. 176–179).

The Boulder program was a second-generation version of the Petaluma one. Boulder adopted its first program in 1976, four years after adoption of the program in Petaluma. The original version of the plan resulted from a citizen initiative and was named the Danish plan after citizen activist and later city council member, Paul Danish. The original plan imposed an annual limit of 1.5 percent on the increase in the number of dwelling units in the city; the current plan allows a growth rate of 2 percent. During the early years of the growth management program, Boulder even hired the Petaluma planning director as its own.

As in Petaluma, public facility capacity is not the basis for the Boulder growth limit. In a court challenge to a related city policy (but not to the growth management program itself), the Colorado Supreme Court sustained a lower court ruling that required the city to provide sewer and water service to land outside the city limits for which the city had denied service on the basis of its growth policy.[4] The case is discussed in Kelly (1976). There was no indication in the findings in the case that the city was unable to serve the developer. The Boulder program remains in effect in 1992. As in Petaluma, actual growth in the city has remained below the rate permitted by the program (see Table 4.2). Although there growth has shifted to other areas of the county, the total growth in the county has also remained below the city's 2 percent annual growth goal.

Presumably a program like the one in the Evergreen Area of San Jose, in which public officials adjust the growth limit annually, based on actual capacity, should be tied more closely to actual service capacities. Perhaps the one in Evergreen is. However, in observing a similar system in operation in San Juan Capistrano, Dubbink noted that a technical report prepared by the local planning staff seemed to be largely irrelevant to the actual decision about growth allocation for the year:

My impression was that the technical findings of the report had long been eclipsed by the hours of public hearings associated with setting San Juan's yearly growth quota. This seemed to be an essentially political event where the unrest of the protectionists was balanced against the unrest of those with land to develop and the costs of extending services was balanced against the cost of litigation for withholding them (Dubbink 1983, p. 129).

It is interesting that Boulder and Petaluma have taken separate but similar steps to simplify their programs. Both originally included "merit" reviews, in which development projects competed for scarce permits through complex and comprehensive reviews that awarded "points" for quality of architectural design, site planning, energy conservation and a multitude of other issues, with building opportunities in tight years allocated to those projects achieving the most points (see, generally, James Duncan and Associates and Kelly 1991a; the Boulder point program is described in Cooper 1986). Both Boulder and Petaluma amended their programs in the 1980s to simple proration programs, requiring very little administration and greatly reducing the burden on private developers. Under the simplified programs, each city simply divides the available permits in a particular period prorata among the competing developers.

In a question-and-answer format in its *Residential Growth Management System: User's Guide,* Petaluma noted succinctly that: "The biggest difference between the present system and its predecessor is the elimination of the point system used to rate projects to determine whether or not they qualified for allotments. That process had become a burden for both staff and the developer, and had been regularly criticized for being too subjective in its scoring procedure" (Petaluma, City of 1991, not paginated, Chapter 3, answer to question 2).

A background memorandum prepared by the Boulder planning director to explain the revised program to the Boulder City Council, similarly noted that the pro-rated allocation method was a change "made at Planning Board, based upon the almost unanimous support for the sole use of the prorated method by the building community" (Gawf 1985, p. 1). A Boulder builder, complaining of the "hassle involved, . . . the time to process a development, [and] the complexity of the ordinances," helps to explain the support for the simpler program in comments about the old program:

The growth control ordinance tries to deal with issues of quality in a quantitative way—by putting numbers on things and saying, "You can only do this and that at this or that rate." It is impossible to deal with qualitative issues in a quantitative way; this practice, quite simply, detracts from good planning. The experience in Boulder has been that the planning department has deteriorated in quality because it has had to concentrate on counting numbers and on administering a highly bureaucratic system. Boulder's is not a lousy planning department—its staff members are good planners. Perhaps under the newest system, they will even be able to get back to planning (Leach 1986, p. 35).[5]

Clearly the political and philosophical basis for a rate-of-growth program is quite different from the pragmatic ones that lead to adoption of adequate public facilities controls. The author of the original Boulder program noted in an article that

The first attempt to pass a growth control ordinance in Boulder came about in 1971, when the Boulder chapter of Zero Population Growth (ZPG) put a proposed dwelling-unit cap of 40,000 to a vote by the initiative process. This move sufficiently frightened the prevailing local establishment that the latter persuaded the city council to put an alternative advisory question on the ballot, urging the city government to keep the growth rate "substantially below the rates experienced during the 1960s" (Danish 1986, p. 27).

It is interesting, but not particularly surprising, to note that this proposal from Zero Population Growth in Boulder came at a time when the studies for the Club of Rome Report (Meadows et al. 1972) and the Douglas Commission Report (Commission on Population Growth and the American Future 1972) were under way and just a year before Finkler's publications on "non-growth" planning options appeared (1972, 1973). The timing of this early proposal, as well as the ultimate program itself, illustrates the significant difference in apparent motivations behind rate-of-growth programs and other growth management programs that are more clearly based on community growth capacity. Although Boulder voters did not pass "the Danish plan," as it was often called, until 1976 and although it sprang from the roots of the city's own advisory question on the 1971 ballot and not from the ZPG proposal, the concerns addressed were clearly the same: the actual rate of growth or change in the community. Even if there was plenty of water and a substantial excess of sewage treatment capacity, the majority of people in Boulder simply felt that a 5 percent annual growth rate represented too much change (note that this is half the annual growth rate that preceded the adoption of the Petaluma program). Although any growth management program is likely to slow the rate of growth at certain times, Snyder (1982) illustrated the difference between the types of programs. In contrasting Westminster and Boulder, twenty miles to the north, he found continuing acceleration in the rate of growth during the early years of the Westminster program and a dramatic slowing of the rate of growth in the early years of the Boulder program (pp. 286–288).

COMPREHENSIVE PROGRAMS

Most of the programs cited so far, and in fact most of the programs in effect, are not comprehensive programs of managing community change but single regulatory tools directed at particular local issues. The Boulder and Petaluma programs address the rate-of-growth issue without particular regard to the availability of public facilities, while adequate public facilities controls address only the public facilities issues. The programs in San Jose, Boulder, Livermore, and Petaluma regulate only residential growth.

Although some of these programs operate as part of a larger plan, many do not. A 1991 national survey of seventeen communities (an eighteenth was the control) regarded as "growth management communities" found that

- only three of them had both development timing requirements and adequate public facilities ordinances (Boulder, Livermore, and Westminster);
- three of the communities had neither;
- two had only development timing controls, and nine had only adequate public facilities controls;
- the control community, Montgomery County, Maryland, had both (James Duncan and Associates and Kelly 1991c).

Note that the response of Livermore to the question was somewhat deceptive, because its development timing control *is* its adequate public facilities ordinance. Thus from the surveyed group, a group identified as communities with some sort of active growth management program, only Westminster, Boulder, and Montgomery County clearly had programs with both adequate public facilities and development timing elements in 1991; in Boulder, the timing requirements apply only to residential uses, although in Westminster and Montgomery County they apply to most land uses.

Boulder provides a useful illustration. The city council adopted its adequate public facilities requirements separately from the growth management program in 1977, and they remain separate from the growth management program (James Duncan and Associates and Kelly 1991c). The city has engaged in joint planning with Boulder County for more than two decades. It has actively used its control of crucial public facilities in fringe areas as a control tool (see, generally, early discussion of *Robinson* and Chapter 5; as well as specific discussions of Boulder in Gleeson et al. 1975, pp. 10–11; also, Cooper 1986; Lewis 1990). It has also invested millions of dollars of dedicated sales tax revenues in the acquisition of a large greenbelt around the community, to halt urban sprawl and to limit the encroach-ment of other communities into the area (Cooper 1986; also, Walker 1978; program described in last section of Chapter 5).

The Westminster program is the simpler of the two comprehensive growth management programs. It measures the capacity of the com-munity to provide service at a given time in "service commitments"— one service commitment being equal to the system demand imposed by a single-family detached home. The city council, on the basis of recommendations of staff, annually determines the capacity of the city to provide service for the following year and then allocates that capacity among six categories of potentially competing users: (A) active residential projects; (B) other residential projects; (C) nonresi-dential projects; (D) service contracts with users outside the city; (E) other projects, including government-sponsored housing and some very small project exceptions; and (F) contingency and public use (Westminster, City of 1990).

The city created the two categories of residential uses in the origi-nal program in 1977 to give preference to partially-built but still-active projects, for three reasons: first, developers of such projects clearly had the most current commitment to their projects and thus would suffer the greatest harm if stopped; second, such developers were the most certain to use the allocations promptly, thus providing needed "tap fee" revenues to the city; and, third, the city wanted to reduce as rapidly as possible the backlog of approved but partially-built projects (see, generally, earlier discussion, and Westminster, City of 1978b; Kelly 1982). Category E included in the program a reserve for allocations that are the subject of exemptions in other programs such as those in Boulder and Petaluma. Within Category C, economic base industries received a high priority. Snyder (1982) found several years later that Westminster had achieved significant success in attracting new jobs (pp. 219–222).

In Westminster, as in Petaluma and Boulder, growth pressures from the mid-1980s into the early 1990s fell far below those of the past and thus below the growth permitted under the programs; thus, the program has not been subject to significant recent pressure. Like the programs in Petaluma, Ramapo, and elsewhere, however, it was challenged in court. The city won in each of the challenges (for dis-cussion of all the challenges, see Kelly 1982; the principal case was decided by the Colorado Supreme Court in 1982).[6]

Unlike many other communities involved in growth management, Montgomery County, Maryland, containing a number of northwest-ern suburbs of Washington, D.C., continued to grow rapidly through the 1980s and into the 1990s. The county thus continued to test the limits of its growth management program.

The "annual growth policy" is the key to the Montgomery County program. The county's planning board adopted the first such policy in 1974 (Montgomery County Planning Board). That policy document noted that it followed by ten years the adoption of a general plan intended "to provide for consolidated development with the least amount of sprawl, the most coordinated form of transportation, and the most accessible open space" (p. 34). It also noted that an adequate public facilities ordinance already applied to the subdivision process and that a limited "staging" (phasing) concept applied to plans for individual communities (p. 38). However, the 1974 report represented the first comprehensive approach to addressing growth in the booming suburban area. Serious limitations on sewage treatment capacity were a major concern in Montgomery County then, with additional capacity not expected to come on line for four years or more (pp. 52–53, 107–112). The report noted the existence of separate sewer capacity allocation policies and commented, "In summary, it seems reasonable to conclude that much of the growth rate of the suburban ring nodes in the next six years will be dependent upon whatever sewer allocation policy is established for the Rock Creek interim plant" (p. 111).

Although the later growth policy documents served as regulatory tools, the original one really updated the general plan. It reaffirmed the three goals of the plan:

(1) To channel the bulk of long-range growth in the County to the I-270 corridor in the form of satellite cities which have both jobs and housing in a balanced ratio and which reduce travel demands.

(2) To focus a more limited amount of growth in "nodal" areas, or activity centers, within the suburban ring.

(3) To build a network of bus and rail transit lines to serve movements through this area and, in so doing, to reduce traffic congestion and air pollution (p. 117).

To implement those policies, it outlined a series of recommendations for both regulation and capital investment by the county. It specifically recommended construction of major highways and of the Rockville treatment plant because, "Improving access to the corridor is the prime requisite to make it attractive to new jobs, and job increases there are the key to achievement of a balanced growth pattern in the corridor that can lessen auto travel needs and take the pressure off the suburban ring nodes" (p. 125).

The growth policy again acknowledged that most growth in the near future would take place in the area in which the county was allocating sewer capacity and thus recommended transit and other improvements in that area in order to accommodate the inevitable growth in ways compatible with the plan (pp. 125–126). Finally, the policy recommended increased coordination among governmental agencies influencing and serving growth—including multiple county agencies (pp. 127–135).

From that early planning document, Montgomery County has developed its annual growth policy into a sophisticated and complex regulatory tool. Simply adopting the policy is a relatively complex process that begins nine or ten months before a new policy will become effective. The county bases its capital investments on the growth policies, but the capital improvements program itself also affects the allocation of growth within the county (see, generally, Montgomery County Planning Board 1990b, pp. 13–20).

The growth management program divides the county into seventeen policy areas, and the annual policies phase growth differently for each area, on the basis of its capacity to absorb growth and other policy considerations. A key element in the program is the "staging ceiling" for each policy area, defined by the county as "the maximum amount of land development that can be accommodated by the existing and programmed public facilities serving the area, at an assigned level of service standard" (Montgomery County Planning Board 1990a, p. 4). Simply put, in computing public facilities capacity under its adequate public facilities policies, the county considers not only existing facilities but also those that the county has included in its adopted capital improvements program. That is a realistic policy approach, because development of most proposed projects will occur over a period of months or years after the approval date and such projects thus do not require all facility capacities immediately.

According to the *FY92 Annual Growth Policy*, as adopted by the planning board, the annual policy "tests the adequacy of four types of facilities: transportation; schools; water and sewerage facilities; and police, fire and health services" (Montgomery County Planning Board 1990b, p. 3). Sewer service was the most scarce resource and thus the critical determinant of the location of new growth in the original 1974 program, but by 1992 transportation had become the key element countywide (see, generally, Clancy 1986).

Another major element of the annual growth policy is a section establishing policies for the administration of the adequate public facilities requirements. Although such guidelines may not be necessary for sewer and water facilities, for which engineering computations can determine capacities, they are essential for other facilities for which the determination of capacity involves policy judgments. For example, a traffic level that is totally unacceptable in one community may be entirely acceptable in another, because the second community is willing to tolerate stop-and-go traffic at rush hour and the first is not. Montgomery County, for example, is willing to accept heavier projected traffic loads on roads near transit stations. Such a policy serves two purposes: it acknowledges that people driving to the train create local traffic, although they help to reduce regional traffic; second, and perhaps more important, it creates a situation in which road conditions make the use of mass transit more attractive.

Although raising some concerns about a new requirement for traffic impact projections for some development, a developer termed the Montgomery County program "strict but reasonable, and a known quantity" (Clancy 1986, p. 97).

There is more to the Montgomery County program than the pieces described here. The county implements its planning program, of which the growth policy is a major part, through a series of sector plans (for geographic sectors) and local master plans within the separate cities in the county. The 1992 growth policy itself identified interrelationships among a total of eight different sets of county policies: land use policy, economic policy, housing policy, transportation policy, community facilities policy, natural resources policy, social policy, and fiscal policy.

The county also has a program of traditional planning in established communities and an aggressive program to protect agricultural land. In Montgomery County, as in Boulder, the growth management program is simply one piece of a complex array of planning and development controls (Hamblen 1991).

No single growth management or other land use control technique can address all of the concerns of a rapidly growing community. Thus, a few communities with serious commitments to managed growth have adopted comprehensive programs consisting of multiple coordinated techniques addressing all types of new development.

THE ROLE OF EXACTIONS

"Make growth pay its own way" is a call heard perhaps more often than "manage growth" among citizens concerned with rising taxes and, in many cases, declining levels of service. In response to that call and to a variety of local fiscal pressures, by the early 1990s most local governments in growing areas had adopted broad policies for "exactions" through which developers are required to pay for the infrastructure improvements required by new growth.

Although most local governments have long required developers to pay for such on-site improvements as street paving and utility lines within a subdivision, exaction requirements go further. They may require that a developer improve a road leading up to a site or a drainage way leading away from it. Traffic impact analyses may lead to requests (or demands) that a developer install a traffic light at an intersection near the development project or construct adjacent turning lanes to improve access into and out of the development. Through *impact fees* (the most common term, although there are many others), a community may assess a developer for a share of a larger facility, such as a major arterial roadway or a new sewer plant.

Clearly the subjects of exactions and growth management overlap in principle, in politics, and in practice. A comprehensive growth management program can and should include rational policies on exactions. However, far more communities have exaction policies than have growth management policies, and the two are typically adopted and administered separately.

Exactions, of course, have their own effects on urban form, the fiscal position of the municipality, and the availability of public facilities. Operationally those are quite separate, and sometimes quite different, from the effects of growth management. For example, a community may have an impact fee policy related to roads and also an adequate public facilities standard related to roads. Simply paying the impact fee may not guarantee the developer that there is sufficient road capacity to permit the proposed project, because financing of the project may depend on the payment of such fees by several developers.

The literature on exactions is broad. Some starting points for one who is interested would include books edited by Robinson (1990) and by Frank and Rhodes (1987). Nelson (1988) edited a comprehensive work on impact fees. Not everyone accepts exactions enthusiastically, in significant part because of the tendency for them to increase housing costs (see, generally, Babcock 1987).

OTHER REGULATORY TECHNIQUES

This chapter describes four major regulatory types of growth controls: adequate public facilities requirements, rate-of-growth controls, urban growth boundaries, and growth phasing regulations—along with examples of more comprehensive programs that include elements of more than one of those techniques.

Some analysts include more techniques under the general heading of "growth management." Schiffman listed twenty-six, including a number of zoning techniques, some nonregulatory techniques such as those discussed in the next chapter, and some other regulatory techniques that are simply not included here (1989). This book is limited to actions intended to direct the timing or location of growth or both. Other sources provide a thorough treatment of zoning and other regulatory techniques that can affect the quality of growth (see, generally, So and Getzels, 1988, and sources cited there).

LATER LITERATURE

The later (post-1975) literature is in some ways not as interesting as the early literature. There were several dissertations, a dozen or so books, and a large number of articles. Several provided useful case studies. Others updated the early literature. A few contained some interesting evaluative material (discussed separately in Chapters 7 through 11). What has been surprisingly missing from the later literature is any sort of comprehensive look at growth management programs in general and how those programs affect the communities that adopt them. That deficiency was noted repeatedly in papers offered at a conference on research needs in the field (Brower, Godschalk, and Porter 1989).

The Urban Land Institute continued its series of publications on the subject. It included in the series a 1976 publication on the complexities of the regulatory process (Bosselman, Feurer, and Siemon 1976), although for reasons that are not clear it reserved the next volume number in the series for a later publication. The Institute published Volume 4 in the Management & Control of Growth series in 1978 with the subtitle, *Techniques in Application* (Schnidman, Silverman, and Young). That book, like the earlier ones in the series, contained a series of useful essays on various aspects of growth management. Innovative approaches to land use management, many of them quite separate from growth management, were the subject of the first section of the book. Other sections covered practical aspects of administering growth management, fiscal impact analysis, environmental issues, and, in a brief section, the implications of growth management for housing.

In 1979, ULI published *Growth and Change in Rural America,* a thoughtful analysis of the demographic, economic and other changes taking place in non-metropolitan areas (Fuguitt, Voss, and Doherty). It included some recommendations for improvement under the general heading of "growth management" (pp. 75–90). However, as in some later studies, the authors used the phrase broadly and included within that chapter tax incentives, infrastructure investment policies, land purchases, innovative zoning tools, and, interestingly, mobile home regulation (pp. 88–89).

Although the ULI discontinued the designation of books as parts of the Management & Control of Growth series after 1979, it published additions to the collection in 1986 and 1989. The 1986 book, *Growth Management: Keeping on Target?* was clearly an update of the earlier studies (Porter). It revisited several of the communities included in the earlier studies (Petaluma, Boulder, Boca Raton, and Montgomery County) and added some new ones. It included a broader look at the social and equity issues involved in growth management than any of the earlier reports. One of the most interesting parts of the book was a short but thoughtful essay by Paul Niebanck (pp. 215–216) in which he assessed the benefits and "byproducts" of growth management. He noted great concern about one particular byproduct, summarized here. "Most dramatically, the decline in residential opportunity for poor people, for people of color, and, yes, for middle-class people, resulting from the decidedly negative effects of growth management on housing prices" (Niebanck 1986, p. 216).

Three years later, ULI published *Understanding Growth Management: Critical Issues and a Research Agenda,* based on papers from a September 1988 conference sponsored by ULI and the Center for Urban and Regional Studies at the University of North Carolina, Chapel Hill (Brower, Godschalk, and Porter 1989). As the title suggests, the focus of the book was on what society does not know about growth management and the need for further research. Most striking perhaps is the fundamental question left open, as stated by one of the participants. "Moreover, despite the plethora of Boulder studies, there has been no research analyzing whether Boulder is a better place to live as a result of its growth management program" (Godschalk and Brower 1989, p. 162).

In the same publication, in a concluding chapter outlining a proposed research agenda, Porter noted that quality of life as an area of research "has hardly been touched" (Porter 1989, p. 187). He went on to note that the field even lacks measurable standards for quality of life, in order to provide the basis of a study. In a chapter called "The ecology of 'quality of life' and urban growth," Myers noted that "the poor state of knowledge about quality of life has hampered negotiations about growth management" (1989, p. 87) and that, because "few can agree on its definition . . . it is very difficult to measure quality of life in any comprehensive fashion" (p. 87).

The principal post-1975 contribution of the American Society of Planning Officials and its successor, the American Planning Association, to the library of books on growth management was an excellent introductory legal work entitled *Constitutional Issues of Growth Management* (Godschalk et al. 1977). Developed as a teaching tool, it included a dozen illustrative case studies, with clear and careful discussions of the law related to each. It also included a good discussion of the policy issues involved in growth management, noting that, "In the final analysis, growth management plans will be judged by the people of the region and, in some cases, by the courts. Each plan will be looked at in terms of its impact on a particular local and regional situation and in terms of its internal logic and consistency" (p. 218). The authors provided three guidelines for effective growth management plans:

- Methods employed for benchmark technical studies, impact analyses, and plan making should be systematic, rigorous, and replicable.
- Internal consistency of growth management approaches is as important as accuracy. There must be a clear relationship between the findings of the basic studies, the public purposes to be served, the plan adopted, and the regulations used to carry out the plan.
- Explicitness is a third fundamental for growth management plans. . . . such plans cannot afford to be broad-brush, general collections of possible futures (pp. 218–219).

The International City Management Association published another collection of essays, edited by John DeGrove (1991). It consisted almost entirely of short articles on major programs, most of them originally published in popular and trade journals like *Planning* and *Governing.* Although the collection included no new analytical material, it did include a useful, if somewhat disjointed, collection of articles on current issues in the field.

One work likely to be listed in the catalog of works in this field should probably not be there. Schiffman's short book, *Alternative Techniques for Managing Growth* (1989), might more appropriately be called *A Land Use Controls Primer.* It provides a succinct introduction to a variety of land use control techniques, ranging from zoning to historic preservation. It is a useful book, but it deals only peripherally with growth management as defined in this book.

This period saw the publication of a number of significant works on the state role in growth management. Chapter 6 includes its own literature review and citations to works on that subject; those are not repeated here. However, two are worthy of particular note. Robert Healy wrote an in-depth analysis of the state role in land use, first published in 1976 and updated by Healy and John Rosenberg in 1979. The two overlap considerably. Both provide a broad examination of the role of the state in land use and in depth analyses of the statewide programs in Vermont and Florida and the coastal zone program in California.

Popper also contributed an interesting work to the literature on the state role in planning and growth management in 1981. It contained the broadest policy analysis since that of Bosselman and Callies (1971). It also included a short section on the politics of state land use control.

Several dissertations examined particular growth management

programs in depth. Abe provided a rather cursory review of the state of growth management and a very brief look at the Petaluma program in her 1977 dissertation at the Claremont Graduate School. In his 1982 dissertation at Colorado State University, Snyder suggested an evaluation of state efforts ("An Evaluation of Colorado's Attempts to Cope with Rapid Growth") but actually offered an interesting and useful comparison of the growth management programs in Boulder and Westminster. He examined both the political and the practical aspects of the programs and reviewed data on their effectiveness after approximately five years of experience in Westminster and nearly ten years in Boulder.

Knaap made a careful analysis of the effects of the Portland urban growth boundary on land prices (1982) and subsequently adapted the material into an article (1985). Others have cited his work extensively (see, for example, Fischel 1990, pp. 23–24), and it provides the basis for some of the analysis in Chapter 9 of this book.

Dubbink first encountered growth management as a regional environmental planner for the California Coastal Commission (1983, p. 26). He later completed doctoral work and prepared a dissertation on growth management in one of the communities with which he had previously worked, Bolinas, and one with which he had no prior experience, San Juan Capistrano. He based the dissertation largely on personal interviews, attempting to find the motives of those implementing growth management programs, as well as some of the results. His analysis balances empathy for the subjects of his study with a critical view of the results of their efforts. He concluded that growth management largely represented futile preservation efforts of newcomers to semirural communities. He characterized the results as "anti-suburb suburbs." Because of its broad perspective, it is a particularly important contribution to the literature.

For a 1986 dissertation for the University of California at Berkeley, Greenberg conducted an extremely thorough analysis of the growth management programs of Livermore and other communities in the Amador valley. It provided a detailed history of the ups and downs of growth management politics in several communities that share a geographical location but differ greatly in their politics. The comparative political histories were particularly interesting.

A later academic contribution to the field came in the form of a working paper prepared by LeGates and Nikas for the Public Research Institute at San Francisco State University (1989). It provided a review of eleven different growth management programs in effect in cities and counties in the Bay Area. All fell within the definition of growth management used in this book. The authors also provided one of the few attempts prior to this book to place the programs in categories. The categories there ("flexible systems, point systems, first come first served systems, and flexible criteria systems") seem less descriptive and thus less useful than those proposed in this book, but the effort of the authors to compare particular programs to similar programs in other communities is very useful.

Glickfeld and Levine, in a study sponsored by the Lincoln Institute of Land Policy, prepared a statistical analysis of the demographic and other characteristics of communities adopting growth management programs in California (1992). Although their definition of "growth management" included standard zoning techniques such as building height limits, the study provides useful demographic data on growth managing communities.

Researchers at the University of California at Berkeley contributed a number of working papers on growth management issues in the late 1980s and early 1990s. Particularly notable is a 1991 contribution of Landis. A problem with his work in using it to analyze programs in other jurisdictions is that his working definition of growth management is one that this author would apply to land use controls. It included zoning and subdivision controls, fees, and annexation and infrastructure policies (p. 5). Works by Teitz and Innes from the same Berkeley series are cited earlier under later literature on the state role (Innes 1991b).

A number of articles and books on particular aspects of land use control, such as housing policy, joined the literature in this period. The topical chapters that follow include appropriate references to significant literature on those topics. Although there has been surprisingly little literature that attempts to provide any sort of broad evaluation of growth management efforts, the last chapter cites a substantial portion of what exists. Short reports by Landis (1991) and Fischel (1990) are particularly noteworthy, as is a brief article by Benjamin Chinitz (1990).

CONCLUSION

Each of the four growth management techniques addresses somewhat different community concerns and has somewhat different effects.

Adequate public facilities requirements directly control the impacts of development on public facilities and ensure that capacity will be available to serve new development as it occurs. Such requirements indirectly phase growth because they make development most feasible in areas that already have most urban services, generally areas contiguous to existing development; for that reason, such requirements help to reduce sprawl. However, in many communities, some (or many) public facilities are available in locations relatively remote from the community or areas that for other reasons may be low on the list of the community's priorities for development. Adequate public facilities requirements will not prevent development in such locations, nor will they halt development in a high-growth market in any location to which developers can afford to pay most of the costs of extending facilities.

Growth phasing programs directly control the timing of growth in particular locations, generally based on the availability of public facilities. Such a program can be used to reduce sprawl and is more likely to be effective in reducing sprawl than are adequate public facilities standards. However, as the examples illustrate, growth phasing programs used alone may result in the approval of projects for which most facilities are available but for which some are not.

Urban growth boundaries most effectively define the limits of urban growth and thus create a clear delineation between developed and undeveloped lands. Although such boundaries reduce contiguous sprawl, they may, if too tightly drawn, promote leapfrog development.

Rate-of-growth programs, which are the least common of the types discussed here, directly regulate the community's growth rate without particular regard to capacity. Development under such a program may occur more slowly, or more quickly, than public facility capacities would otherwise permit. Such a program does not necessarily control the location of development, and it may or may not affect the pattern of urban growth.

These regulatory techniques are analyzed in subsequent chapters of the book, together with the nonregulatory techniques presented in Chapter 5.

NOTES

1. Colo. Rev. Stat. Sec. 30-28-133(6).

2. *Associated Homebuilders of Greater Eastbay, Inc.,* v. *City of Livermore,* 18 Cal3d 582, 135 Cal Rptr 41, 557 P2d 473 (1976).

3. *Reed* v. *Planning and Zoning Commission of Chester,* 208 Conn 431, 544 A2d 1213 (1988).

4. *Robinson* v. *City of Boulder,* 190 Colo 357, 547 P2d 228 (1976); the lower court opinion, which rejected a challenge to the original, "interim" growth policy, is reproduced at pp. 237–252 in Scott, Brower, and Miner 1975b.

5. The publication date is deceptive; the article was based on remarks made at a 1985 conference. The context of the article, including the last sentence included in the quotation, make it clear that the quoted remarks are about the old system that had been replaced by the prorated system some months before the conference.

6. *P. W. Investments* v. *City of Westminster,* 655 P2d 1365 (Colo 1982).

5

Nonregulatory Techniques to Manage Growth

Some of the most important activities that control the rate, timing, and location of growth by a local government entail actions outside the exercise of its regulatory powers. The most common nonregulatory such activity is spending money. The annexation of territory or the purchase of land is also an activity that, from the perspective of a local government, does not involve its regulatory powers. This chapter includes several such activities under the general heading of nonregulatory techniques. These techniques may, of course, be regulated by other levels of government; few activities in the contemporary United States are totally free of regulation. However, from the perspective of the actor, these activities are not regulatory.

Activities described in this chapter include building new highways and sewer lines, agreeing to make land part of a city through annexation, and purchasing strategically located land to prevent or control its development.

ANNEXATION

Annexation is the process through which a city or other municipal government expands its territorial boundaries. As Galloway and Landis concluded, "Throughout the 1970s, as earlier, municipal annexation was the primary means by which local governments, particularly those in metropolitan areas, regulated their physical expansion" (1986, p. 41).

The purpose of annexation finds its roots in the structure of American local government, discussed briefly in Chapter 1. Citing North Carolina law, a 1989 study noted that the express purpose of annexation is to "make municipal that which is urban" (Mumphrey, Wildgen, and Williams 1990). Although all territory within a state is subject to the jurisdiction of some form of local government, local governments vary greatly in their purpose and authority. In the majority of states, the form of local government with jurisdiction over the largest land areas is the county (Louisiana's parishes are similar). The county was created as a branch of state government, the county courthouse serving as the local office for a variety of state functions when, lacking twentieth-century transportation and communications systems, residents found the state capital relatively inaccessible (see, generally, Sands and Libonati 1981, sects. 2.13, 8.01; Sengstock 1985, pp. 1–9). Counties continue to handle such state operations as maintaining land records, assessing property for taxation, registering voters, serving legal process (through the sheriff), building and maintaining roads, managing social service (welfare) programs, and registering vehicles. All these require, or at least function better with, some degree of geographical convenience to citizens, something unavailable if the services are offered only from the state capitol.

Some county officials who are elected by county residents have express duties to the state; the sheriff and, in many states, the local prosecuting attorney are primary examples. Judges, who are often housed in the county courthouse, are typically officers of the state, not the county (Sands and Libonati 1981, sect. 8.01).

Counties in most states have been given at least limited authority over their own territory. For example, the authority for county zoning and subdivision control in the "unincorporated" territory is common. However, counties in most states lack general ordinance (local lawmaking) power and the authority to operate a police force. Although counties in some states have the authority to offer such urban services as street lighting, sanitary sewer, and potable water service, counties in others do not. Further, even where counties have such authority, there are difficulties in implementation. If a county has an urbanized area next to a city within its general jurisdiction, it faces conflicting pressures regarding service and equity. Should it provide sewer, water, street lighting, and police services throughout the county in order to accommodate the needs of residents of the urbanized area; provide different levels of service in the two areas and attempt to adjust for the differences through user fees or other fiscal policies; or continue to function largely as a rural form of government, offering few if any municipal services? Although some counties have elected to provide significant urban services, the reasons for not doing so are many.

Thus, new development typically occurs within the boundaries of municipalities. Many municipalities have significant undeveloped areas within their borders. New development may take place on such land. In some cases it may be possible for a developer or group of developers to incorporate a new municipality (see discussion in Mumphrey, Wildgen, and Williams 1990, p. 15; also in Rahenkamp 1991). It is more difficult for a developer to incorporate a new municipality in states like California that provide rigorous administrative or quasi-legislative review of proposed incorporations (Mehay 1981).

However, an easy way for a developer to ensure the availability of urban services is through annexation to an existing municipality. Not surprisingly, a detailed study of the motives behind annexations in two cities found that a substantial number were initiated by "builders and Realtors" (Fleischmann 1986, p. 133). That study found that 25 percent of the requests for annexation to Milwaukee over a thirty-year period and 42 percent of such requests to the City of San Antonio were initiated by builders and Realtors. Why do developers want territory annexed? To obtain urban services. Fleischmann cited the desire for services as a recurrent theme and found that in virtually all cases there was in fact an increase in services after annexation. The desire for services is a perfectly logical motivation for developers (see Goldberg and Ulinder 1976 and material presented later in this section).

A municipality initiates or consents to annexation for a variety of reasons: to ensure the availability of land for future development or to secure an improved tax base. In their study of annexations to Charlotte, North Carolina, Mumphrey, Wildgen and Williams found that annexation in fact improved the public fiscal circumstances, resulting in reduced taxes with a steady level of services (1990). Gonzalez and Mehay reached a similar conclusion in a broader study (1987), although Coe noted that not every annexation has a positive fiscal impact (1983). The existence of property tax rate limits may accelerate municipal desires to annex (Johnson 1989). Sales tax revenues from new commercial development also provide significant motivation to annex territory in states where local governments receive a portion of sales tax revenues directly.

Some annexations are defensive in the sense that the best defense is a good offense. Thus, annexation wars in growing metropolitan areas may lead to annexation of increased amounts of territory, perhaps far beyond current needs to absorb development (see, generally, Johnson 1989, pp. 39–42; for data about an example, see Westminster, City of 1978b). A city may also annex territory simply to assert zoning and regulatory control—to ensure that such high-impact uses as feedlots, adult entertainment establishments, or salvage yards are not established on the urban fringe without municipal control. Such an annexation may be necessary because the county either lacks land use control authority or has not exercised it or because different political values in the county may lead to decisions different from those the city might like. Such a protective annexation is less necessary in states that permit some form of "extraterritorial" zoning or land use control, allowing a city to assert regulatory control along its borders without annexing the territory.

What does all this have to do with growth management? A great deal. If a developer needs or wants annexation in order to obtain municipal services, a denial of annexation may leave a proposed development without urban services and consequently unbuilt. The corollary is that annexation in many cases makes development a good deal more likely. Once territory has been annexed to a city, the city may as a matter of course provide urban services. In some states, property owners and potential developers have a right to demand services similar to those provided in other areas of the same city. Politically it is difficult for a city not to provide services to an area that has been paying city taxes. For these and other reasons, Stahura and Marshall concluded that "It is likely that suburbs which annex territory acquire the space for residential development which attracts in-migrants" (1982. p. 21).

Thus, simply by constraining its borders, a municipality may be able to influence significantly the location of growth around it. That concept forms the basis of state growth management programs in Hawaii and Oregon (see Chapter 6), but it also provides a lesson for other communities. Refusing to expand territorial boundaries, however, may have little effect on urban form if there are other communities nearby and if one of them is willing to annex territory rejected by another.

Annexation policy can be an effective growth management tool, but it is not one that falls entirely under local control. According to Galloway and Landis, only Idaho, Nebraska, and North Carolina allow unilateral municipal annexation. Six other states give the municipality control subject to consent of the annexed area, and three more give the municipality control subject to consent of both the annexed area and the municipality. Five states require judicial review of annexation proposals, while ten others have quasi-legislative bodies that review annexations against stated criteria. Sixteen states require a vote of the people for annexation, and five require an act of the legislature (1986, p. 32; their classification of types of procedures was based on the earlier work of Sengstock [1985]).

DeGrove found the cumbersome annexation procedure in Washington to be a significant impediment to the state's growth management strategy. Although the state's policy of urbanization and use of "urban growth boundaries" suggest that most development should take place within city limits, the "triple majority" requirement of state law makes annexation very difficult by requiring approval by a majority of the residents of an area, a majority of the land parcels involved, and a majority of the assessed valuation involved (1984, p. 271).

Although a municipality does not exercise complete control over annexation matters, in virtually all states the municipality can prevent an annexation by refusing to approve it; only in the five states where the legislature makes the determination does the system create a mechanism that can force territory on a community, and such an action seems unlikely even in those states. In other states, the annexation process includes an act of the municipal governing body. If the governing body does not approve the annexation, the proposal goes no further. The additional procedures in those states simply provide an outside review or veto on annexations by a municipality. Thus, in most states a municipal government retains the key element of control of annexation, and that is the power to say no.

Limiting the amount of annexation will not automatically limit the growth of a community. However, careful management of annexation practices is an important element in an effective growth management program because extensive annexation of undeveloped territory can reduce rather than increase the degree of control a community has over the location of growth.

THE GROWTH SHAPERS

The title of this section comes from a 1976 study subtitled "the land use impacts of infrastructure investments" (Urban Systems Research & Engineering, Inc. 1976). The author was first exposed to the concept several years before that, when a realtor in southern New Jersey advised him to buy land near proposed interceptor sewer routes because "growth follows sewers." As Clawson noted, "The nominal planners are often not the real planners; sewer builders, transportation agencies, and other units of government often usurp the role assigned to the planning agency" (1971, p. 6).

An econometric model of development patterns in the Denver, Boston, Washington, and Minneapolis–St. Paul metropolitan regions during the period 1960–1970 concluded that "public investments in transportation and wastewater facilities have identifiable and measurable effects on urban growth" (Environmental Impact Center, Incorporated 1975, p. 67). The study suggested that from 10 to 15 percent of single-family construction was correlated with either highway or sewer construction. However, it found that in some locations, depending on other conditions, up to 40 percent of development decisions might be attributable to such investments. Other variables in the study included land availability and price, zoning and land use controls, income levels of existing residents, existing levels of access, and sewer service and vacancy rates. The impact of sewer investments in the study is particularly notable because the data all arose before the adoption of the Federal Water Pollution Control Act Amendments of 1972 (see discussion later in this section).

Growth does follow sewers and highways. Although it may be difficult to see the effects of sewers without a map of the lines, observing the effects of highways is considerably easier. The concentrations of intense commercial activity in a ring around Washington, the concentration of development in the Denver Technological Center area south of Denver, the elliptical shape of the Des Moines metropolitan region, and the enormous growth between Dallas and Fort Worth all follow the paths of freeways built before most of the development occurred. In his detailed study of suburban growth in the San Francisco region, Dowall found that "land development in the 1950s set the pattern for the years to come. Growth spread outward along all major transportation corridors; small towns within commuting range of employment centers became major cities in a few short years" (1984, p. 17).

Construction of the Tappan Zee Bridge opened Rockland County to suburban commuting from New York, resulting in the growth pressure that led Clarkstown to adopt its early growth management program (see Figure 5.1 and Chapter 3). A decade later, in 1965, the opening of the New York State Thruway through Ramapo extended the Rockland County development pressure to that community, leading to the adoption of Ramapo's own growth management program within four years (Hammer, Siler, George 1977, p. 1).

The pattern identified in *The Growth Shapers* was not new, nor is it limited to contemporary experience. Warner described the relationship between infrastructure investment and suburban Boston development patterns in the last third of the nineteenth century. He told how the development of streetcar systems by private companies and water and sewer service by public entities made possible the private development of land in the suburbs. Transportation (streetcars) opened the area to suburban development. Water service then made that development possible, and sanitary sewer service followed development pressures. Warner described the "consequences" of the expansion of infrastructure to a suburban area covering a ten-mile

Figure 5.1
Southern Rockland County, New York, Showing Ramapo, Clarkstown, the Tappan Zee Bridge, and New York Thruway

Source: Map adapted by Jerzy Lewicki from original Rockland County Planning Department, 1991, "County of Rockland."

radius from city hall. "Once a dense merchant city clustered about an ocean port, Boston became a sprawling industrial metropolis. In 1850 it was a fairly small and unified area, by 1900 it had split into two functional parts: an industrial, commercial, and communications center packed tight against the port, and an enormous outer suburban ring of residences and industrial and commercial subcenters" (1962, p. 153).

Spengler (1930) analyzed the relationship between transit improvements and land values in New York City in the 1920s. He found the transit facilities to be a significant factor in facilitating development although he did not find a direct and certain increment in land values resulting from transit improvements. Despite some reservations, Spengler's study found essentially the same thing that other studies did half a century later, the construction of transportation improvements clearly influenced development pressures and related land values.

In addition to influencing the location of development, infrastructure investment also influences the type of development that will take place. Thus, one finds intense commercial or residential development near critical freeway interchanges and mass transit stations. Not surprisignly, an international study found a high degree of correlation between urban densities in general and use of mass transit, with a corresponding negative correlation between urban densities and highway use (Newman and Kenworthy 1989). The study made no attempt to analyze cause–effect relationships between urban form and the availability of transit facilities or highways.

The Transportation Link

There are a variety of models of the relationship between transportation and land use patterns. A 1989 study examined a number of models based in microeconomics, macroeconomics, and spatial theory and encompassing the experience in a number of countries (de la Barra 1989). Wingo (1961), whose work was cited by de la Barra, developed a model based on the premise that a consumer would spend a fixed amount on the combination of transportation and housing, including in the cost of transportation the value of commuting time. Without citing Wingo, in a work based in large part on field research, Meyer, Kain, and Wohl noted that "in urban areas, transportation expenditures and housing costs are substitutable in varying degrees" (1965, pp. 119–130). One of the clear corollaries of such a substitution model is that commuting cost must vary inversely with housing cost.

Another major, early work in this field was William Alonso's *Location and Land Use* (1964). That frequently cited book developed an economic model of urban land values, with location and the related transportation costs as key variables. Although Alonso's model shared a similar conceptual basis with that of Wingo, whom Alonso cited, the actual models were quite different. Wingo was interested in personal expenditures and Alonso in land values in general and land rents in particular. Alonso used transportation costs to project the relative value of different pieces of land. Under Alonso's model, the parcel nearer the urban center would have a higher price than a piece further from the urban center; all other things being equal, the land further from the urban center would have a value lower than the more central piece by exactly the difference in transportation costs between each piece and the urban center. Wingo's model started from the same conceptual base, but it modeled the choice of housing location for the individual consumer rather than modeling the entire local land market. That is quite a different model. However, for purposes of this book, the important factor in both is that they recognize the critical link between transportation and the use and value of land.

A simpler model than Wingo's, if indeed it can be called a model, is the transportation planner's "circle" around a city, which is not a circle at all but an "iso-time" line. A 1951 Planning Advisory Service report described the analysis of the journey to work through the use of "iso-times," each of which is a "line connecting all geographic locations which are removed from an employment center by the same distance in time by the same means of transportation" ("journey to work: relation" 1951, p. 19). Although a geographer may be interested in the distance from the center of the city, a transportation planner uses these strange lines to reflect commuting time. The iso-time lines, of course, extend outward from the center along expressways and remain closer to the center where access is not as convenient. They reflect the simple concept that commuting time is more critical than geographical distance to the commuter. Figure 5.2 shows iso-time lines on routes leading to Washington, D.C., from Montgomery County, Maryland. The figure illustrates how a highway makes land near it more accessible in minutes, even if the land is no closer to the city.

Consider the effect of opening a new freeway either under Wingo's model or a simple model that simply reflects commuting time. Under Wingo's model, the new freeway will in most cases reduce transportation time and resulting cost, thus making areas along that route more desirable for development than they previously were. Existing housing along the route would, presumably, rise in value as market forces restore equilibrium; this notion derives easily from Alonso's model, if one substitutes the more critical time for the distance that he used for the sake of simplicity. More important, the undeveloped land along that route would become economically attractive for development. It is obvious that the new road changes the travel-time curves, reducing travel times to some areas and making them more attractive for development.

All this explanation may belabor the obvious. In a busy society, convenience is critical. Chains of convenience stores and fast-food restaurants profit greatly by catering to the desire of consumers to save time. Clearly, a new road link that increases the accessibility of

Figure 5.2
Montgomery County, Maryland, Commuting Times to Washington, D.C.

Source: Map from Montgomery County Planning Department, 1987, *Alternative Transportation Scenarios and Staging Ceilings: A Background Report for the FY89 AGP*, unnumbered map at p. 212 (original credits Douglas & Douglas, Inc., Gorove/Slade Associates, Inc., and Dynamic Concepts, Inc.)

an area, particularly when measured in commuting time, will significantly influence the behavior of developers and of the consumers whom they ultimately serve.

Sewer and Water Service

The relationship between sewer lines and land development patterns is perhaps simpler to explain, if somewhat less obvious, than the relationship between highways and development.

Although few homeowners are likely to inquire about the availability of sewer lines when selecting a new residence, most prospective homeowners buy residences from entities that do concern themselves with such things. A 1975 study summed up the relationship succinctly:

Residential development is dependent on the availability of essential public services. Sewerage, along with highways and water supply, is among the most capital intensive of these services and, therefore, is frequently the most in demand. In the past, the provision of interceptor sewers often trailed behind other services because of low political priorities for environmental quality. Developers of residential housing dealt with the problem of waste disposal through the provision of septic tanks, local package treatment systems, or discharges of raw sewage into local receiving waters.

In recent years, rising public concern for environmental quality has led to strict new water quality regulations. Ad hoc solutions to the pollution problems of new residential development have been severely restricted through the enforcement of zoning restrictions on septic tank use, bans on new connections to existing collection sewer systems, and requirements for advanced wastewater treatment. As a result of these environmental standards, the lack of sewerage has become a real bottleneck to development and, in some localities, has halted residential construction (Binkley et al. 1975, p. 1).

Although the quoted study was several years old when this book was written, the data and analysis included in the study postdated the landmark Federal Water Pollution Control Act Amendments of 1972 and thus remain relevant. That act marked the major national policy shift toward cleaning up the nation's waters, a policy shift destined to affect development patterns. The practical and political issues affecting the relationship between sewers and development have changed little.

The study just quoted, *Interceptor Sewers and Urban Sprawl*, found a positive correlation between excess capacity in interceptor sewers and urban sprawl (Binkley et al. 1975). The authors criticized sewer planning programs for deficiencies that included the tendency of local governments to make overly optimistic population projections. They also criticized several EPA technical requirements that tended to increase projected demand and the resulting facility size. Among the recommendations of Binkley and his colleagues was that new development should pay all capital costs incident to serving it, a policy that has now been widely implemented (see, for example, Advisory Commission on Regulatory Barriers to Affordable Housing 1991; Robinson 1990; Frank and Rhodes 1987; there is a brief discussion of this subject near the end of Chapter 4 of this book).

In a study of land values in Clay, New York, Tabors, Shapiro, and Rogers (1976) found that, all other things being equal, a parcel of land with sewer service would sell for 1.8 to 3.0 times the price of a

piece of land without it. The authors commented, "We did not determine the significance of either local roads or water or other utilities
because within Clay, these facilities already existed. Sewers were,
therefore, the final step in the process of providing required infrastructure for development" (p. 161).

Tabors and his colleagues also traced the history of sewer lines as
a control mechanism in Fairfax County, Virginia, an area which has
long felt the effects of growth around the nation's capital. A sewer
moratorium there began under a state mandate resulting from water
contamination in the area. Early in the process, the task of allocating
the limited capacity available fell entirely to the engineers, with
some participation from the board of supervisors (governing body).
Facing a growing concern among residents about the impacts of
growth, however, the county subsequently used its sewer moratorium as a method to delay growth pressures while it designed and
implemented a new "Planning and Land Use System" (Tabors, Shapiro,
and Rogers 1976, pp. 133–145; note also quotation on p. 1).

A 1989 study suggested that technology may limit the effectiveness
of sewers as a growth management tool. In their study in Wisconsin,
Hanson and Jacobs (1989) found that the improving technology of
private sewage treatment systems offers developers a practicable
alternative to public sewers, even with contemporary pollution control requirements. However, such systems are not feasible every-
where, and some state health departments are less receptive to them
than others.

The relationship between water supply and growth has received
much less study than the relationship between sewer supply and
growth. Two studies in the 1970s did examine how water affects
growth patterns. Both concluded that there was no correlation between the availability of public water service and regional growth.
One (Llewelyn-Davies Carson, Ltd. 1978) examined the growth of the
Denver metropolitan region; and the other (Carson, Rivkin, and
Rivkin 1973) examined growth of selected counties in four states:
Georgia, Minnesota, Pennsylvania, and Oregon.

The similar conclusions in the two studies are hardly surprising
for, as Deakin and *The Growth Shapers* correctly pointed out, the influence of all of these facilities is on the location of growth within a
region, not on whether the region grows at all (see discussion later
in this chapter). Because both studies simply examined the effect of
water supply on total county or regional growth, they found none.
In short, those studies asked a different question from the one considered here. There are two other problems with the cited studies.
First, the Denver study was prepared for the Army Corps of Engi-

neers as a defense of its plans to build the proposed Foothills Dam and Reservoir. The report responded to allegations of critics that the project would contribute to regional sprawl and the resulting air pollution. The other study is puzzling because it examined only - counties in wet states. Clearly the influence of water supply is greater in arid states like Nevada and Colorado than in states like Georgia and Pennsylvania, which have extensive surface water supplies and accessible groundwater systems.

One suspects, although the author found no studies to prove it, that the locational effects of the availability of water in arid states would be similar to the locational effects of sewer service in wet states. In wet states, water is often relatively accessible from shallow and inexpensive wells or from low-technology private systems. That would result in circumstances similar to those found by Hanson and Jacobs when they determined that the availability of private sewage treatment technology reduced the growth effects of sewer lines (Hanson and Jacobs 1989). In general, it is in those same wet states that sewage disposal is the most difficult because high water tables and extensive surface water systems create greater risks of contamination from septic tanks. In the wet states, sewer service is the scarcer and thus more valuable commodity. Viewed from another perspective, in those states a consumer or developer who has difficulty obtaining water can realistically consider drilling and using a well, but that same consumer or developer may find few alternatives for sewer service.

In contrast, in the arid states the priority system of water rights limits the legal ability of many people to drill wells, and the depth at which good water is found limits the practicability of wells. The same system limits the use of surface water to those who own the rights. However, in those states there are comparatively large land areas on which septic tanks are unlikely to threaten water supplies, even in cases of marginal soils. In the arid states, water is the rarer commodity. A developer in an arid state who has a water supply can probably find a way to handle sewage, but a developer (or consumer) without water may not be able to build.

Note that there is an operational difference between the effects of sewer and water service on development patterns and the effects of highways. In most cases, highways simply increase the convenience of a particular location and thus make development there more convenient and more attractive. In contrast, the availability of water and sewer service is, in many locations and for many types of development, a prerequisite to development. Even in circumstances where a developer may be able to provide on-site sewer systems or use wells to provide water, it is rare for a developer to be able to do both. Thus, the combination of utility services does not simply make development more convenient; it makes it possible.

The Roles of Consumers and Developers

No single authority decides that the location of a new sewer line or new highway will change the patterns of growth in the region. In fact, transportation and utility planners often deny that their decisions affect growth. They are correct—in a technical and narrow sense. For example, Brand (1991) argued that it is difficult to establish the link between transportation and land use because the equation includes a third factor, the behavior of individuals. Certainly this behavior is implied either in Wingo's model or in the simple transportation planning iso-time lines.

A study that is now somewhat dated still seems entirely plausible in explaining why new transportation links can influence development patterns so significantly. Given the choice of living in a city of more than 500,000, a city with a population between 50,000 and 500,000, a smaller city within commuting distance of a large city or a small city further away, a majority of respondents (55 percent) preferred the small city within commuting distance of the larger city. Although 51 percent of those then living in a large city preferred to remain in a city, either large (36 percent) or smaller (15 percent), another 37 percent chose the alternative of living in a suburb near a city. A majority of those living in smaller cities preferred the suburban alternative (Fuguitt and Zuiches 1975).

Tiebout (1956) developed a model that, among other things, attempted to explain the consumer choice involved in determining what community within a metropolitan area would become home for that consumer. Tiebout created an idealized model in which different communities would offer different mixes of public goods, ranging from recreational facilities to basic public utility services. Each consumer would then select the community that provided the mix of public goods that best fits that consumer's needs and pocketbook. There are three problems with trying to apply Tiebout's model nearly four decades after it was published. First, some public goods are essential to providing the opportunity for anyone to reside in a community. As suggested in this chapter, those include, at a minimum, sewer and water service and reasonable access. Those are not readily available in all communities in a metropolitan area, and the market thus skews toward those which have those basic public goods. Second, there are at particular times and in particular communities shortages in some public goods. Those lead to moratoriums and other market limitations that further constrain consumer choice. Third, as the following material explains, an individual consumer does not simply pick a community in which to live.

Any attempt to analyze urban form or the urban land market based on consumer behavior assumes that consumers may choose freely among all locations within the metropolitan region. That is simply not the case. Few consumers buy land and develop their own homesites. In fact, most consumers of new housing buy houses from homebuilders.

The location where a consumer buys a house depends heavily on where houses are built. Thus, the behavior of builders is important. In a survey of Phoenix-area builders, Hepner (1983) found that the availability of services was a key element in the selection of locations for development. It ranked behind zoning and attractiveness and prestige of area. However, the survey was somewhat confusing because it listed "availability of services" as one item and "utility extension not required" as another. The two are, of course, closely related. If some respondents listed only one of those items in preference to the other, then the two should be partially or wholly combined; that revision to the tabulation would increase the rank of "service" to first or second on the list. The only surprising thing in the Hepner study was that "near freeway" ranked relatively low among criteria for selection. Hepner's findings were entirely consistent with an earlier survey of developers around Vancouver, British Columbia, which concluded that "developers require adequate supplies of zoned and sewered land *before* development can be considered" (Goldberg and Ulinder 1976, p. 364).

A separate study suggested one reason why highways may not have ranked higher in either survey:

Although analyses of pooled data [from four case studies] indicated that new highways have an impact on single-family housing construction, analyses of individual regions did not show any strong or consistent effect. In part this was probably because most of the regions analyzed had relatively good highway accessibility even before 1960. Each new highway in a region brings a successively smaller improvement in accessibility. These diminishing marginal changes imply diminshing marginal effects on location decisions and land use (Environmental Impact Center, Incorporated 1975, p. 6).

However, a Minneapolis study concluded that highway access was still important, even by the late 1970s. It found that "general accessibility" was a "limiting factor" at the last two of a developer's three-stage site selection process and that roads and public and private utilities were limiting factors in the third stage, in which the developer typically selects a specific parcel of land (as opposed to a general area in which to develop) (Baerwald 1981, see table at p. 350 and accompanying text).

The explanation for the need for zoning relates to the uncertainties of the political process. The explanation for the need for sewer and other services is simpler still, money. As Peiser (1989) noted, "As a practical matter, extending utility services more than a mile or so from the end of existing lines is not economically feasible except for the largest developments" (p. 202). *The Growth Shapers* explained the process simply:

Infrastructure influences local land use by changing the supply of developable land, the demand for development, or both. . . .

It is easiest to look at land use changes from the point of view of developers. They are the chief actors in the urbanization process, and deal with the market forces of supply and demand in the most direct and practical way. Developers acquire land, remove or modify any existing structures, build their projects and then seek tenants or buyers. They are, of course, interested primarily in profits. . . .

Infrastructure investments can lead to local increases in demand for development or reductions in development costs, and thus create a strong incentive for developers to locate their projects nearby. The presence of infrastructure can both reduce risk and increase profits for developers. While this is obvious, it is seldom adequately considered by infrastructure planners (Urban Systems Research & Engineering Inc. 1976, p. 18).

Deakin noted, perhaps unnecessarily, that highways do not produce (population) growth; they simply shift it from other locations within the region (1991). A University of Iowa study team found that highway construction alone would not produce economic development, although good transportation is clearly important to economic development (Forkenbrock et al. 1990). Deakin's assertion and the University of Iowa findings are, of course, entirely consistent with the discussions here of developer behavior and consumer behavior. None of the discussions reviewed here analyzed the decision of a consumer choosing a new job and a new community in which to live; all the studies tacitly but clearly assumed that the consumer had a job or other reason for being in the region and was selecting a location for a home within that region. Similarly, the decision of a developer about whether to develop in a particular region must be based on complex market analyses of the region. *The Growth Shapers* acknowledged that "growth seems to be created by the installation of new infrastructure; actually, the infrastructure merely concentrates growth which might otherwise have been located elsewhere in the region" (Urban Systems Research & Engineering Inc. 1976, p. 5).

Having considered all this, it is important to recognize two things. First, for a particular community within a larger region, a highway may indeed "produce" growth. In economic or regional planning terms, it will simply attract growth that would occur somewhere in the region, anyway. Further, the highway may very well induce growth in travel totally separate from growth in population. By making travel more convenient, the highway encourages people to travel longer distances or to make new trips. Thus, the highway does indeed "create" certain types of growth. However, neither a highway nor a utility line will actually create regional population growth. They simply influence its location.

Although the capacities of the transportation and utility systems are powerful determinants of growth patterns within a region, they have relatively little impact on the total amount of growth in the region as a whole. It was the developer's selection of a location within the region, not the selection of a region within which to be active, that was the subject of the studies in Phoenix and Vancouver.

In short, the direct impact of the location of sewer and water lines and freeways is not on growth itself or even on consumer behavior. The direct impact affects the behavior of developers, who play the most active role in determining urban form. Individual consumers simply buy from those developers or from builders who buy lots from the developers and then build houses on them. Consumer desires influence developer behavior; but it is the developer, not the consumer, who decides to build next to the new sewer line or highway and not on the other side of town. The developer selects a site near a highway because the convenience is important to sales. The developer selects a site with water and sewer service because local government will generally not approve building houses without those services, and it is cheaper to tie into existing systems than to build new ones.

Clearly sewer lines and freeways are "growth shapers." They can be powerful elements of a growth management program. Perhaps more typically, the construction of such facilities without regard to growth management and other plans of the community can thwart, or at least substantially impede, those plans.

One important variable not considered in any depth up to this point is the issue of who makes important decisions about these facilities. Local growth management programs are generally implemented by local governments interested in local issues. Although the city councils and other governing bodies of those governments generally control their own comprehensive plans, zoning ordinances, and subdivision regulations, in many cases they do not have direct control over other crucial decisions. Local officials typically have little if any influence over highway decisions. The most important highways are built by state agencies, using federal funds and following state and federal guidelines. Political decisions regarding the relative priority of roads, and even the location of roads, are generally made at the state level.

That may be changing. Land use will play a greater role in transportation planning in the mid-1990s than ever before. The Intermodal Surface Transportation Efficiency Act of 1991 (its acronym, ISTEA, is widely pronounced as a homonym for *iced tea*) included strong planning provisions, with specific reference to land use issues.[1] The title of the act itself is important, because it suggests a significant departure from the "highway bills" of past years. "Intermodal" indicates the emphasis of the new act on multiple modes of transportation, including bicycle and pedestrian ways; bus, light rail, and other forms of mass transit; and automobiles. It is "intermodal" rather than "multimodal," because the modes should connect to one another as part of a total system. "Surface transportation" simply distinguishes it from separate bills addressing air transportation. The emphasis on "efficiency" should result in increased planning for those modes of transportation that are more efficient than the single-occupant automobile.

The new act continued the provision for regional planning by designated "Metropolitan Planning Organizations" and required the designation of an MPO for each urbanized area of more than 50,000.[2] The law authorized $225 million for planning by MPOs, more than double the amount available for planning in the last transportation act (Morris 1992, p. 2). The act also broadened the planning requirements to be considered by the MPO. Among the fifteen "factors to be considered" in developing a metropolitan transportation plan are

3. The need to relieve congestion and prevent congestion from occurring where it does not yet occur. . . .

4. The likely effect of transportation policy decisions on land use and development and the consistency of transportation plans and programs with the provisions of all applicable short- and long-term land use and development plans;[3]

The act added a new requirement for state-level planning function. The states will be responsible for coordinating metropolitan-level planning activities and developing a state implementation plan.[4] Among the factors to be considered by the states are

3. Strategies for incorporating bicycle transportation facilities and pedestrian walkways in projects where appropriate throughout the State. . . .

6. Any metropolitan area plan. . . .
12. Methods to reduce traffic congestion and to prevent traffic congestion from developing in areas where it does not yet occur, including methods which reduce motor vehicle travel, particularly single-occupant motor vehicle travel.
13. Methods to expand and enhance transit services and to increase the use of such services.
14. The effect of transportation decisions on land use and land development, including the need for consistency between transportation decisionmaking and the provisions of all applicable short-range and long-range land use and development plans.[5]

As the title suggested, the act was not just another highway bill. Of the $151 billion authorized in it, $31.5 billion was specifically designated for mass transit. Of the $119.5 billion remainder, $23.9 million was allocated to the "surface transportation program," from which funds can be used for highways, transit, or bicycle and pedestrian ways. States with Clean Air Act "nonattainment" status related to ozone can use all those funds for mass transit, and others can use. up to 75 percent of them for that purpose (Morris 1992, p. 1). Of the total appropriation, $3 billion, or about 2 percent, was designated for a "transportation enhancement program." Those funds may be used for acquisition of scenic easements and historic sites, pedestrian and bike trails along abandoned rights-of-way or as part of new projects, and control and removal of billboards, among other purposes (Morris 1992, p. 4).

Highway planning, one of the most powerful determinants of growth patterns has, since the beginning of the federal highway program, been largely beyond the control of local officials concerned with land use, growth management, and related issues, although they have had limited input through the old MPO planning process. With its emphasis on intermodal transportation and coordination with local planning, ISTEA provides a very different scenario through the mid-1990s. Although the effectiveness of its provisions have not been tested as this book is published, they offer the potential for local officials to influence transportation planning and to bring it more closely into alignment with local land use plans, opportunities, and concerns.

The control of sewer and water systems is more complex. Some sewer and water systems belong to regional entities that make decisions much as highway departments do. One factor that led to the ultimate failure of the Ramapo growth management program was the fact that Ramapo did not control its own sewers. Sewer construction by the regional authority fell behind the schedule outlined in the original plan, posing major problems for the growth management

program. Ramapo officials then elected to solve that problem by ignoring sewers as a factor in the program, an ironic twist indeed
(Hammer, Siler, George 1977, p. 11).

Engineering and cost considerations are major factors used by
regional authorities to make decisions about sewer system expansion.
A dominant consideration in such decisions is the desire of engineers
to ensure that sewage all flows downhill by gravity to a central treatment plant (Tabors, Shapiro, and Rogers 1976, beginning at p. 1, offers a description of the design process). Many local governments
control their own sewer and water systems. Unlike the zoning and
subdivision regulations and other growth-influencing tools, however,
such systems typically do not remain under direct control of the
policy makers. They are operated by "enterprise departments," run
by technical experts charged with the duty to operate them safely,
effectively, and at a profitable or breakeven level (Pierce and Rust
1991). Thus, money drives everything. Engineers can easily make
sewage flow uphill if there is a reason to do so, but it costs more.
Thus, money, in the form of a profit from the enterprise department,
is more important than many of the engineering considerations. A
candid utilities director in a southwestern community once told the
author, asked why he was willing to provide utility service in an
area shown on the comprehensive plan as inappropriate for growth,
"I am running an enterprise department. I will provide service anywhere that I can make a profit. I will continue to do that until the city council tells me otherwise."

In theory, effective planning should eliminate conflicts between
infrastructure construction practices and growth management plans.
In practice, the planning processes are separate, even when a single
local government makes most of the decisions. Plans for local roads
and for sewer and water lines are typically included in a capital improvements program (CIP). A good CIP is a rolling five- or six-year
plan for construction of new facilities, ranging from swimming pools
to a new city hall to roads and sewer lines. The CIP is largely budget
driven. The governing body, together with the chief administrative
or executive officer and the chief budget official, typically control
the process. They establish costs and priorities on the advice of the
technicians responsible for the projects. Those technicians then
control the implementation.

In contrast, growth management programs typically evolve from
the comprehensive planning process. Responsibility for the comprehensive plan lies with the planning commission. The planning director
typically assists the commission in the process. Early model legislation, still in effect in most states, called for the planning commission
simply to deliver the finished plan to the governing body. That process

is not likely to generate any real interest in the document on the part of the governing body. Although many jurisdictions now wisely involve the governing body in developing the comprehensive plan, the process is still too seldom linked to the CIP and budgeting processes.

Thus, dollars and engineering studies drive critical local decisions about the location and capacity of new sewer and water lines, just as dollars and engineering studies drive critical state decisions about the location and capacity of new freeways. There is nothing inherently wrong with that fact, except that it will often lead to results inconsistent with local growth management plans and may at times serve to thwart those plans.

If the only consideration of the local government is ensuring adequate highway and sewer capacity, then the loop will close nicely. Growth will follow the sewers and highways, which will become available to serve the growth. However, if the new highway goes north of town and the new interceptor sewer line flows southwest from town, problems arise. If the growth management plan calls for directing development to the east of town, where capacity in schools and parks is best, the problems are substantial indeed.

Even where the governing body decides to use infrastructure construction policy as a growth management tool, it may encounter problems in doing so. First, within the city limits, it may be legally difficult to refuse to extend service. Outside the municipal boundaries, the community typically has more flexibility to set policy, although that flexibility is not unlimited (see, generally, Stone 1982; "Note: public utility land" 1978). Boulder lost a court challenge to its refusal to grant service to a developer whose property adjoined a city-controlled system outside the city limits (discussed in Kelly 1976; the opinion of the trial court was published in Scott, Brower, and Miner 1975b, pp. 237 ff.).[6]

Although a community may not be as free as it might like to be to deny service when there is adequate capacity or to refuse to connect users to existing lines, water and sewer lines can still be important tools in growth management. Courts in Colorado, including the Colorado Supreme Court, sustained Westminster's growth management program when it refused service because it lacked adequate capacity (Kelly 1982; see general discussion of principles in Kelly 1984).[7] Callies (1992) cited the lack of infrastructure in large areas of Hawaii as one of three major factors that have contributed to maintaining 95 percent of the land in that state in nondevelopment categories despite substantial pressures for tourist development.

What can the growth managing community learn from all this? In deciding to extend sewer and water lines into undeveloped areas, community officials should consider seriously whether the community wants those areas to develop. Although it has been relatively rare in the 1980s and early 1990s for local governments simply to extend such services to undeveloped territory, it is not at all unusual for them to extend services through undeveloped areas. A line may pass through undeveloped areas on the way to a new airport or a new industrial park or as a shortcut from one part of town to another. In some cases, the intervening lands are entirely suitable for development; in others they are not. Those suitability factors should be considered in the decision to extend the services through such an area. As the authors of *Interceptor Sewers and Urban Sprawl* found, one of the major problems is the existence of excess capacity in lines (Binkley et al. 1975). A community could choose to serve a new airport with a line that has exactly enough capacity for the airport. As the cited study indicates, however, engineers typically prefer larger lines with the capacity to serve future needs although providing for future needs is likely to become a self-fulfilling prediction. Thus, whether development is desirable along the route of a line is a critical question that should influence both the location and the size of the line.

The scope of the problem can be great indeed. Airports and residences are fundamentally incompatible, and communities take many steps to buffer airports from residences. Extending major water and sewer lines to an airport or an adjacent industrial park, however, opens the area to all types of development and creates just the problems the community hoped to avoid. Building a good access road to the airport simply compounds the problems. Officials in metropolitan Washington, D.C., tried to avoid that problem by building an expressway to Dulles Airport that had no exits to Reston, Virginia, or other residential areas on the outbound lanes and no entrances from them on the inbound lanes. After years spent watching commuters take the roadway to the airport in order to turn around and drive to Washington, officials gave up in the early 1990s and created a parallel commuter toll road in the original airport expressway right-of-way. Infrastructure-induced development will continue around the airport, increasing the probability of future conflicts between the airport and its neighbors.

Sometimes project planners themselves create the problems. In their zeal to minimize operating costs and problems by ensuring that everything flows by gravity, engineers seek the lowest possible location for each link in a sewer system. Interceptor sewers, the major lines in the system, thus wind up in the river bottoms. Those lands, of course, are the centers of floodplains. Thus, public officials simultaneously discourage development in floodplains and allow the people who work for them to build major growth magnets in the middle of those problem lands.

There is obviously no perfect solution to these complex problems. Clearly, interceptor sewer lines should not run along high ridgelines just to avoid floodplains. Equally clearly, a good airport must have good road access. However, by understanding the growth-shaping role of infrastructure investments and considering the secondary impacts of those investments, a community can make far better decisions. By understanding the process and attempting to implement a rational planning program, a local government certainly has the opportunity to do better than those in California's Amador Valley. According to Greenberg, these officials facilitated virtually uncontrolled growth through the provision of transportation, sewage collection and treatment, and other public facilities "but within a fragmented political structure in which there was virtually no overall coordination and planning" (1986, p. 152).

LAND ACQUISITION

Both Boulder and Montgomery County have recognized that owning land or rights in land can be an important element of an effective growth management program (Hamblen 1991; Walker 1978).

Boulder has used land acquisition to establish a city-owned greenbelt around the city (Walker 1978). Using revenues from a special sales tax passed by the voters in 1967 and from several subsequent bond issues, by 1992 the city had spent $59 million acquiring 22,000 acres of open space (Boulder, City of 1992b). The city leases some of the open space to farmers for continued agricultural use and maintains other areas of open space as part of its active park and recreation system. Some open space is simply passive (Boulder, City of 1992a). Open space owned by Boulder County, as well as mountain parks owned by both the city and the county, link with the open space to provide green space on most of the mountain backdrop to Boulder and for several miles to the south, blocking suburbanization from the sprawling Denver suburbs. As of 1991, the open space system also included lands to the north and east of the city, forming a nearly complete greenbelt around the city (see Figure 5.3; Boulder, City of 1991).

A publicly owned greenbelt stops continuous sprawl more effectively than any other technique because it absolutely precludes development. In order to ensure that their greenbelt will continue to function as intended, Boulderites approved an amendment to the city charter in 1986 severely restricting the ability of the city to sell

Figure 5.3
Publicy-Owned Greenbelt around Boulder, Colorado

Source: Map adapted by Jerzy Lewicki from Boulder, City of, 1991, "Boulder Open Space, Parks and Trails Map" (Zia Maps); and Boulder County, 1991, "Boulder County Road Map" (Boulder County).

open-space land. Under the provision, any proposed sale of open land requires the affirmative vote of three of the five members of the open space board as well as approval of the city council. Even after such approval, citizens have a period of sixty days within which they can force a referendum on the sale by obtaining signatures of 5 percent of the eligible voters on a petition seeking such a referendum.[8]

Although a greenbelt is the strongest tool in the local arsenal for attempting to control urban form, it is not perfect. If the greenbelt is too narrow or the area within it too constrained, it may cause leap-frog development (see discussion in Chapter 7). There is evidence in Boulder County that the combination of growth management programs in Boulder and the effective programs precluding growth on the fringe of the city have redirected some growth to nearby Louisville, Longmont, and Lafayette ("Growth masks out-migration" 1992; see more general discussion in Chapter 10). However, Boulder itself has a well-defined urban edge without the contiguous sprawl characteristic of many communities.

Montgomery County has used a combination of land acquisition and development rights acquisition to attempt to shape its urban areas. It has tried to preserve both greenways along creeks and major agricultural areas (Hamblen 1991). Other communities have used the acquisition of development rights to preserve farmland (Hamblen 1991; Strong 1991; Peterson and McCarthy 1977). Strong (1975) described the efforts of a private group to preserve parts of the Brandywine Valley through development rights acquisition. Although the project was not a complete success, her documentation of it provides valuable lessons for others interested in using similar techniques. Private groups have also been active in land acquisition in other communities, including Palm Beach County (Abberger 1991).

The purchase of property is relatively simple, although it can also be expensive. Boulder has dedicated revenues from a special sales tax for that purpose. The acquisition of "development rights" may offer a less expensive alternative. The theory of purchasing development rights is that the acquiring entity does not purchase the entire bundle of the owner's land interests; rather, it acquires simply that part of the owner's interests representing the ability to develop the land. That transaction leaves the seller with the residual land interest, which typically permits an agricultural use. The acquisition cost of development rights should consequently be less than the acquisition costs of the land by the amount of the residual value (Strong 1991; Peterson and McCarthy 1977). The acquisition of development rights makes the most sense where agricultural (or other residual) values are relatively high and in areas where public services and growth pressures have not placed a high value on the land for development (see Strong 1979).

Although the term *development rights* is used rather freely by planners, it does not refer to anything in particular. Water rights and mineral rights have been well defined through the common law in this country and in England, from which U.S. property law originally came. In contrast, development rights are a modern invention. The legal mechanism through which they are acquired, however, is based on another common law concept, the *easement*. Under an easement, the holder of the easement (the *dominant estate* in legal terms) has the right to make limited use of another's property; the holder of the property (the *burdened estate*) has free use of the property except to the extent that it would interfere with the rights of the dominant estate holder. Classic uses of easements are those for roadways,

waterways, and utility lines. William H. Whyte suggested the application of easement law to the acquisition of partial interests in open
space in a short but influential publication in the late 1950s (Whyte
1959). Since that time most states have adopted legislation permitting
the use of "conservation easements" or something similar, and the
Internal Revenue Service has adopted regulations under which the
value of the gift of a conservation easement is recognized.

One problem with property (or development rights) acquisition as
a control technique is that the budget in any given year is limited,
and the short-term impact is thus limited, even in cases, such as
Boulder, where the long-term impact is significant. One device that
communities in many states might consider to make land acqustion
programs more effective is the *Official Map Act*, originally included
as part of the *Standard City Planning Enabling Act* (Advisory Committee on City Planning and Zoning 1928). Under that act, a local
government can reserve property for future acquisition without acquiring it immediately. Although this device over the years has
primarily been used for reserving enlarged rights-of-way along existing roads, the act as adopted in many states includes "open space" or
is otherwise broad enough to permit its use to reserve open space. A
carefully drafted local ordinance can create an acquisition "trigger"
that is pulled by a development application, thus forcing the community to acquire the property within a specified period. Such a
device could in effect give a local government a broad option on
targeted lands, with the priority always given to those lands threatened by development.

There are two disadvantages to the proposed scheme. First, as
Strong pointed out, it is desirable and logical to try to acquire agricultural and other rural property before development pressures
occur in order to avoid paying the inflated price that development
pressure brings to land (Strong 1979). Second, under a series of U.S.
Supreme Court decisions, a local government that establishes such
a system and then fails to acquire reserved property after the event
triggering the reservation is likely to be held liable for "interim dam-
ages," representing the value of the loss of use of the property for
whatever period use or development was delayed by the failure of
the government to act.[9] A local government can mitigate the impact
of those decisions, however, by providing a prompt determination
of whether it intends to buy the property or forgo its "option" in response to a development application.

The acquisition of land or development rights can play an important part in an effective growth management program. Both Boulder
and Montgomery County provide good examples. Land acquisition
is the most effective technique for drawing a firm urban edge around

a community. Because of its cost, it is not likely to become a dominant growth management tool, but it will remain an important one for those communities that have the fiscal will and the ability to use it.

CONCLUSION

The question communities must face is not whether these nonregulatory techniques will affect the timing and location of growth but whether they have the power and the political will to use these tools to influence the timing and location of growth. Some authors routinely include such tools in their definitions of growth management (Glickfeld and Levine 1992; Landis 1991). Two years before *The Growth Shapers* called attention to the important role that infrastructure improvements play in shaping communities, Clawson recognized that they not only could be inadvertent growth shapers but that, "Extension of various public improvements, such as roads, sewer lines, water lines, schools, and others, and even such privately provided services as electricity, gas and telephones, in coordinated fashion into suburban areas ripe for development could be a powerful tool affecting the location and rate of such suburban development" (1971, p. 347).

A community that has the authority to control all these techniques clearly should use them to implement planned growth strategies. The growth-shaping power of infrastructure investment is so great that infrastructure investments may overwhelm regulatory efforts to direct growth. Similarly, the legal and political pressure to provide services to annexed lands is so great that the decision to annex should be viewed as a decision to develop. Conversely, the decision to purchase land is the most certain way to ensure that the land will not be developed without public sector support.

Some communities control virtually none of these nonregulatory tools that affect their growth patterns. Those communities clearly have less opportunity to manage growth than do communities with more techniques under their control. However, every community should coordinate the nonregulatory decisions that it does or can make with its total strategy of community planning and growth management.

NOTES

1. H.R. 2950.
2. H.R. 2950, Sect. 1024(a); 23 U.S.C. 134.
3. H.R. 2950, Sect. 1024(a); 23 U.S.C. 134(f).
4. H.R. 2950, Sect. 1025; 23 U.S.C. 135.

5. H.R. 2950, Sect. 1025; 23 U.S.C. 135(c).
6. *Robinson* v. *City of Boulder*, 547 P.2d 228 (Colo. 1976).
7. *P. W. Investments* v. *City of Westminster*, 655 P.2d 1365 (Colo. 1982).
8. Charter, City of Boulder, Sec. 177.
9. *Lucas* v. *South Carolina Coastal Council*, 112 S. Ct. 2886 (1992); *First English Evangelical Lutheran Church of Glendale* v. *County of Los Angeles*, 107 S. Ct. 2378 (1987); also *San Diego Gas & Electric Co.* v. *City of San Diego*, 101 S. Ct. 1287 (1981).

6

Statewide Efforts to Manage Growth

The complexity of most metropolitan regions makes it difficult for local governments to manage some aspects of growth effectively. With the broad extent of their territorial controls, states have a greater opportunity to address such growth-related issues as the actual shape of the metropolitan area. This chapter examines briefly the implementation of several state-level programs to manage growth.

THE LITERATURE ON THE STATE ROLE

In 1971, Bosselman and Callies wrote, in *The Quiet Revolution in Land Use Control,*

The *ancien regime* being overthrown is the feudal system under which the entire pattern of land development has been controlled by thousands of individual local governments, each seeking to maximize its tax base and minimize its social problems, and caring less what happens to all the others.

The tools of the revolution are new laws taking a wide variety of forms but each sharing a common theme, the need to provide some degree of state or regional participation in the major decisions that affect the use of our increasingly limited supply of land (p. 1).

There was a flurry of interest in state land use activity in the mid-1970s. Under contract with the Department of Housing and Urban

Development, the American Institute of Planners (1976) prepared a comprehensive review of state planning activities in all fifty states. That study included state planning and budgeting activities, as well as land use enabling powers and broader state land use programs.

Also under contract to the Department of Housing and Urban Development, the Council of State Governments prepared a report called *State Growth Management* (1976). That report was interesting because it included both economic development programs and regulatory programs, the latter ranging from energy facility siting legislation to zoning. It thus provided an extremely broad, if brief, examination of the growth management issue at the state level.

In July 1976, the Urban Land Institute devoted an entire issue of its monthly newsletter, *Environmental Comment*, to the topic: "The States Manage Growth." It provided an interesting look at policies in two states that are not typically viewed as growth management states: Texas, which had very limited state activity; and Wyoming, which was in the process of creating a statewide land use plan and had required local governments to undertake comprehensive planning. It also examined the current policies in Florida and Hawaii.

In the same year, Rosenbaum (1976) prepared a report called *Land Use and the Legislatures*. It examined three major areas of activity: "growth management"; siting legislation for power plants, surface mines, and other large-scale activities; and natural areas legislation protecting such areas as wetlands and shorelines. Rosenbaum's use of the term *growth management* was broad and included state laws requiring that local governments engage in planning, zoning, or subdivision regulation.

Also in 1976, Resources for the Future published the first edition of Healy's *Land Use and the States* (1976), updated three years later by Healy and Rosenberg (1979). The first edition provided the first in-depth view of several state land use programs and an examination of their common themes. It focused on Vermont, California, and Florida. In the same period, the Conservation Foundation sponsored a series of short publications on state programs, including Vermont (Myers 1974) and Hawaii (Myers 1976).

Callies and Bosselman's original report featured statewide programs in Hawaii and Vermont, along with specialized and regional programs in other states. The Hawaii system remains little changed since the report was published. Vermont has added a new piece to its state control program. Florida and Oregon joined them in adopting strong statewide programs during the 1970s. Georgia adopted a state planning law in 1990, and Washington began implementation of a new state planning program in 1991. Other states have tinkered with their enabling acts, some of them strengthening the role of planning. States with a strong presence in land use control and growth management, however, remain a distinct minority.

The revolution is not one that has swept the nation, as some thought it would. Even by 1979, Healy noted of the quiet revolution, "This early momentum has been lost. . . . State legislatures are reluctant to pass more laws that seem 'comprehensive' in affecting all lands in the state or a wide range of types of development" (pp. 1–2).

The development of the literature on state planning paralleled the development of both the initial state programs and the influential growth management literature (see material in Chapter 3). As the examples just cited suggest, most of the literature on the state role was published in the 1970s. At first impression, John DeGrove's 1984 book, published by the American Planning Association (Planners Press), appeared to be an exception. However, most of the interviews and source materials in the book dated from the late 1970s; a small proportion of the material came from 1981 and 1982. Thus, the book substantially overlapped the time covered by Healy and Rosenberg. It was a far different book from theirs, with far more emphasis on the politics. It contained thorough analyses of the politics of state land use control in Vermont, Florida, California, and Oregon, as well as Colorado and North Carolina, which have far more limited programs. Callies updated the literature on Hawaii with a book (1984) and a short chapter on land use controls in a larger book about Hawaiian politics (1992). Popper (1981) contributed a political analysis of state land use reform efforts. He focused on the efforts of New York, Pennsylvania, and Maryland, states not typically considered to be in the forefront of the "quiet revolution," as well as on Florida, Vermont, and California, states more typically included in such studies.

Three 1991 working papers from the University of California at Berkeley provided interesting, if limited, perspectives on issues in state-level growth management. Teitz (1991) analyzed the practical and policy issues confronting California in his plea for development of a state growth policy. Innes examined the role of state growth management programs in increasing planning coordination among different levels of government (Innes 1991b) and for enhancing the role of citizens in planning decisions (Innes 1991a).

It is unfortunate that the only broad examination of the state role in growth management based on information dating later than the period around 1980 was a 20-page article by John DeGrove (1989). Although the "quiet revolution" did not spread across the nation as some anticipated that it might, the implementation of evolutionary controls continued in the "quiet revolution" states and in several others. An updated report on state growth management activity would be a useful contribution to the research literature and to planning practice, particularly if it had the breadth and depth of Healy's and DeGrove's earlier works. This chapter does not attempt to fill that need. It simply includes an examination of the state role in growth management to broaden the context in which the reader considers local growth management.

THE STATE OPPORTUNITY IN GROWTH MANAGEMENT

Despite the limited number of statewide programs of planning and growth management, it is important to examine these programs. One of the difficulties facing local governments in developing growth management programs is that they generally do not control enough territory to manage growth on a meaningful scale. Petaluma and Ramapo, famous for their growth management programs, are both exurbs of major metropolitan areas that faced regional growth pressures beyond the control of any single municipality. Boulder is somewhat more independent, lying outside the "normal" commuting range of Denver. However, it is still less than a half-hour's drive from the north Denver suburbs; and commuters travel from Boulder to the Denver area and vice versa every day.

Clearly a state, with its broad area of control, can address some issues that a local government simply cannot touch. It is important to examine, at least briefly, some significant state programs and their apparent effectiveness.

Although the vast majority of states have not adopted comprehensive planning or land use policies, every state significantly influences local land use patterns and practices through amendments to enabling acts, investments in highways, and regulation of air and water pollution. Thus, even in a state where there is no express policy, the state does play a role. That role can perhaps best be understood by examining, however briefly, the experience of several states with express land policies. Further, local governments can learn from, and even use, some of the techniques applied by those states. There are lessons from some of the programs even for local governments that prefer not to have the state intervene further in their land use affairs.

HAWAII

Hawaii does not call its program "growth management"; but it works like a growth management program. Its statewide program originates in a "land use law" that antedates the current interest in growth management. The land use program, which is called that, looks a lot like statewide zoning and controls the timing and location of growth more effectively than any form of local zoning. It thus constitutes a statewide growth management program, regardless of the name.

To understand why Hawaii had the earliest statewide control system and why it remains one of the strongest, it is important to understand Hawaii. It is unique in more ways than just being the island state. It was a monarchy until 1890, and concentrated land ownership and strong central authority were a part of the Hawaiian tradition. According to Myers, by the 1950s, "72 major landholders (owners of more than 1,000 acres) held title to 47 percent of the land. The state owned 38 percent of the land, and the federal government, by lease or ownership, controlled 10 percent (including 25 percent of the island of Oahu)" (pp. 16–19). That leaves only 5 percent of the land for the other 99.9 percent of the population. The land ownership pattern created a unique set of circumstances.

Technology created the other. Agricultural commodities, particularly sugar cane and pineapple, were the mainstay of the Hawaiian economy through the 1950s. Although there was some tourism, it was not a large factor. However, at about the time that Hawaii achieved statehood, the jet aircraft made Hawaii considerably more accessible to tourists than it had been. Speculators began to acquire inexpensive agricultural land, with the apparent intent to develop it. Many saw excessive tourist-driven development as a threat to the economic base. From that political source, support for the strong state land use law arose (see, generally, Bosselman and Callies 1971; Myers 1976, pp. 5–7; DeGrove 1984, pp. 9–11).

The Land Use Law, adopted just two years after Hawaii became a state in 1959, created a state Land Use Commission.[1] The governor appoints the nine-member commission. The commission determines the boundaries of four types of districts in the state:[2]

Urban. Lands in this district fall entirely under local control. Local governments may permit all sorts of urban uses. Local planning and zoning within these districts are similar to those activities in other communities in the mainland states.

Rural. Rural lands permit residential uses on relatively large lots of one-half acre or more. The Land Use Commission establishes permitted uses within this district. The original law did not include this kind of district, which was added in a 1963 amendment.

Agricultural. The agricultural district contains lands most suitable for the principal agricultural activities of the islands, sugar cane and pineapple plantations, and for less intensive agricultural uses and agricultural industries, such as sugar mills. The commission also establishes the permitted uses within this type of district.

Conservation. The Department of Land and Natural Resources regulates uses within this kind of district. The initial district boundaries contained only public land, but the Land Use Commission subsequently enlarged them to include significant areas of private land (Callies 1992, pp. 132–133; Bosselman and Callies 1971, pp. 7–10; DeGrove 1984, pp. 15–17).

Figure 6.1 shows boundaries on Oahu established by the commission.

The Land Use Commission has the sole authority to make boundary changes. That process appears to differ little from rezoning pressures in other communities. Bosselman and Callies may have understated the problem somewhat when they noted that "applications for boundary changes and special permits keep the Land Use Commission quite busy" (1971, p. 10). During the ten years after the commission established the initial boundaries (1964–1974), it granted boundary change requests that increased the urban district by 30,000 acres, or 25 percent (Healy and Rosenberg 1979, p. 186). During that period, the commission considered petitions to change the classification of 133,438 acres and approved a change for 66,670, or 50 percent of the amount included in the petitions (DeGrove 1984, p. 32). Cooper and Daws examined the files of the commission over its first twenty years and found 264 applications for boundary changes involving at least five acres and a presumed profit motive (the authors ignored petitions from public and nonprofit agencies); of those 264 petitions, the commission granted 202 (1990, pp. 98–99, 110). DeGrove (1984) gave the commission generally good marks for its role in implementing the act ("a creditable job in the face of substantial handicaps" [p. 32]) in its first several years, somewhat mixed reviews for the next five years, and a reservation of judgment for the following five years, which was the last period included in his book (1984).

Cooper and Daws alleged that the boundary change process is highly political and documented the relationship of public officials with major landowners affected by the process. They found a 91 percent approval rate for those 185 applications (of the 264 cited above) with which public officials had direct ties as officers, trustees, lawyers, or otherwise (1990, p. 110). However, the problem may not be as severe as they allege. An official report for Oahu (Honolulu County) shows that thirteen amendments approved during the previous year removed as many acres from the urban zone as they added, thus resulting in no net change (Honolulu, City and County of 1991).

Has the Hawaii program worked? Healy concluded, "The record shows that Hawaii's land use law has been relatively, but not completely, effective in stopping the urbanization of agricultural lands. . . . Nevertheless, the law has had a striking effect on the pattern of Hawaii's growth, making urban expansion far more compact and

Figure 6.1
City and County of Honolulu (Island of Oahu) Land Use Districts Established
by Hawaii Land Use Commission

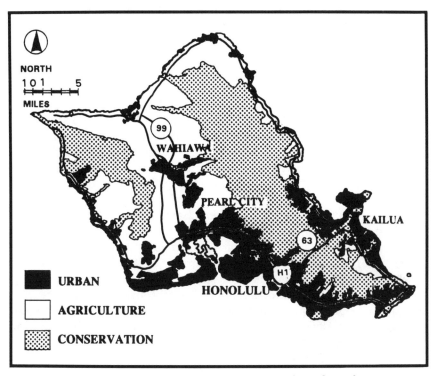

Source: Hawaii Land Use Commission, 1992, "State Land Use for Oahu."

orderly than it would have been without the law" (Healy and Rosenberg 1979, p. 186). In 1992, after more than three decades of operation of the new law, 95 percent of the land in the state remained in the rural and conservation classifications (Callies 1992).

The effect is dramatic on Oahu, where the high density of Waikiki Beach lies within two or three miles of areas showing no signs of development (see Figure 6.1). However, DeGrove suggested that the policies underlying the state law require reconsideration because of the significant decline of agriculture as a factor in the economic base and because of pressures for increased housing opportunity. By 1991, a City and County of Honolulu report noted that "Oahu's economy is currently dominated by tourism and defense expenditures." The fact remains, however, that the state of Hawaii has exercised far more effective control over patterns of development than any of the other forty-nine states.

VERMONT

The second state to join "the quiet revolution" was Vermont. In 1970, some ten years after Hawaii adopted its landmark Land Use Law, Vermont adopted Act 250. That law, the first in a series of land use reform measures adopted in the state, established a statewide development-permitting system, with substantial control at the regional level.

Each state is in a sense unique. However, Vermont and Hawaii, the first two states in this movement, are particularly so. Vermont is one of the smallest states in the nation in both land area and population, with a 1990 population of 582,758 (Bureau of the Census 1991). Myers noted that "one symbol of change, according to some observers, came in the early 60s, when for the first time, Vermont had more people than cows" (1974). Its largest city, Burlington, had a 1990 metropolitan area population of 137,079 (Bureau of the Census 1991a). In short, Vermont is unique in part because of its rural character and lack of major urban areas.

It is also unique in its form of government. The town meeting remains a form of government for a number of its 292 municipal and township governments. It is noteworthy that, disregarding Burlington, the average population served by one of those local governments is roughly 1,500 people, a fact bound to affect the style of government (see, generally, DeGrove 1984, pp. 66–67). Not surprisingly, planning and zoning were not widespread in Vermont as the quiet revolution began (Healy and Rosenberg 1979, pp. 41–43).

Act 250: The First Shot in the Vermont Revolution

Vermont did share one thing with Hawaii in the quiet revolution, and that was the circumstances leading to the adoption of its revolutionary legislation. The threat of tourism development to agriculture clearly fueled the drive for the new land use law. In particular, a 1968 proposal by International Paper for a second-home development on 20,000 acres created a political outcry that led the 1970 legislature to adopt Act 250 (Bosselman and Callies 1971, pp. 54–56; Healy and Rosenberg 1979, p. 41). Healy also cited a proposal to add 2,000 condominium units to Wilmington, a town of 2,000, and a survey of Wilmington and adjacent Dover that found "a total of seventy-three developers in business, one for every twenty-five residents" (1979, p. 41). Despite some early opposition, the act, which had been proposed by a study commission appointed by the governor, finally passed the state senate by unanimous voice vote (DeGrove 1984).

The new law required a development permit for industrial or commercial development on tracts of greater than ten acres (or one acre where the town has not adopted zoning or subdivision controls), housing projects of ten or more units within a five-mile radius, and any development above 2,500 feet. It also required a permit for any subdivision into ten or more lots of less than ten acres each.[3]

Primary control of the issuance of development permits falls to nine district commissions created under the law, with a coordinated review process at the state level. The law is clearly supplemental to local regulation. Thus, approval through the state process does not ensure approval by the town under its zoning ordinance or other regulations.

The act included ten standards for approval of development permits. Five of them amounted to the first statewide requirements for adequate public facilities in the nation. The law permits a local government to approve a proposed development only if it finds that the development meets these criteria:

2. Does have sufficient water available for the reasonably foreseeable needs of the subdivision or development.
3. Will not cause an unreasonable burden on an existing water supply, if one is to be utilized. . . .
5. Will not cause unreasonable highway congestion or unsafe conditions with respect to use of the highways, existing or proposed.
6. Will not cause an unreasonable burden on the ability of a municipality to provide educational services.
7. Will not place an unreasonable burden on the ability of the local government to provide municipality or governmental services.

The other standards addressed environmental issues and conformance with plans. Thus, in order to approve a development, the local government also is required to find that five other conditions are met:

1. Will not result in undue water or air pollution. . . .
4. Will not cause unreasonable soil erosion or reduction in the capacity of the land to hold water so that a dangerous or unhealthy condition may result. . . .[4]
8. Will not have an adverse effect on the scenic or natural beauty of the area, aesthetics, historic sites or rare and irreplaceable natural areas.
9. Is in conformance with a duly adopted development plan, land use plan or land capability plan.
10. Is in conformance with any duly adopted local or regional plan or capital program. . . .[5]

Act 250 required the adoption of three plans, all of which required ultimate legislative approval: an interim plan, a land capability and development plan, and a state land use plan. The legislature and the governor approved the interim plan in 1972 without apparent difficulty. They approved the land capability and development plan two years later. That plan established stronger environmental standards but also increased local control over issues within the borders of a particular community. The state land use plan failed in two major legislative efforts. DeGrove provided a good political history of the political activity surrounding all three (1984, pp. 80–94; see, also, Healy and Rosenberg 1979, pp. 61–66; and Myers 1974).

Although Act 250 created a strong system of statewide development control, note that two major types of development are exempt: small commercial development (under 10 acres in most circumstances) of the type that generally creates commercial "strips" along highways; and subdivision of land into parcels larger than ten acres. Healy and Rosenberg referred to these as "gaps" in the law (1979, pp. 54–56), and DeGrove cited examples of developments with lots of "10+ acres" (1984, pp. 94–96). From a policy perspective, exemption for parcels greater than ten acres is particularly troublesome because it encourages the worst developers (those who want to avoid regulation) to consume the most land per unit sold.

Has Act 250 worked? It certainly increased the control of development in a state where many communities lacked basic zoning and subdivision controls before its adoption. DeGrove offered this assessment:

Certainly as a growth-management measure capable of directing growth into desired areas and preventing it in areas marginal or unsuitable, Act 250 has yet to be fully utilized and probably cannot be so utilized without changes in the law. . . .

Within the framework of its objectives, there is broad consensus that Act 250 has been successful. Observers and participants agree that while the law has not had a significant impact on the rate of growth in the state . . . it has significantly improved the quality of the growth that has taken place (1984, p. 94).

Healy offered a slightly different perspective. He agreed with DeGrove's assessment that it affected the quality of growth more than the quantity. He also found it to be "more effective in regulating second homes and suburban tracts than in stopping commercial sprawl" (Healy and Rosenberg 1979, p. 72), a result not surprising in light of the fact that the pressure of second-home developments led to its adoption. However, Healy also noted, "Perhaps the most interesting feature of Vermont's experience is that the policy has evolved over time. . . . For the future then, the question is not how to revamp Vermont's land regulatory process, but whether it can continue to evolve as the process itself uncovers new kinds of issues" (Healy and Rosenberg 1979, pp. 73–74).

Myers found that the early days of implementing Act 250 were characterized by a process of negotiation that generally led to project approvals. However, she cited anecdotal evidence that the law provided more protection than might appear through the imposition of large numbers of conditions on most permit approvals. (Myers 1974).

Writing six years after its adoption, Strong assessed Act 250 as follows, correctly anticipating the need for further action. "Act 250 has resulted in creation of a permit system applicable to some development. It has not resulted directly in preservation of any prime farmland, one of the Act's stated objectives" (Strong 1977, p. 25).

Strong saw it as "part of an effective farmland retention program." The type of broader program she suggested emerged some eleven years later with the adoption of Act 200. As Healy correctly predicted, the system has continued to evolve in Vermont. The land gains tax, discussed in the next section, was included in Healy's assessment of the Vermont program, but the adoption of Act 200, discussed later, proved the accuracy of his prediction that the system would continue to evolve.

The Land Gains Tax

In 1973, Vermont adopted a unique progressive land gains tax under which the tax rate varied depending on the length of time the owner held the land and the amount of the gain. The maximum rate is 60 percent of the gain for land held less than one year with a 200 percent or greater gain in value. The tax declines to 5 percent for property held more than five years on which the gain is less than 100 percent, and it disappears after six years.[6] The legislature adopted the tax as part of a tax reform package that included property tax credits and a change in the method of assessing agricultural property. Buildings and other improvements, as well as the site of a principal residence, are exempt from the tax. The land gains tax is clearly an antispeculation tax. Because it applies both to subdividers and developers and to those who simply hold land for its unearned gain, it may affect the amount of subdivision and development activity. However, the evidence on that issue is not clear (DeGrove 1984, pp. 69–72).

Act 200

Renewed development pressures in the 1980s led to the adoption of Act 200, a statewide planning act (Fulton 1991). Adoption of the act followed the 1988 publication of the *Report of the Governor's Commission on Vermont's Future: Guidelines for Growth*, prepared by a commission appointed by Governor Madeleine M. Kunen and chaired by Douglas Costle, former administrator of the U.S. Environmental Protection Agency and then Dean of the Vermont Law School (Governor's Commission on Vermont's Future 1988). Citing concern over the failure of the planning aspects of Act 250 and the continued growth of the state, the commission made a number of legislative recommendations. These included streamlining the development review process; improving planning at local, regional, and state levels; and adopting statewide planning guidelines.

The legislature acted on the recommendations, but as is often the case, the legislation represented a compromise. The legislature did adopt twelve statewide goals.[7] Compliance with those goals is mandatory for state and regional agencies although an agency can disregard a specific goal if it expressly determines that it should not follow that goal in particular circumstances.[8] However, the law failed either to make planning mandatory[9] or to require that local plans be consistent with state goals.[10] The act does provide a financial incentive for communities to follow state goals. It authorizes impact fees as a form of exaction only for local governments with plans that have been confirmed by the regional planning commission.[11]

DeGrove said of Act 200, "The new Vermont law goes a long way toward establishing an integrated policy framework to guide growth in Vermont, but it fails to take the final, and crucial, step of mandating municipalities to prepare plans and implementing regulations" (1989, p. 38).

On the date of publication of this book, Vermont state, regional, and local governments are just beginning to implement the new state planning act. It is thus difficult to tell whether it will significantly improve planning in Vermont. However, Vermont remains a good example of a state that has taken an active role in attempting to manage growth.

FLORIDA

Florida joined the revolution later than the others, but when it did join, it moved quickly on many fronts. This state, which was not included among those featured in *The Quiet Revolution in Land Use*

Control, now arguably has the most comprehensive statewide land use program.

The revolution in Florida began differently than it did in Vermont and Hawaii. The state had a century-long history of promoting growth. Florida had used massive land grants in order to attract railroads into South Florida and to encourage draining of the swamplands. However, rapid growth began to overwhelm the state. It grew from twentieth among the states in population in 1950 to eighth in 1976 (DeGrove 1984, p. 102). Healy offered other figures that put the growth in perspective. "At times during the 1970s as many as 25,000 persons a month have moved to Florida. . . . In 1973, for example, one out of every seven new homes built in the United States was built in Florida" (Healy and Rosenberg 1979, pp. 126–127).

As an indication of the scale of the growth, Healy noted the proposed Palm Coast development in Flagler County, which then had a population of about 4,500. ITT's Palm Coast originally proposed enough housing for 750,000 people (Healy and Rosenberg 1979, p. 128).

According to DeGrove (1984, pp. 105–106), the change of heart in Florida began in 1969 when environmental groups successfully mobilized to stop a proposed new jetport west of Miami in the Everglades. Increasing concern with growth and the actual and potential environmental destruction from it, combined with a serious drought in 1971, led to the adoption of the Environmental Land and Water Management Act in 1972. That act combined new regulatory concepts with a proposal to float state bonds to finance the acquisition of certain areas. The voters subsequently passed the $200-million bond issue (1984, pp. 106–114).

The new regulatory concepts in the 1972 act addressed "areas of critical state concern" and "developments of regional impact." Both concepts were based on the *Model Land Development Code* prepared by a committee and distributed by the American Law Institute (ALI) (American Law Institute 1975). "Areas of critical state concern," as the name implies, are designated land areas of particular concern: these include environmentally sensitive areas, areas "affected by or having a significant effect on" a major public facility, or a "proposed area of major development potential."[12] The Big Cypress Area, Green Swamp, Apalachicola Bay, and Florida Keys were the subject of subsequent designations as critical areas under the revised process.[13]

The targets of the "developments of regional impact" regulations were, on the other hand, large projects such as power plants, large commercial centers, or particularly large housing projects likely to have an impact on an area greater than the communities that controlled them. The state law defined such a development as "any development which, because of its character, magnitude, or location, would have a substantial effect upon the health, safety or welfare of citizens of more than one county."[14]

The law regarding developments of regional impact remains in effect in essentially its original form. The Florida Supreme Court struck down the law regarding areas of critical state concern as an unconstitutional delegation of authority (the designation of the areas) to an administrative agency. It was, however, readopted with provisions for legislative action on future designations and with some other revisions (DeGrove 1984, pp. 126–128). Both concepts remain in Florida law today.

The basic idea behind the regulation of critical areas and developments of regional impact is similar. Both are based on the concept that although land use control should remain largely a local affair, certain types of activities and certain areas affect a region or the state as a whole, which thus should have some participation in the regulatory process beyond that of the local government.

However, the regulatory approach to the two is quite different. "Areas of critical state concern" are subject to a "designation" process, created in the ALI *Model Land Development Code* (1975, Article 7, Part 2) and involving the state. Once such an area is designated, the state supervises local preparation and enforcement of regulations and can step in to take over the process if the local government does not adequately protect the area. In contrast, the development of regional impact, or DRI, process is simply a procedural one. The DRI regulation is also based on the same article of the ALI model code (1975, Article 7, Part 3). Projects meeting the regulatory definition are subject to review by designated regional agencies, which then submit their comments to the local government that has regulatory authority over the project. The local government retains the final approval or denial authority, but the state law requires that it give serious consideration to regional concerns as reflected in the comments of the regional agency.

Although the critical areas and DRI provisions remain law in Florida, in many ways the most interesting provisions of Florida law are ones adopted in 1985. There were several legislative acts regarding planning and growth management in the 1984–1986 period, including the adoption of a state comprehensive plan as Chapter 187 of the Florida statutes (deHaven-Smith 1991, pp. 92–95, Table 4.1, at pp. 74–77, provides a chronological history of all planning-related legislative actions in Florida since 1960). In 1985 Florida amended Chapter 163 of the Florida statutes, governing local planning and development regulation, to

- Make local comprehensive plans mandatory;[15]
- Specify in some detail the required elements of local plans;[16]
- Require completion of such plans on a specified schedule, beginning on July 1, 1988, and concluding July 1, 1991;[17]
- Require that each county and municipality "adopt or amend and enforce land development regulations that are consistent with and implement their updated comprehensive plan" within one year after completing the plan;[18]
- Establish a process for state review of both the plans and the development regulations to determine whether they comply;[19]
- Give the state strong enforcement authority; and
- Require that local governments develop regulatory requirements limiting the approval of new developments unless there is evidence that adequate public facilities to serve such new development will be available "concurrently" with the demand generated by the development.[20]

Other states have established mandatory planning requirements and eliminated the confusion from the old enabling acts by requiring that local zoning and subdivision regulations be consistent with adopted plans (Innes 1991b; DeGrove 1984). However, with that act in 1985, Florida became the first (and as of 1992 the only) state to require affirmative acts by local governments to bring their local regulations into conformance with new mandatory plans. Although it may seem entirely logical that a local government updating its plan would also update its regulations, that is frequently not the practice. For example, a major study of the implementation of plans within the Portland, Oregon, urban growth boundary found that some communities had failed to update their zoning and had thus approved developments inconsistent with state-mandated plans (Ketcham and Siegel 1991). As the later discussion indicates, Oregon is a state with a strong commitment to planning, and such a finding there is particularly significant.

Even where a local government has the will and the means to continue working on planning issues after a major planning effort, and many do not have the will or the means, there are often political difficulties in implementing a new plan. For example, the new plan may suggest that certain areas should be "downzoned," or zoned to a less intense or otherwise less valuable category than they hold under current zoning. Adopting such a policy in a typically nonbinding plan is easier for most local governments than actually amending the zoning map to tell the landowner that she or he can no longer build apartments or industry on his or her property. Further, many good ideas in comprehensive plans remain unimplemented. Policies favoring increased open space and new bufferyards are provisions that local governments often include in plans but less often include in actual regulations.

In some ways, however, the concurrency requirements of the updated Florida law are even more significant than the planning requirements (see, generally, Pelham 1992).[21] The requirements for concurrent availability of public facilities with new development, of course, amount to adequate public facilities standards (see Chapter 4) imposed on a statewide basis (for a general description of this requirement, see Boggs and Apgar 1991). There was precedent for that. Vermont's Act 250 required affirmative findings regarding the availability of water and road access in its development permit review (see earlier discussion). Colorado had earlier required that counties make affirmative findings regarding the availability of water supply and waste treatment in approving subdivisions.[22]

However, Florida went further in two respects. First, the requirement in the Florida law applied to every type of project reviewed by any local government. In contrast, the Vermont provision applied only to those larger projects subject to the regional review process, and Colorado's requirement applied only to new subdivisions under county jurisdiction. Florida also went further in another respect. It tied the standards for facilities and improvements to a mandatory capital improvements element in the local comprehensive plan.[23]

Although that requirement is a little unusual, there is nothing particularly radical about it. It simply requires that a local government develop specific standards to define adequate public facilities or adequate levels of service as part of its capital improvements program. Local governments have long engaged in such activity. Establishing street widths, requiring 4 percent or 8 percent of an area to be open space, and requiring that water pressure provide a minimum "fire flow" are all typical standards contained in local regulations and affecting the design of public improvements.

The twist in the Florida law is the complementary provision that requires that the capital improvements element that set these standards also include "principles for correcting existing public facility deficiencies, which are necessary to implement the comprehensive plan."[24] That provides a very significant balance to the standard-setting procedure. The general trend of local government practice has been to increase standards over time. Thus, a project approved in 1991 typically faced greater improvement requirements than one approved in 1981; increased street widths, increased open space requirements, and requirements for such amenities as street trees have been typical additions (see, generally, Advisory Commission on Regulatory Barriers to Affordable Housing 1991). However, a community in Florida considering an increase in the amount of park land it requires for each resident must also consider how to acquire and pay for enough additional park land to bring existing areas of the community up to that standard. There is a nice symmetry to the Florida approach that seems likely to bring considerable balance back to the establishment of development standards.

DeGrove, who has been heavily involved in the implementation of growth management in Florida, published his book including the assessment of the Florida situation shortly before the latest legislation was passed in the mid-1980s. He posed the question of whether the growth management program then in place was adequate and answered his own question with a no. He cited as a "critical issue" the "lack of an integrated planning and policy framework that can assure that clear state policies frame regional policies and equally clear regional policies frame local government plans and policies" (1984, p. 171).

Although the 1985 act included exactly that sort of structure and the legislature adopted the first state comprehensive plan at about that time, the jury remains out some seven years later. Writing four years after its adoption, Fulton noted that the fiscal impacts of growth and their solutions remained major issues in the state (1991, pp. 122–123). DeHaven-Smith, in a somewhat radical critique of growth management in Florida, wrote in 1991 about "why growth management failed" (pp. 106–108). His thesis was that growth management is misdirected at the rate and amount of growth (a thesis for which he provides little documentation) and that it has thus failed to address the critical issues. To deHaven-Smith, those critical issues were the location and patterns of growth. He argued that the only real problem that faces Florida is urban sprawl and its side effects, including the negative fiscal impacts of sprawl (pp. 71–103). He urged the adoption of statewide zoning based on the Hawaii model in order to create development patterns that are efficient to serve and that are less threatening to the natural environment (pp. 109–110). He also recommended the adoption of urban service area boundaries (pp. 42–43). The consulting team led by James Duncan reached the same conclusion in their recommendations regarding more efficient development patterns (James Duncan and Associates 1989a, p. 21).

Those involved in implementing Florida's program may not agree with deHaven-Smith's proposed solution, but they recognize the problem. The Department of Community Affairs promulgated a document called "Techniques for Discouraging Urban Sprawl" in 1989 (Florida

Department of Community Affairs 1991). Also that year, the state commissioned James Duncan and Associates to conduct a major study called *The Search for Efficient Urban Growth Patterns* (1989a; see also James Duncan and Associates et al. 1989b).

As figures at the beginning of this section indicate, Florida's growth rate has been daunting. Some may question whether Florida can manage its growth without some type of limitation. The fact that much of the state's growth consists of retirees limits the impact on schools, a fact that makes it easier for the state to absorb growth. On the other hand, the substantial immigrant population places an extra burden on schools and social welfare programs in urban areas like Miami. Perhaps implementation of deHaven-Smith's suggestion of a state income tax might have some growth-limiting effect by limiting the number of retirees. An income tax would do nothing to stem the number of immigrants, although it would generate revenues to help to provide services for them.

On the one hand, the fact that Florida has absorbed virtually a tripling of its population from 1960 to 1990 and continued to operate at all is a remarkable achievement. On the other, the issues of the fiscal and environmental impacts of continued growth, at least in present development patterns, remained in 1992 much the same as they were when the first major Florida legislation was adopted twenty years before. Just as DeGrove urged that the state take additional initiatives to manage growth when he wrote his major assessment of growth management in Florida early in the 1980s, Florida must through the 1990s continue to seek improved and more effective solutions to managing the environmental and fiscal effects of growth on the state. Whether the state can accomplish that through the existing structure of local control under state supervision or whether it will take a stronger state hand, as deHaven-Smith urged, is not clear.

OREGON

Oregon adopted a statewide land use law in 1973, two years after the publication of the Bosselman and Callies work. The coalition that led to the adoption of the Oregon law included environmentalists concerned about logging in the eastern part of the state and others concerned about typical growth issues around the urban areas along the Pacific coast and in the Willamette Valley. DeGrove said that, of those issues, the concern about the loss of farmland to urban growth around Portland was perhaps the greatest (1984, p. 236).

Oregon's law, which remains in effect in 1992 substantially in its original form, contains some unique features. It established a state Land Conservation and Development Commission (LCDC) with the duty to adopt state goals and guidelines.[25] Local governments then had one year to bring their local plans into compliance with the state goals and to submit them to the commission for review and "acknowledgment" or rejection.[26]

The commission adopted the initial goals in December 1974 DeGrove 1984, p. 251). The process of reviewing local plans for compliance took far longer than projected. After seven years, the state had acknowledged about half the local plans and reviewed another 30 percent without accepting them. Roughly 15 percent of local governments had submitted no plans at all by that time (DeGrove 1984, p. 263).

Probably the most interesting features of the Oregon program are its dual emphases on the preservation of agricultural and forest lands, on the one hand, and the control of urban form, on the other. Goal 14 required that each community establish an "urban growth boundary" in a perimeter around the city. Figure 6.2 shows the urban growth boundary in the Portland metropolitan region. Land within the boundary was to be sufficient for twenty years of urban development. Goal 3 provided an extremely limited set of uses in the agricultural areas. Those restrictions are, in part, tied to the suitability of the land for farming, based on Soil Conservation Service classifications.

The program bears some philosophical resemblance to the Hawaii system because it provides a method of limiting sprawl and containing urban development within a limited area. However, there are some marked differences. First, the local government establishes the initial boundary and retains control over any changes in it, subject to LCDC review. That is very different from Hawaii, where the state Land Use Commission establishes the boundaries of the urban districts. Perhaps because the boundaries were established to include so much land or perhaps because of a lower rate of growth, Oregon has not faced the problem of constant amendments, as Hawaii has. Kasowski noted in 1990 that, "So far, only a handful of disputes have arisen in regard to whether or not to expand [urban growth boundaries], but this may be due in large part to the sluggish economy in Oregon" (1991, p. 128 [reprint date]).

The next chapter contains a discussion of the effects of the Oregon program on urban form. It has been far more effective than most in determining the shape of metropolitan areas. It has also resulted in increasing the intensity of development in some communities (Ketcham and Siegel 1991; see also discussion in Chapter 7).

Has the Oregon program worked? DeGrove found it a political

Figure 6.2
Portland, Oregon, Urban Growth Boundary as Established by Metropolitan Service District

Source: Map adapted from Jerzy Lewicki from Portland Metropolitan Service District, 1990, "The urban growth boundary and incorporated cities."

and practical success (1984; 1989). Kasowski gave this anecdotal evidence of his assessment of the program as "one of the most successful statewide programs":

Drive south on I-5 from Portland, a city of 1.3 million, to Salem, the state capital less than 50 miles away, and you won't see the typical commercial strip sprawl, runaway roadside development and far-flung subdivisions that characterize many other highly-traveled corridors in the U.S. What you see instead are pastoral landscapes of farms and fields in the fertile Willamette Valley, broken by occasional copses of evergreens.

   Make no mistake about it: the fact that much of the countryside is still rural can largely be attributed to Oregon's statewide land use planning program, which restricts development to areas within urban growth boundaries (1991, pp. 125–126).

OTHER STATES

There are other states in what Fulton has called "the second revolution" (1991). Several are worthy of brief mention.

Georgia

The development of the state role in Georgia will be interesting. In 1989, the governor signed legislation that he had urged the legislature to adopt. It created a three-tiered planning structure.

At the state level, the law created two new state bodies:

- **Governor's Development Council,** a body chaired by the governor and including representatives of key state agencies. It is responsible for long-range planning at the state level and for the location of public facilities by state agencies.[27]
- **Board of Community Affairs,** a reconstituted body appointed by the governor. Its role is to establish state planning guidelines, both procedural and substantive, and to establish the territories of each of the regional bodies.[28]

To carry out regional planning functions, the law created regional development centers (RDCs) and required that every local government become a dues-paying member of one of the centers.[29] The RDCs have the duty to coordinate local plans, resolving differences among them, and develop bottoms-up regional plans.[30] "Bottoms-up" planning generally refers to a process in which a comprehensive plan is built from recommendations from constituents rather than coordinated and dictated from a central planning authority. It often refers to plans assembled from recommendations of citizen committees. In this case, the bottoms-up planning synthesizes the concerns of each local government within a region into a regional plan. Although bottoms-up planning is politically attractive, because of the participatory process, it is often difficult to bring such divergent interests together into a meaningful and coordinated plan.

Local governments retain the primary authority to plan and regulate land use and development under the new law. Development of a comprehensive plan, including elements on land use, infrastructure, environmental issues, and economic development, became mandatory under the law. However, implementation and enforcement remain entirely matters of local discretion. The mandatory planning requirement will be enforced through denial of Department of Community Affairs grants to local governments that are not "qualifying," that is, that do not adopt plans as required by the law.[31]

The Georgia experience will be interesting for two quite different reasons. First, most of the experience with strong state programs has been acquired in coastal states with relatively high growth rates. Although Georgia has a limited coastline, it is quite different in character from states like California and Florida. Further, its major population center (Atlanta) is not along the coast.

Second, the program is a unique middle–United States blend of local control and regional and state planning. It lacks the strong state controls of Hawaii, Florida, and Oregon; but it includes the same basic goal: to accomplish regional and state coordination of diverse local activity.

Washington

Also joining "the second revolution" was the state of Washington, with the adoption of its Growth Management Act in 1990.[32] That act included mandatory planning requirements for the fastest-growing counties and cities in the state and a requirement that zoning be brought into conformance with comprehensive plans. Like the Oregon law, it included requirements for the designation of agricultural and forest lands and for the establishment of "urban growth areas."

In September 1990, the Washington State Growth Strategies Commission published its report. The commission had been appointed by the governor in 1989, before the adoption of the Growth Management Act. Its report provided broad recommendations for planning and growth management in Washington, including proposals for amendments to the just-passed act.

Although many of the commission's recommendations are similar to those cited in discussions of actions in other states, a few are worthy of particular note. The commission recognized the significance of state actions in one of its first recommendations. "All state agencies must plan and carry out actions consistent with the growth strategy goals. The state must develop a coordinated strategy that uses state spending as an incentive to accomplish the goals" (Washington State Growth Strategies Commission 1990, p. 4). Noting that 69 percent of recent growth in Washington had taken place outside cities (p. 11), the commission determined that "cities are the preferred places for urban growth: In areas required to develop comprehensive plans, urban growth areas should be cooperatively identified by counties and the cities within them. Development within the urban growth area should be coordinated and phased through joint county and city planning agreements" (p. 10).

The commission adopted a philosophy similar to Florida's "concurrency" requirement in determing that "paying for public facilities should be a shared burden between today's citizens and those of the future. New development should pay for its own impacts, and the broad community should fund the cost of improving, over time, existing facilities that are inadequate to meet present needs" (p. 13).

As the system in Washington evolves, it will be interesting to compare its effectiveness with that of neighboring Oregon.

Maryland

Maryland is a small state that includes portions of two major Metropolitan Statistical Areas, Baltimore and Washington. It also includes such innovative local governments as Montgomery County (see description of program in Chapter 4) and Howard County.

At the state level, however, Maryland's record for studying issues is better than its record for taking action. As noted in Chapter 3, its legislature failed to adopt an innovative and farsighted development code prepared for it in 1969. More than two decades later, the 1991 session of the legislature rejected legislative recommendations of the Governor's Commission on Growth in the Chesapeake Bay Region (1991a). Among the legislative recommendations of the report were the establishment of a statewide land classification system to designate developed areas for concentrated growth (p. 8).

Protecting Special Lands

A number of state programs provide special protection for special lands. California's coastal zone management program is a prime example (Healy and Rosenberg 1979, pp. 80–125; DeGrove 1984, pp. 177–234; DeGrove 1989, pp. 26–28). All coastal states have adopted programs under requirements of a federal law, although not all go as far as California's.

New York has adopted a management program for its Adirondack Park area which, despite the name, includes 3.7 million acres of private land along with 2.7 million acres of public land (Healy and Rosenberg 1979, p. 178; see, generally, Banta 1989; and Bosselman and Callies 1971, pp. 295–298; Popper 1981). A joint federal–state partnership resulted in a large-scale plan for preservation of New Jersey's Pine Barrens, which also contain a mixture of public and private land (DeGrove 1989; Healy and Rosenberg 1979, p. 178; Babcock and Siemon 1985).

Other states have adopted mandatory planning requirements. Those include, but are certainly not limited to, Maine, Rhode Island, and Delaware (Abberger 1991). Whether those laws, like one that has long been in effect in Wyoming (Gilmore and Duff 1975; Sanborn and Logan 1976), will create growth management systems or just better planning is uncertain at best.

REGIONAL PLANNING: THE REAL ISSUE?

A principal advantage of planning at the state level is that it offers the opportunity to control the complexity of the metropolitan regions within a state. The statewide land use planning effort in Oregon is really not about statewide land use planning. It is about providing some order to the regions around Portland, Eugene, and a handful of other growing urban areas.

Clawson long ago recommended a regional solution. Under the heading of an "ideal planning process," the first of five recommendations was, "Planning that deals with major land use in the whole of an urban area should be on a metropolitan or SMSA scale since land use planning for only part of an economic area is inevitably only partial in its answers. This does not deny that some problems are local or that planning for their solution cannot be local" (1971, p. 182). In the concluding chapter of his work, Clawson recommended the development of "larger units of government of metropolis-wide scope. Unless some unit of government has the responsibility for planning and action on problems which involve the whole metropolitan area, such problems will simply go unattended" (p. 353).

Several years earlier, Chapin had recommended a metropolitan regional plan, metropolitan public works policy, and an "urban development code" to serve an entire metropolitan region (1963). Writing before the federal government preempted most pollution control activity, he wrote, "The urban development code would reorganize and codify in one metropolitan area instrument the regulations presently scattered through different ordinances in each jurisdiction that relate to land development and the construction, use, and occupancy of structures on the land. Such a code would also include controls in the use of land, water, and air in the larger region" (p. 84).

Bain proposed an interesting approach in an apparently little-noticed paper in a compendium prepared for the report of the 1969 National Committee on Urban Growth Policy. He suggested creation of an "urban development district" as a regional agency in a metropolitan region. His proposed agency would temporarily supersede local land use controls in the region, but it would also actively engage in both land development and economic development activity. In short, it would take a pro-active role in causing the kind of development shown in the regional plan. Ultimately, after the development of its designated region was substantially complete, the agency would be abolished (1969). More recently, Porter cited the need for regional government and called it "the missing link in relating transportation and land use" (Porter 1991).

An individual local government can easily implement adequate public facilities standards without the intervention of either the region or the state. However, enforcing such standards may require the cooperation of both. It does little good for a particular community to decide that traffic on its arterials should be at level of service (LOS) "D" (heavy traffic but still moving) or better at rush hour if adjoining communities allow development to load the same roads to LOS "E." Addressing the issues of sprawl and urban form and even the timing of development are issues that can best be accomplished at the regional level.

Widespread mergers of local governments seem unlikely to be more common in the 1990s than they were in the 1970s when Clawson recommended such mergers. However, creating some stronger forms of mandatory regional planning, as Oregon has done, may be more practical and politically realistic in many states than implementing statewide land use planning, as Oregon has also done. The budget problems and resistance to tax increases facing many local governments in the early 1990s may contribute to increased regional cooperation out of financial necessity. State governments may begin to mandate regional planning or cooperation as a condition of state financial assistance for local projects.

Clearly in some cases the problems are statewide. In Hawaii and Vermont, the pressures of tourist and second-home development affect wide areas of the state, many of them outside logical metropolitan regions. In Florida, population growth is occurring throughout the state. In those states, statewide programs seem clearly necessary. However, in other states a modified form of the Oregon approach, with strong, state-mandated regional agencies, may offer a more interesting approach. In that context, it will be interesting to observe the Georgia experience as it implements its mixture of bottoms-up and top-down planning, with a strong regional emphasis.

CONCLUSION

How important is state growth management? It depends on what one is trying to achieve.

Only a state or a strong regional agency with authority delegated from the state can use techniques like urban growth boundaries or "state zoning" to control urban form. If the goal is to stop sprawl or to protect certain lands, such as agricultural lands or wetlands, while still accommodating development, only the state can do a fully effective job. If regional efficiency of services is a goal, again only the state or a regional body empowered by the state can be effective. Even the adequacy of public facilities can be regulated better at a regional level than at a local one.

Innes argued that state growth management programs are "systems for sharing power" (1991a, p. 3). In characterizing state programs in a separate publication, she noted that, "In each state there is some arbiter of conflicts" (1991b, p. 6). She also cited as a coordination strategy the requirement for planning as applied to state agencies as well as local ones (1991b, pp. 6–7). She noted the significance of the fact that developers, environmentalists, and state and local governments have joined to make growth management a reality in most of the states that have adopted programs and remarked that, "These interests have decided they prefer rules of the game to endless controversy" (1991a, p. 3).

Regional or statewide planning offers a considerable improvement over the status quo in most states because it offers some chance of coordinating the diverse activities of the multiple local governments within a typical growing metropolitan area. Although it seems unlikely that a significant number of additional states will, in the foreseeable future, adopt strong statewide programs like those in Vermont and Hawaii, many of the issues addressed in this book realistically cannot be solved by individual local governments. Encouraging or mandating regional planning may be the most politically practicable form of state role in growth management in most of the United States.

NOTES

1. Haw. Rev. Stat. Sect. 205-1.
2. Haw. Rev. Stat. Sect. 205-2, 3.
3. 10 Vt. Stat. Ann., Sect. 6081; see also definition of "development" at Sect. 6001(3).
4. 10 Vt. Stat. Ann., Sect. 6086(a).
5. Ibid.
6. 32 Vt. Stat. Ann., Sect. 10001, et seq.
7. 24 Vt. Stat. Ann.., Sect. 4302.
8. Ibid.
9. 24 Vt. Stat. Ann., Sect. 4381.
10. 24 Vt. Stat. Ann., Sect. 4382.
11. 24 Vt. Stat. Ann., Sect. 5200.
12. Fla. Stat. Sect. 380.05.
13. Fla. Stat. Sects. 380.055, 380.0551, 380.0552, 380.0555, and 380.0558, respectively.
14. Fla. Stat. Sect. 380.06(1).

15. Fla. Stat. Sect. 63-3177.

16. Ibid.

17. Fla. Stat. Sect. 163-3167(1).

18. Fla. Stat. Sect. 163.3202(1).

19. Fla. Stat. Sects. 163.3167, 163.3213.

20. Fla. Stat. Sect. 163.3202(1)(g).

21. The term *concurrency,* does not appear in the statute but rather in the Department of Community Affairs Regulation 9J-5, which provided the regulatory basis for implementing the 1985 act. See Reg. 9-J5.003(19) and (20). The term has subsequently come into relatively wide use. See, for example, Boggs and Apgar 1991.

22. Colo. Rev. Stat. 30-28-133(6).

23. Fla. Stat. 132.3202(1)(g).

24. Fla. Stat. 163.3177(3)(a)(1).

25. Ore. Rev. Stat. Sect. 197.005 et seq.

26. Ore. Rev. Stat. Sects. 197.005k, 197.040, and 197.250.

27. Code Ga. Ann. Sect. 45-12-201.

28. Code Ga. Ann. Sect. 50-8-4.

29. Code Ga. Ann. Sect. 50-8-33.

30. Code Ga. Ann. Sects. 50-8-34, 35.

31. Code Ga. Ann. Sect. 50-8-2(a)(18).

32. Wash. Code Ann. Sect. 36.70A.010 et seq.

7

Growth Management and Urban Form

Urban form is a complex subject that can encompass everything from the skyline to the urban landscape to the actual shape of a city. Urban form is both directly and indirectly a concern of growth-managing communities. Some communities, such as Boulder and Montgomery County, adopt growth management programs in part to manage the shape of urban growth. Many communities that adopt growth management programs do so hoping to reduce the cost of serving new development. Those costs are in part a function of urban form (James Duncan and Associates et al. 1989a; Real Estate Research Corporation 1974; see Chapter 9). Finally, urban form can affect housing costs, both directly and indirectly. Thus, to understand fully the effects of growth management programs on the land and housing markets and on the public treasury, it is important to understand whether and how such programs affect urban form.

In certain respects, the answer to the question posed here is self-evident. Any conscious attempt to regulate the location of urban growth is bound to affect urban form in some way. An adequate public facilities requirement ensures that most new development will take place reasonably close to existing facilities. That is an effect on urban form. It may or may not be an effect consistent with the goals of the community adopting the growth management program, but it is nevertheless an effect on urban form.

In discussing urban form, it is important to remember the context in which most growth management programs take place. As the discussion in Chapter 2 indicates, most growth-managing communities are parts of metropolitan regions in which dozens, or even hundreds, of local governments and special districts make decisions that influence the patterns of growth. In that typical context, it is difficult for a single community to make a significant difference in the overall pattern of urban development. It can, of course, make a difference in its own shape, but that is only a small part of the typical metropolitan region.

Dowall described the competition among communities in the San Francisco metropolitan region, first for each to obtain as much growth as possible and later for each to push as much growth as possible onto other communities (1984, pp. 14–33). Greenberg documented the very specific competition among communities within the Amador Valley, which includes Livermore. He showed how the willingness of officials of the county and of nearby Pleasanton to approve projects facilitated the continuation of the rapid residential growth that Livermore tried to slow down in the region. Those attitudes also created political pressure that threatened the viability of the Livermore program (1986).

URBAN FORM AND SPRAWL

Treatment of the broad subject of urban form goes far beyond this book. However, some growth management programs do address one very significant aspect of urban form: the shape and extent of the urban area.

It is almost a truism among planners and others that sprawl is bad and that the ideal urban form consists of a central city with relatively intense development surrounded by less intense development, all separated from nearby communities through open space, whether public or private. In a 1958 piece, William H. Whyte noted that *Fortune* and *Architectural Forum* had recently convened a group of nineteen experts for a "two day conference on urban sprawl." In that piece, he noted that the problem was not a shortage of land:

The problem is the pattern of growth, or rather the lack of one. Because of the leapfrog nature of urban growth, even within the limits of most big cities, there is to this day a surprising amount of empty land. But it is scattered; a vacant lot here, a dump there, no one parcel big enough to be of much use. And it is with this same kind of sprawl that we are ruining the whole metropolitan area of the future. . . .

Sprawl is bad aesthetics; it is bad economics. Five acres are being made to do the work of one, and do it very poorly. This is bad for the farmers, it is bad for communities, it is bad for industry, it is bad for utilities, it is bad for the railroads, it is bad for the recreation groups, it is bad even for the developers (1958, pp. 116–117).

A dozen years later, in his landmark work, *Suburban Land Conversion in the United States* (1971), Marion Clawson noted the inefficiency of sprawl and particularly of what he called "subdivision discontiguity," or "sprawl on the subdivision scale" (1971, p. 320; see, generally, Chapters 8 and 9 of Clawson). He also traced the history of sprawl and the role of infrastructure construction, federal policies on housing finance, and other governmental influences on creating the sprawling metropolises of the last part of the twentieth century. In 1969, the National Committee on Urban Growth Policy attributed the pattern of sprawl to three factors: "prosperity, automobility, and public policy" (published in Canty 1969, p. 18). The committee cited two public policies that contributed significantly to sprawl: federal mortgage policy, which facilitated the purchase of single-family houses; and federal highway policy, which "spread automobility." In 1980, the federally appointed Council on Development Choices for the 80s listed as one of its principal concerns an increase in the consumption of land by urbanization, in part because of a reduction of the intensity of use (Council on Development Choices for the 80s 1980, pp. 10–13). The council made six recommendations for the 80s, two of which directly addressed sprawl:

1. Increase compactness of metropolitan fringe and nonmetropolitan areas;
2. Accelerate the process of infill and redevelopment in existing communities (1980).

More recently, Benjamin Chinitz, in an article challenging some of the premises of those who oppose sprawl, gave this example of "USING LAND THE WRONG WAY. . . . Urban sprawl that encourages automobile use and results in an inappropriate pattern is illustrative" (Chinitz 1990, emphasis in the original).

Although a number of economists challenge some of the economic bases on which Clawson and others have found sprawl to be "inefficient" (see later discussion in this chapter), the issue remains important in establishing urban development patterns. Thus, to the extent that growth management programs do attempt to influence urban form, they are likely to attempt to limit sprawl. Boulder has addressed the issue of contiguous sprawl directly with its greenbelt. Montgomery County has similarly tackled sprawl within its focus on preserving "wedges and corridors" of green space as well as large areas of agricultural land while allowing substantial development in other areas.

The model of a reasonably compact community surrounded by open space (often in the form of agricultural land) is not a modern invention. It finds roots in the independent rural communities that dotted the United States before the automobile facilitated commuting. It resembles the types of compact towns that tended to cluster around commuter railroad stations near nineteenth-century New York and Philadelphia.

That idealized form of development certainly owes some debt to the work of Ebenezer Howard, a British court reporter whose small book, *Garden Cities of Tomorrow*, remains in print nearly a century after it was written (Howard 1902). It has, directly or indirectly, influenced many planners and accounts directly for the designs of both Radburn, New Jersey, and Sunnyside, located in the Queens borough of New York City, both built in the 1920s. It also influenced the construction of the federal greenbelt towns of Greenbelt, Maryland, Green Hills, Ohio, and Greendale, Wisconsin, in the 1930s (Parsons 1990; Mields 1973). The same idea underlay the promotion of new towns by the Department of Housing and Urban Development in the 1970s (Mields 1973). In creating the new communities program, the Congress made specific findings related to this issue:

The Congress further finds that continuation of established patterns of urban development, together with the anticipated increase in population, will result in: (1) inefficient and wasteful use of land resources which are of national economic and environmental importance; (2) destruction of irreplaceable natural and recreational resources and increasing pollution of air and water; . . . (4) costly and inefficient public facilities and services at all levels of government.[1]

One of the reports available to Congress when it adopted the new communities legislation was the 1969 report of the National Committee on Urban Growth Policy (published in Canty 1969). Among its findings, many of which related to inner cities, were these related to suburban growth patterns:

But our concerns extend to the suburbs as well. They are the fastest growing areas of this nation, yet the way they are growing is wasteful and destructive of environmental value. Their residents' taxes increase steadily, yet yield decreasing benefits in terms of the amenities these people came to the suburbs to find. Uncontrolled development is consuming at random the irreplaceable resource of land and steadily polluting the life-giving resources of air and water. Man-made elements of the environment, transportation facilities, water and sewage lines, are being stretched and overburdened by sprawling development. The process is wasteful of money as well: Each extension of these facilities entails a "sprawl tax" of costs that could be reduced by rational planning (p. 169).

Private developers operating without federal subsidies built the original portions of both Reston, Virginia, and Columbia, Maryland, in that period. Both are part of a large metropolitan area, but both include concentrated employment centers, relatively high densities, and significant amounts of open space (Mields 1973).

Similar concepts of urban form clearly influenced those who developed the programs in Boulder, with its tight urban edge defined by a thirty-five-square-mile greenbelt, and Oregon, with state-mandated urban growth boundaries.

In a chapter called "General Development Plans" in a standard planning reference book (So and Getzels 1988), Barnett outlined four historical periods of urban design as the basis for modern planning ideas. Two relate primarily to the built environment of the inner city and thus do not relate to this discussion. The other two were garden suburbs and garden cities, distinguishing the free-standing cities proposed by Howard from the garden suburb movement in this country; and "modernist city design," a concept for complete design coordination of a city surrounded by a greenbelt (Barnett 1988, pp. 177–185). Bair described a scheme of urban design that he called the "open space net" (1979, pp. 161–188). It is not surprising that it included nodes of relatively intense development separated by areas of linked open space and surrounded by a greenbelt.

Other ideas of urban form are typically based on concepts of efficiency, minimization of capital or operating costs, or both. Those models also call for relatively compact and contiguous forms of development, although the high-density center and the surrounding greenbelt are not essential to those models (see, generally, James Duncan and Associates et al. 1989a; Real Estate Research Corporation 1974).

Of course, one can reach the same type of urban form simply from principles of land preservation. If one believes that the optimal urban development form is one that affects the least amount of land, clearly a tightly contained, relatively dense urban area best meets that ideal (Whyte 1958).

In their mid-1970s survey of communities involved in early growth management efforts, Brower et al. found that 78 percent of the communities surveyed listed "reduction of urban sprawl" as an objective of growth management (1976, Table 5, p. 109). That objective was second only to "provision of adequate public services" (84 percent). It tied with "environmental protection," and was followed by "preservation of open space" (66 percent), clearly a related topic. Audirac et al. noted, "Redirecting future growth to a more compact urban form has emerged as the all-encompassing vision of Florida's growth management policy" (1990, p. 577).

Whether growth management programs can effectively limit sprawl is the question addressed in the rest of this chapter. The question of whether it makes sense to do so is largely left to Chapters 9 and 10.

Two Aspects of Sprawl

The relationship between sprawl and efficiency in the use of land raises two separate issues. One is the general density of development. If the growth trends of a community indicate a need for 2,000 additional dwelling units over the next several years, accommodating that growth at eight dwelling units per acre will consume 250 acres of land, whereas accommodating it at more typical suburban densities of three or four dwelling units per acre will consume 500 or more acres of land. Most studies of the fiscal impacts of development (the focus of Chapter 9 of this book) compare the relative efficiency of various densities of development.

The other aspect of sprawl, however, is so-called "leapfrog" development, which economists are more likely to call "discontinuous development." As the alternative names suggest, such a pattern of development skips over land next to the community and takes place on land separated from the community by unused or underused land. Chapter 9 also examines the fiscal impacts of leapfrog development. This chapter contains additional discussion of the debate over other economic effects of leapfrog development.

GROWTH MANAGEMENT AND SPRAWL

Can growth management programs stop sprawl? As a practical matter, yes. However, doing so may require more political will than many public officials have.

Effects on Discontinuous Development

Almost any growth management program is likely to limit leapfrog or discontinuous development, at least to the extent of the effective jurisdiction of a community. However, if that jurisdiction adjoins or overlaps the jurisdictions of other communities, as is typically the case in a metropolitan area, a growth management program in one community may simply force development to leap further, beyond the control of that community. Although Boulder limited its growth in housing units in the 1980–1990 decade to almost exactly 20 percent, the number of housing units in Boulder County increased by more than 26 percent (from 74,638 to 94,621) during that period (see Figure 7.1 which shows the decrease in Boulder's share of the county population). The figure is even more dramatic when placed in the context of some of the communities that absorbed the growth: the number of housing units in Louisville increased 111 percent (2,264 to 4,785); the number in Lafayette by 55 percent (3,703 to 5,775). Longmont, with a much larger base, increased its housing stock by 25 percent (16,346 to 20,480) (Bureau of the Census 1991a, 1982; see also Figure 7.1). Because household size decreased over that decade, Boulder's rate of population increase was only about 1 percent. Further, its share of the county population has decreased consistently under its growth management program (see Table 7.1).

Fischel cited an unpublished study of Fairfax County by George Peterson for data showing that even within a jurisdiction restrictive controls in one area can force development further out within the same jurisdiction (1990).

Clearly regional urban growth boundaries such as those imposed directly and indirectly by the states of Hawaii and Oregon, can minimize the problem of having discontinuous development leap further out. However, even such techniques have their limitations. Ketcham and Siegel examined development patterns around Portland to date and concluded that there will not be enough land within the urban growth boundary to absorb all projected growth under current zoning over the planning period (1991, p. 8). Unless development patterns change, local governments change the zoning, or the state permits the regional government to move the growth boundary, the only choice available to those wanting (or wanting to provide) additional housing may be leapfrogging.

Further, if a growth boundary of any sort is as impermanent as a line on a zoning map, it is likely to have little effect on leapfrogging. Bair described the difficulty faced by Montgomery County in adhering to the strong open space component of a 1965 plan when the county faced massive urban development pressure around the nation's capital (1979, pp. 108–119). In a study of the price effects of Portland's urban growth boundary, Knaap (1985) found that the outer boundary significantly affected land prices but that an inner, interim boundary had little discernible effect. He concluded that the reason for the difference was that the outer boundary was viewed as a rela-

Figure 7.1
Growth Trends in Boulder and Three Other Communities in Boulder County,
with County as Reference

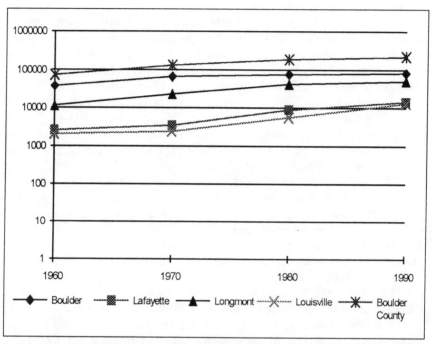

Sources: Bureau of the Census, 1991, *Census of Population and Housing: Summary*
Population and Housing Characteristics, Part 7, Tables 15 (county) and 16 (cities);
Bureau of the Census, 1981, *Census of the Population: Characteristics of the Popula-*
tion, Chapter A, Number of Inhabitants, Part 7, Tables 4 (county) and 5 (cities); and
Bureau of the Census, 1972, *Census of Population, Vol. 1, Characteristics of the Pop-*
ulation, Part 7, Table 10; graph by author.

tively permanent constraint on the market. The corollary of that
conclusion is, of course, that those involved in the market apparently
did not take the inner boundary very seriously (Fischel 1990). Because
a state agency controls the ability of the region and local governments to change the more permanent outer boundary in Portland, it
is both procedurally and politically more difficult to change than
the inner boundary, which remains under regional control. If the
permanence of a growth boundary is not taken seriously enough to
affect land prices, it probably will not survive long enough to make
much difference in the shape of the community. Clearly the Boulder
approach of owning the greenbelt is the only one certain to ensure
the preservation of that part of Ebenezer Howard's "garden city"
concept.

Table 7.1
Boulder Population as Percentage of County Population 1960–90

Population	1960	1970	1980	1990
Boulder	37,718	66,870	76,685	83,312
Boulder County	74,254	131,899	189,625	225,339
City population as percentage of county population	50.8	50.7	40.4	37.0

Sources: Bureau of the Census, 1991, *Census of Population and Housing: Summary Population and Housing Characteristics*, Part 7, Tables 15 (county) and 16 (cities); Bureau of the Census, 1981, *Census of the Population: Characteristics of the Population, Chapter A, Number of Inhabitants*, Part 7, Tables 4 (county) and 5 (cities); and Bureau of the Census, 1972, *Census of Population, Vol. 1, Characteristics of the Population*, Part 7, Table 10 (includes 1960); percentage computations by author.

Subsidizing Leapfrogging?

It can be argued that if the installation of such public improvements as freeways and interceptor sewer lines to or through an area makes leapfrogging possible, the public sector actually subsidizes leapfrog development. That is probably true regarding freeways, which are typically constructed with federal and state funds. Hanson has calculated the substantial direct and indirect subsidies to automobile use in one community in Wisconsin (1992). Because of widespread policies of "making growth pay its own way" through exactions (Robinson 1990; Witt and Sammartino 1990; Frank and Rhodes 1987; see discussion in Chapter 4), communities clearly subsidized sprawl less in the 1980s and early 1990s than in earlier periods. Parker noted that by the early 1990s it was not uncommon for developers to participate even in financing major freeway improvements (1991).

Nevertheless, there are circumstances in which a community still subsidizes sprawl, whether or not it intends to do so. New freeway and other major road construction, carried out for a variety of community purposes, will certainly encourage development along them. When a community builds such a road away from existing urban areas, something that it may do simply because of the cost of right-of-way, it is likely to encourage sprawl. A road or interceptor sewer line to a new industrial park outside town will attract development along it. As is urged in the conclusion to Chapter 5, it is important to understand that phenomenon not to stop building public works with public money but simply to do so with a full understanding of the secondary impacts.

Effect of Growth Management on the Intensity of Development

Can growth management make a community more dense? Although Downs, Audirac, and others argue that doing so conflicts with consumer desires (see discussion and citations in the last section of this chapter), there is evidence that at least one program has done so.

A major study of the Portland program found, among other things, that

- The *volume* of multiple-family and attached single-family development increased dramatically;
- The *proportion* of multiple-family and attached single-family housing increased dramatically; and
- The *proportion* of smaller and more affordable developed single-family lots increased (Ketcham and Siegel 1991, pp. 6–8).

The study was a joint project of 1000 Friends of Oregon, widely viewed as an environmental organization, and The Home Builders Association of Metropolitan Portland, a trade group.

The Oregon program, however, consists of more than the simple urban growth boundary. Under the Oregon growth management law, local jurisdictions had to develop plans to meet state goals (see program description in Chapter 6). One of the state goals, Goal 10, requires that local governments plan and implement an affordable housing program. Further, because the urban growth boundary was a long-term limit on urban growth, state policy required that local governments accommodate long-term housing needs within that boundary.

One of the other findings of the Ketcham and Siegel study was that "in providing the 'opportunity' for development to occur at targeted densities, most local governments predicated Housing Rule compliance on the assumption that maximum allowable densities (under comprehensive plan designations) could be achieved" (1991, pp. 48–49 and Appendix E). In other words, local governments assumed that an area planned for development of multifamily units at "not more than" twelve units per acre would develop at exactly twelve units per acre. That did not happen, for two reasons, according to the study. First, some of the land was "underzoned." In other words, some local governments had left the zoning on land in more restrictive categories than the new plan required. That is a surprising finding, because it means that the local governments are ignoring their own new plans in preparing their regulations. The Oregon growth management law clearly requires consistency between local plans and local rules. Even before adoption of that law, the Oregon Supreme Court had upheld the application of a developer to build a project at a density greater than that permitted by the zoning but within the density range suggested by a newly adopted plan.[2] Note that Florida is the one state that has addressed the issue of implementation of mandatory state plans, requiring review not only of the plans but also of the implementing regulations (see Chapter 6).

Development also fell short of that planned in some parts of the Portland region, according to the study, for a second reason: "underbuilding," in which developers built less intense projects than local plans and zoning would have permitted. For example, 12 percent of single-family subdivisions developed during the study period were built on lands zoned for multifamily housing (Ketcham and Siegel 1991, p. 9). The study found that the principal causes of "underbuilding" were market demand factors and site constraints, both natural and human-made. The primary market demand factor influencing decisions to build at less than planned density was the continued demand for single-family detached homes on relatively large lots (1991, pp. 53–54). Site constraints ranged from power-line easements to wetlands and floodplains (pp. 57–58). It is surprising that the study found citizen opposition to the increased density to be a relatively minor factor in underbuilding (pp. 59–60).

Perhaps the most interesting of eight major recommendations of the 1991 Portland report is that local governments be required to include minimum densities in their zoning ordinances (Ketcham and Siegel 1991, p. 69). Zoning ordinances have always contained density standards, but those have been maximum density standards. As the Portland study showed, it is not unusual for actual development to fall below the maximum permitted density.

Specific recommendations for implementing the minimum-density rule in Oregon include a prohibition of single family homes on land zoned for apartments, rather than the more typical, "cumulative" approach that permits in each residential zone any type of residential development up to and including the primary intensity for that zone (for a discussion of cumulative zoning, see Kelly 1988, p. 269). The Portland study also proposed a limit to the subdivision of higher-density single-family zones into large lots and a requirement that in multifamily zones development occur at no less than 75 percent of the maximum permitted intensity (Ketcham and Siegel 1991, p. 69). Presumably the authors of the report would also recommend that in determining the size of a twenty-year growth boundary planners should calculate the development capacity of the area within the ur- ban growth boundary at 75 percent of the permitted density rather than 100 percent.

A minimum-density requirement attacks directly one of the con- cerns about sprawl: the low-intensity use of land. That might seem to limit the range of housing opportunities available. The Portland study found that it has done so (that aspect of the study is discussed in Chapter 10 of this book). However, a University of Wisconsin study found a surprising amount of overlap in the types of dwelling units theoretically buildable at various densities (Alexander, Reed, and Murphy). The authors determined that single-family detached resi- dences could be built at as many as twelve units per acre, while at- tached dwelling units (townhouses) could be built up to fifty-seven units per acre (1988, pp. 34–40). Target density ranges for communi- ties in the Portland area range from six to ten units per net buildable acre.[3] Thus, according to the Wisconsin study, it would be possible for the communities to meet their *density* goals with a mix that in- cluded few apartment units. Because Goal 10 primarily addresses affordability, Oregon would probably not permit that. However, where the reduction in the consumption of land is the primary con- cern, it would be possible to implement similar density goals without significantly disturbing the diversity of housing types in the market.

IS SPRAWL ALL BAD?

There remains the question of whether the influences of growth management on urban form are beneficial. Advocates of compact, contiguous patterns of development argue that higher densities combined with contiguity result in lower housing costs for consumers and lower service costs for the public. The arguments and their cri- tiques are presented in Chapters 9 and 10. However, it is important to consider here another aspect of the issue. Is a compact, contiguous development pattern generally beneficial?

Some persuasive voices argue that it is not, for somewhat different reasons. Peiser raised one of the most interesting arguments in favor of leapfrog development, although he criticized low-density urban development as "inefficient. It increases transportation costs, con- sumes excessive amounts of land, and adds to the cost of providing and operating public utilities and public services" (1989, p. 193). Nevertheless, in the same article, Peiser built a theoretical and em- pirical argument favoring discontinuous development. His argument was that, over the long run, such development will encourage greater densities. He hypothesized that land prices on the omitted parcels (the land over which the early development leaps) would increase faster than those at the urban fringe. That is a perfectly logical argument because land surrounded by development (the original community and the "leaped" area), would presumably have most or all urban services. The very fact that it would be surrounded by development would increase its market value. Peiser next argued that the higher land prices would force developers to build higher densities on the omitted parcels, resulting in higher infill densities on the omitted parcels than would have occurred with continuous patterns of development. In other words, in order to recover the higher land costs, developers would find ways to increase the intensities of use on those parcels omitted by the leap of early development.

Peiser tested the hypothesis with data from Fairfax County, Virginia; Dallas, Texas; and Montgomery County, Maryland. Montgomery County's regulations thwarted his hypothesis by prohibiting higher densities on the omitted parcels. However, he found that the data from Fairfax County, which had permitted increased densities on infill parcels, generally supported his theory. The data from Dallas were mixed. Despite the limited relevant data, he concluded, "The regressions indicate that for cities which allow higher densities on infill parcels, discontinuous development may lead to higher densities than are likely to occur where discontinuous development is prevented" (1989, p. 201).

Peiser ignored an important variable in this process, the political process. In a careful study of Sacramento County, a team from the University of California-Davis found that implementation of an urban services boundary was easier than encouragement of infill development (Johnston, Schwartz, and Tracy 1984). Citizens involved in the plan implementation process forced the reduction of infill densities below those projected by planners in Sacramento County. Peiser's model would permit the ultimate infill site to be surrounded by neighbors who, as developers know, frequently become opponents of intense development. Thus, although Peiser's economics appear to be sound, it is essential to account for the political aspect of the process.

In a separate article, Peiser acknowledged exactly such concerns, although in a different context (1984). He acknowledged the logical corollary of his argument regarding land prices and densities: if urban growth boundaries increase land prices, they should lead to increased ·densities. He would presumably support minimum density requirements, such as those included in the urban growth boundary program in Portland. He did argue in favor of exactions and adequate public facilities requirements. "New residents should bear their fair share of costs associated with urban growth" (1989, p. 202). He continued, in the same article:

While sprawl may be unjustly maligned for generating low density develop-ment, the potential benefits of discontinuous growth nevertheless depend on the full-cost pricing of development. If discontinuous development is subsidized by utility companies, highway programs, or municipal contribu-tions, sprawl patterns of development may be spread over so large an area that inefficiencies associated with sprawl would outweigh any potential benefits from higher density infill development (p. 203).

Some studies have argued that the best way to reduce sprawl is to encourage the development of higher density, mixed-use projects that are often called "planned unit developments" (Council on Devel-opment Choices for the 80s 1980; Real Estate Research Corporation 1974) or simply "planned developments." Peiser argued in a separate article that there are institutional reasons why there is not more construction of planned (unit) developments in the United States. His analysis tacitly recognized that construction of "planned develop-ment" typically requires one developer willing to undertake an entire large-scale project. He cited the risks inherent in large projects with long build-out times, including the risk of market changes, the diffi-culty in obtaining financing, and the threat of regulatory barriers in the community. Finally he noted the significant risk that with a long-term building project, new residents who move in may begin to exer-cise political power to oppose completion of the project as planned (1984, esp. p. 430). In short, although Peiser acknowledged some ad-vantages to planned development rather than sprawl, he has not been optimistic about achieving such patterns on a large scale.

Ohls and Pines (1975), whose work was cited by Peiser, made two arguments consistent with those of Peiser, although one of them is quite different in nature. They argued that commercial development is typically not financially feasible at the urban fringe when residen-tial development first takes place there. Thus, omitted tracts (land over which earlier development leaps) provide opportunities for later construction of convenient and accessible commercial development, leading to a more efficient development pattern than is found if commercial development is forced further out on the expanding urban fringe. That argument is entirely consistent with Peiser's hypothesis of higher values and the need for more valuable uses on omitted land, because commercial development is typically a higher-value and more profitable use than residential development. How-ever, that portion of the Ohls and Pines argument is also subject to the same limitation that Peiser acknowledged for his own work. If the sprawl is so great that it skips over large land areas, those areas may never develop efficiently. The Ohls and Pines argument for essentially using sprawl to "reserve" tracts for convenient commercial development is more persuasive with respect to individual tracts of land than with respect to large tracts around a community.

Ohls and Pines offer a second argument—that "if people prefer lower densities (or if lower costs are associated with lower densities) it may make sense initially to build lower-density housing relatively further from the city center to accommodate this desire for low density as much as possible, while at the same time reserving the central land for its ultimate high-density development" (1975, p. 228). Their model was "based on a trade-off between living space and accessibility" (p. 225). It used a combination of transportation costs and housing costs to determine the housing options available to a family. It thus shared a philosophical base with Alonso's early work and Wingo's integrative model of transportation and land use (see discussion in Chapter 5), although Ohls and Pines did not cite either of those works.

One difficulty in assessing the efficiency or desirability of a particular growth pattern is the increased complexity of the urban fabric. As Pivo (1990) and Cervero (1991) have noted, an increasing number (and proportion) of employment opportunities are to be found in the suburbs. Planners in Montgomery County and elsewhere seek a "jobs-housing balance" within local planning areas to reduce commuting (Montgomery County Planning Board 1990). However, Cervero (1989) found, in a study of San Francisco and Chicago suburbs, that even where such a balance exists, commuting distances and times are greater than ever. Adding even more complexity to the model is the fact that the service patterns of commercial centers have changed and no longer follow traditional, somewhat hierarchical models used by planners (Howe and Rabiega 1992).

Despite these largely theoretical arguments, data presented in Chapter 9 suggest that the fiscal impacts of sprawl on a community may be significant, at least over the short run. That finding is not inconsistent with Peiser's argument, given earlier. His argument is that over the long run infill development will make leapfrog development become efficient. His argument would acknowledge the inefficiency over the short run.

Land as a Scarce Resource

The economic discussion in this section disregards a key point, which is that land is a finite resource. The recognition of land as a scarce resource clearly led to the adoption of the original system of statewide zoning in Hawaii and the similar system of establishing urban growth boundaries in Oregon.

Increasing population threatens the land resource. Although the rate of population increase in the United States has slowed, the rate of growth in new households continues to be significant. The combination of the factors, plus some need for replacement housing stock, drives the residential portion of the development economy. An economist who is a purist would argue that the market will efficiently account for the value of land as the demand for it increases (or shrinks or stays stable). Society, however, may make a different determination. The current market may suggest that the value of nonurban land is not very great, but state or local officials may, as they have in Oregon and Hawaii, decide that the public sector has a stake in protecting that finite resource until society needs it. As long as it remains relatively cheap (and nonurban land is usually relatively cheap when compared to urban land), the market system will not provide that long-term protection.

Note that this issue is different from the issue of protecting particular lands, an issue addressed in the next chapter. The point of this brief discussion is that society may decide to encourage relatively compact development simply to minimize the consumption of land and to reserve as much undeveloped land as possible for long-term use, regardless of the operation of the current market.

CONCLUSION

Many growth management programs affect urban form. Adequate public facilities requirements tend to encourage contiguous, rather than leapfrog, development, except where the community has extended adequate public facilities to some noncontiguous location, such as a public airport. Growth phasing systems that emphasize the location of growth also tend to promote contiguous development. A tightly drawn urban growth boundary creates a clear urban edge and increases the density of development within the boundary, but it is also likely to force some leapfrog development into other communities. A widely drawn urban growth boundary should create a clear urban edge in the long run and may increase densities somewhat in the short run.

Despite the disdain in which "sprawl" is held by most planners and many citizens, it is not clear that efforts to control it through growth management will yield more benefits than costs. Urban growth boundaries in particular may stop one form of sprawl (low-density, contiguous development) while causing another (leapfrog development) that is arguably worse. As the discussion in Chapter 10 indicates, such programs also create significant shifts in the housing supply. The costs and benefits of those shifts must be carefully considered in analyzing the desirability of adopting such a program for a particular community.

Some economists argue that sprawl is actually efficient over the long run. As the discussion in Chapter 9 suggests, one problem with that argument is that the long run may not come, or it may come much further in the future than anyone expects. That is, a community may permit leapfrog development in one year, anticipating that the omitted parcels will develop over the next decade or so. However, if growth suddenly slows, the omitted parcels may not develop for twenty, forty, fifty, or more years. In that case, the short run, during which the leapfrog development pattern is clearly in many ways inefficient, becomes much longer than most planners (or economists) would anticipate.

Nevertheless, the fact remains that sprawl is not a desirable form of development. Or is it?

AFTERWORD: SPRAWL AND THE INTERESTED CITIZEN

Downs analyzed the relationship of housing consumers and sprawl with a twist on the old adage that "in a democracy, people get the government that they deserve." He argued that "in reality the major causes of increased suburban traffic lie in the behavior patterns of the same households who are now complaining about it" (1988, p. 24). He cited as those causes three specific sets of desires and resulting behavior patterns:

- Living at low densities;
- Having access to a wide choice of places both to work and to live; and
- Commuting by private automobile (1988, p. 24).

This argument is, of course, entirely consistent with the conclusions of Fuguitt and Zuiches, who found that people want to live in a small community with access to a big city (1975). It is also consistent with Dubbink's detailed study of two growth management communities in California, San Juan Capistrano, and Bolinas (1984). He found that what the communities sought through growth management was the maintenance of a "rural illusion" (1983, p. 135), or the creation of a "disguised" or "anti-suburban suburb" (p. 139). He noted that both communities had been rural market centers that had suffered, but also enjoyed, years of economic doldrums. During the times of limited economic activity, the communities by default retained older houses, small town character, and expanses of agricultural land around them. He found that the growth management movement in each community was an effort, led by recent arrivals, to retain and/or recapture that small town character.

Similarly, in an assessment of residential preferences among Florida residents, Audirac, Shermyen, and Smith (1990) found that "while there is a small clientele for compact downtown environments in large metropolitan cities, there is a stronger preference for single family homes and rural and semi-rural residence, as well as a willingness to make longer commutes in order to live in such places" (p. 477). Although they did not provide demographic detail sufficient to determine whether one should believe that this preference represents the general population or just the middle class, it is entirely consistent with the findings of several other studies cited here. There is little reason to believe that the dream homes of the urban poor are significantly different from those of the middle class, even if their chance of achieving them is smaller.

Yet it is noteworthy that many of those interviewed by Dubbink in his study of the two California communities were commuters, clearly dependent on the larger metropolitan area. That fact confirms Downs's hypothesis and Fuguitt and Zuiches's 1975 findings. In Dubbink's conclusion, he noted that Bolinas, located in Marin County with some of San Francisco's richest suburbs, and San Juan, located north of San Diego along a booming strip of seaside communities, are "private islands, awash in nostalgia for something they can never be" (1983, p. 199).

Suburban residents have a love-hate relationship with sprawl. Most do not like the idea of sprawl, nor do they like the increased traffic or higher taxes that they perceive as side effects of sprawl. On the other hand, those same suburban residents want to live in single-family detached homes with large yards in a quiet, "semi-rural" community from which they can easily commute by private automobile to a nearby metropolitan center that offers a greater variety of shopping, services, and employment opportunities than they can find in their "anti-suburb suburbs." That pattern of development essentially defines sprawl. The scenario reminds the author of Walt Kelly's Pogo, the comic strip possum, who once remarked, "We have met the enemy and he is us."

NOTES

1. *Housing and Urban Development Act of 1970,* Sect.710(a).
2. *Baker* v. *City of Milwaukie,* 533 P.2d 772 (1975).
3. Ore. Admin. Rules, Sec. 660-07-035.

8

Growth Management and the Natural Environment

This chapter examines the effect of growth management programs on environmentally sensitive lands. Floodplains, wetlands, steep slopes, prime agricultural lands, and forests are some of the kinds of lands that environmentalists, planners, and many interested citizens today seek to preserve (see, generally, *National agricultural lands study* 1981; McHarg 1971; Thurow, Toner, and Erley 1975). Development of such land may represent a hazard to the land itself (as in the case of wetlands), to the development that takes place on it (as in the case of geologic hazards), to the larger community (as in the case of floodplains), or to some combination of those. For example, development of a floodplain may not particularly hurt that piece of soil, but it will increase flooding in the community as a whole and it will subject the buildings on the land and the people in them to an increased risk of damage from flooding.

The issue of protecting such lands is partly, but not wholly, a question of urban form. Concerns with sprawl lead logically to concerns about the efficient use of land and the preservation of the maximum practicable amount of land for nonurban uses. Protecting particular lands is a related but quite different subject.

Environmental issues rank behind issues related to public facilities and more general concern about "sprawl" and community character among the reasons for adopting growth management programs, but protecting such lands is certainly a factor in the adoption of some growth management programs (Brower et al. 1976, pp. 108–112; Greenberg 1986, pp. 260–271). A 1975 study of early growth management programs found, in part, "Concern for environmental damage was a motivating factor in most of the 13 case studies and second only to concern for provision of public services" (Gleeson et al. 1975, p. 109).

All the designated areas of state concern in Florida are environmentally sensitive lands (see Chapter 6). Vermont based its original development-control program on the objective of preserving agricultural lands (see Chapter 6). The joint state-federal effort to preserve the Pinelands in New Jersey was based completely on ecological concerns (Babcock and Siemon 1985; Moore 1986). New York State also based its program to protect the Adirondack Park area on environmental concerns (Ulasewicz 1986). Thus, although environmental issues are not at the forefront of some of the most famous growth management programs, protection of the natural environment is a growth management concern in many areas. Further, a growth management program that sets priorities for growth patterns without regard to sensitive lands would verge on the irresponsible because it would ignore a valuable and often irreplaceable resource of the community. Thus, the protection of sensitive lands is, or should be, a concern in all communities serious about managing growth.

THE CHARACTER OF SENSITIVE LANDS

Like porcupines, sensitive lands contain some built-in protection. Development is often difficult and expensive. The only type of sensitive land on which development is easy is agricultural land. The flat, well-drained character of good farmland lends itself easily to development in patterns required by engineering-driven subdivision regulations and makes drainage problems easy to solve. Prime agricultural soils are typically stable for building (Olson 1981; or see the descriptions of soil suitability in the tables in any local soil survey).

Any type of development on steep slopes, wetlands, or other sensitive lands typically involves extra engineering, earth-moving, and other costs. Developers often skip over parcels of sensitive lands in sprawling metropolitan areas, just because of the cost of developing those parcels. In the 1000 Friends – Home Builders study of the effects of growth management on housing costs, cited in the previous chapter, the authors found that among the principal reasons for "underbuilding" (building less than planned densities) were "site constraints" such as floodplains, creeks, and wetlands (Ketcham and Siegel 1991, pp. 57–60) and "site amenities" such as "hilltop views" and "wooded surroundings" (p. 56). In one sense, the example demonstrated bad planning, because the original Portland plans should have excluded such lands from density calculations. The combination of state pressure to increase density (see discussion in Chapter 7) and the lack of apparent protection for such lands could be devastating to sensitive lands within the urban growth boundary. It is somewhat remarkable that market forces were sufficient to protect some of them in the face of the public pressure to increase densities.

Although both the consumer interest in living on hilltops and in woods and the costs of developing such sites offer some protection to sensitive lands, that protection is not perfect. In the context of today's wide interest in protecting wetlands (Salvesen 1990), it is noteworthy that vast areas of Chicago, Boston, Miami, San Francisco, and other cities sit on fill in what were once wetlands or even bodies of water. Filling those areas was clearly expensive. The fact that it occurred reflected not only a lack of understanding of, or a lack of concern with, the environmental consequences. Those early earth-moving activities also demonstrated a significant need for the land for urbanization.

SENSITIVE LANDS AND THE URBAN COMPLEX

There are serious and unavoidable conflicts in any attempt to preserve sensitive lands from urbanization. Those conflicts are more complex than the straightforward confrontations between local governments and landowners or developers. Many sensitive lands stand squarely in the path of development, and some can be developed easily.

Programs that attempt to preserve prime agricultural land face immediate conflicts because of the location of most cities near rivers. Early settlers in this country, as in others, located towns near rivers because they provided both a source of water to support the population and a means of transportation. As settlement moved west, it remained along rivers, even where those rivers did not offer transportation. Construction first of the railroads and later of highways typically supplied transportation to established population centers, which were generally located along rivers, and thus reinforced the importance of those centers. For a graphic illustration of the effects of those patterns, note the inverted ell around which virtually all the population centers in New York State form. That ell-shape is defined by the Hudson River north from New York City to Albany and then by the route of the Erie Canal west to Buffalo. That path later became the route of the railroad and subsequently that of the New York State Thruway.

What is the character of the river bottoms around which so many cities focus? It is generally very rich soil, deposited by the river. In dry climates where irrigation is necessary for successful agriculture, water is readily available in the river bottom. The land is typically flat and well drained. Those are predominant characteristics of prime agricultural land. River bottoms typically provide such lands. Many, if not most, communities of significant size sit in or surround such river bottoms. Thus, any random development pattern of the city will consume at least some good agricultural land.

Planners often characterize these river bottoms in another way: they refer to them as "floodplains." The founders of these cities sought locations where water would be readily accessible. Sometimes it has been entirely too accessible. Attempts to limit sprawl and encourage infill development put increased development pressure on undeveloped lands within an urban area, including a floodplain. Thus, a growth management program may increase development pressure on floodplains and other sensitive lands within the urban area.

Many floodplains contain growth magnets, making the problem worse. Public works engineers typically design sewer systems to use gravity flow (see discussion in Chapter 5). That design leads to the installation of interceptor sewer lines in floodplains, because the river represents the lowest point in the community. The installation of such a growth magnet in the floodplain reinforces the development pressures on the floodplains. Further, in areas where floodplains remained relatively undeveloped or were developed only in marginal economic activities in the 1960s and 1970s, land prices in the floodplains were often relatively low. The low land costs and the continuity of the riverbed made the floodplains attractive routes for those seeking land for new interstate highways. Those interstate highways are themsevles significant growth magnets. If built in the floodplain, they are likely to attract development there.

Metropolitan areas often include wetlands, steep slopes, and other sensitive lands which often remained undeveloped during early community building because of the higher cost of developing them. Efforts to reduce sprawl or to promote development near existing public facilities may encourage the development of omitted parcels that happen to include wetlands or steep slopes. Thus, growth management programs do not necessarily protect sensitive lands, regardless of the intentions of their creators. They may have quite the opposite effect, encouraging the development of sensitive lands that market forces have essentially protected.

METHODS OF PROTECTING SENSITIVE LANDS

The most effective way to protect sensitive lands, such as floodplains, steep slopes, wetlands, and prime agricultural lands, is to preclude development on them. McHarg (1971), in a book called *Design with Nature*, argued cogently and influentially that in many cases it is possible to do just that—to design around sensitive lands. He suggested and used natural resource analysis as the basis for plans for particular developments and for entire communities. Others have made similar recommendations, in large part based on McHarg's work (see, for example, Kaiser et al. 1974; Thurow, Toner, and Erley 1975). For legal and political reasons, it is often difficult to prohibit all development on private property. In such cases, it is desirable to minimize the amount of development on sensitive lands such as hillsides (Thurow, Toner, and Erley 1975, pp. 570–584). Another approach suggests that development regulations require that a proposed project be designed in such a way as to mitigate the environmental problem. Such mitigation techniques can range from special foundation designs in difficult soils to rock-diversion barriers in areas subject to landslides (Hendler 1977; Shelton and Prouty 1979). Kendig et al. (1980), proposed a system of zoning based essentially on McHarg's techniques.

In an article assessing Florida's attempts to control urban form by limiting sprawl, Audirac, Shermyen, and Smith (1990) argued that sensitive lands should be protected directly by local and state laws rather than indirectly through limits on urban development:

Regulating development to be more dense and compact delays confronting the real environmental impact of rapid population growth and unplanned conversion of land to urban use. . . . Ian McHarg's [citation to *Design with Nature*] organic conception of urban development designed for the carrying capacity of the land seems a more appropriate vision for the future good life in Florida than abstract notions of ideal urban form (p. 477).

Similarly, in a relatively early work on growth management, Finkler and Peterson argued that local planning should be based on carrying-capacity analyses that include the capacity of public facilities, the natural environment, and less tangible human systems (1974, pp. 89–92). They noted that a carrying-capacity approach would best be implemented at a regional level, coincident with regional air and water basins (p. 92). Although they did not cite McHarg, their carrying-capacity concept alluded clearly to the ideas that McHarg had set forth three years earlier.

One community that used the carrying-capacity approach in its comprehensive plan was Hilton Head Island, South Carolina (Hilton Head Island, Town of 1986; Rahenkamp 1986). That island community in one sense constitutes a region by itself because its environment is quite separate from that of the nearby mainland. On the basis of a carrying-capacity analysis, the plan allocated development to various parts of the island based on a combination of environmental and infrastructure capacities (Hilton Head Island, Town of 1985a). Initial work on the plan was developed by John Rahenkamp who like McHarg is a Philadelphia-based landscape architect and whose firm like McHarg's had ties to the University of Pennsylvania.

In proposing the use of a carrying-capacity approach to environmental protection, Finkler and Peterson (1974) included the concept in a list of alternative approaches to growth management. The list also included growth phasing systems, development moratoriums, and other techniques. Thus, they recognized that the protection of sensitive lands was in a sense a separate issue from that of controlling the timing and location of growth, although the two issues are certainly related.

THE EFFECTS OF GROWTH MANAGEMENT

Growth management programs may make the problem of sensitive lands better or worse, or they may make no difference whatsoever. The same 1975 study that found that environmental concerns were second only to those about public facilities in communities adopting growth management programs noted, "None of the case studies evaluated the environmental impact of the proposed systems, nor were such studies done in any other location" (Gleeson et al. 1975, p. 109). The report later noted, "Environmental studies used as a basis for the design of growth management systems are weak or nonexistent" (p. 113).

Little has changed from that early assessment. In 1989, Porter noted, "Environmental concerns sparked much of the early development of growth management systems, but the environmental effects of growth are still not well understood."

The nature and location of the sensitive lands and the type of growth management program determines the effect. For sensitive lands within the primary development area or inside an urban growth boundary, a growth management program is unlikely to offer much protection and may increase development pressure. If one effect of a growth management program is directly or indirectly to discourage sprawl, the pressure to develop vacant infill parcels will increase. If land becomes scarce through such a program, the extra costs of developing a hillside or a wetland may become comparatively insignificant in the market. Thus, an urban growth boundary program or an adequate public facilities program in an area where outlying facilities are limited is likely to increase the development pressure on sensitive lands within the primary development area.

A rate-of-growth program that uses qualitative criteria to rate developments (for reasons explained in Chapter 3, both Boulder and Petaluma have abandoned such criteria) could certainly provide a lower priority to projects that propose the development of sensitive lands. Otherwise, a rate-of-growth program is unlikely to have any particular effect on sensitive lands. A phased growth program could protect sensitive lands if it phased most growth in other directions. However, as Chapter 4 indicates, most communities with phased growth programs base them on the availability of public facilities. The likelihood that the geographical pattern of development most likely to preserve sensitive lands and the one most likely to optimize use of existing facilities will coincide is small. Thus, such programs also are not likely to have a significant effect on sensitive lands.

The best protection for sensitive lands within the primary urban development area, other than outright purchase, is through local land use controls such as performance standards (Thurow, Toner, and Erley 1975). Design regulations requiring that such areas be preserved in the development process (Kendig et al. 1980; Hendler 1977; Kaiser et al. 1974; Land Use Planning Committee 1971) can work well where the sensitive land amounts to a small part of a large parcel. With such a site, it is possible to "cluster" development on developable land, thus preserving the sensitive land at little or no net economic cost to the developer (see illustrated examples in Hendler 1977, pp. 14–65; Salvesen 1990, pp. 69–77; also see Pivo, Small, and Wolfe 1990; Rahenkamp Sachs Wells & Associates, The American Society of Planning Officials, and Stoloff 1977). Communities can implement such controls through zoning and subdivision regulations. Those effective tools are quite separate from a growth management strategy.

Growth management techniques can limit the development pressure on sensitive lands outside the primary development area. Considering the development suitability of lands within the metropolitan area in deciding how to phase growth or where to draw the urban growth boundary can make an enormous difference in the development pressure on sensitive lands.

Nonstructural techniques are also important. Where it is possible to omit environmentally sensitive lands from annexation plans, a community should do so. A community should certainly avoid sensitive lands to the maximum extent practicable in deciding where to locate new roadways, interceptor sewer lines, and other growth-inducing public investments. If there is a large and sensitive area outside a community, such as the steep mountain backdrop west of Boulder, urban growth boundaries and a long-range refusal to annex territory or to provide public services can provide significant protection. However, it is also important to remember that Boulder has not relied solely on refusing to annex and serve such lands. It has also bought many acres of them (see discussion in last section of Chapter 5).

Insofar as sensitive lands fall within the logical area of urban growth, as they often do, growth management techniques simply increase the development pressure on them. Protecting those lands adequately over time requires a combination of strategic public acquisition, performance and other development standards, and incentives to "cluster" development on less sensitive land under common ownership (see, generally, Pivo, Small, and Wolfe 1990; Rahenkamp Sachs Wells & Associates and The American Society of Planning Officials 1977; Rahenkamp Sachs Wells & Associates, The American Society of Planning Officials, and Stoloff 1977). Montgomery County (Hamblen 1991) and a few other communities have used transferable development rights as a method to encourage the preservation of sensitive lands. However, there are major legal and practical difficulties with implementing such a program, and a discussion of it is far beyond the scope of this work.

It is difficult to overemphasize the value of purchasing sensitive lands when possible. Boulder's greenbelt will be green long after sensitive lands in other communities that simply planned or designated those lands for preservation have turned into shopping centers and houses.

CONCLUSION

The growth management proposal rejected by the 1991 Maryland legislature included a program of "visioned growth." Visioned growth was a plan for more compact and contiguous development that would:

I.   concentrate development in suitable areas;

II. protect sensitive areas;

III. establish rural centers;

IV. preserve the Chesapeake Bay;

V.   conserve natural and economic resources; and

VI. do this in a way that allows appropriate financial resources to be directed to appropriate acts and actors (Governor's Commission on Growth in the Chesapeake Bay Region 1991a, p. 73).

The Maryland proposal represented an interesting and responsible combination of growth management and environmental protection. It is unfortunate that the Maryland legislature again lost the opportunity to be a national leader.

The careful reader will note the lack of absolutes in the analysis in this chapter. "The community should consider . . . avoid . . . to the maximum extent practicable." Although there are some who take an absolutist view on the protection of certain sensitive lands, public officials implementing a growth management program must consider many other factors in deciding where and how to direct growth. If a community must choose between permitting development on prime farmland and forcing new development five miles further from town to bypass a large belt of prime agricultural soils, its leaders face a difficult choice. They must choose between immediate damage to the agricultural resource and sprawl, with its potential for other types of long-term degradation. It is the kind of choice that politicians dread, but it is exactly the type of public policy choice that a representative democracy asks its leaders to make. A professional planner or a book author cannot tell officials facing such a decision what the right answer is. All that the professional can do is to provide the basis for the public officials to make a well-informed choice.

The worst results will occur when public officials in a community decide to manage growth without regard to the issues of sensitive lands. In such a community, the growth management program may increase the growth pressure on sensitive lands omitted from development through market forces. In such a community, highway and sewer construction without regard to sensitive lands will provide magnets to development that affect such lands. Only by considering the role of sensitive lands in a community can public officials develop a growth management program that provides a degree of protection appropriate to the community to such lands. Some states now mandate minimum levels of protection for some lands (see Chapter 6), but in others each community must decide for itself what is appropriate. Some people will undoubtedly disagree with any particular choice, finding it too restrictive or not protective enough. However, by making an express and carefully considered decision on the subject, a community can reach a reasonable and appropriate policy regarding the protection of sensitive lands and the priority of that goal in relation to other goals, such as those encouraging efficient, contiguous development patterns.

9

Growth Management and the Cost and Availability of Public Services

This chapter refers to a number of statistical studies that compare the costs of public service for different patterns and types of growth. It is important in considering those studies to retain a common-sense approach to the issue and not to get lost in the numbers. With little analysis (and the analysis will support these assertions), it is safe to assert that

- Any growth management program that limits the approval of new development to an amount that can be served by available public services will, by definition, ensure the availability of public services and will do so better than a program that does not contain such requirements.

- On the other hand, a rate-of-growth program, growth phasing program, or urban growth boundary program that establishes the growth rate, phases, or boundaries based on criteria other than the availability of public services may or may not ensure the availability of public services.

- Over the long run and with good planning, an urban growth boundary program should result in the full availability of services throughout the growth area concurrent with the full development of the area. However, there may be localized or even area-wide imbalances in the short run.

- Any growth management program that requires or encourages new development to take place in areas with existing services (which will typically, but not always, be adjacent to existing development) will result in a lower cost of services than would result if there were no limitations on the location of development.

- Increased capital costs resulting from increased distance, for example for longer roads or larger pumps, will usually mean increased operating and maintenance costs.

Nothing in the studies cited in this chapter contradicts these common-sense principles. Some of the studies confirm them. Like most studies with large numbers of figures, however, the ones cited here can become confusing.

EFFECT ON PUBLIC SERVICE AVAILABILITY

An adequate public facilities program, properly administered, should result either in a balance between the demands on public facilities and the capacities of those facilities or in a surplus of capacity.

When Westminster established its growth management program, based largely on the availability of public facilities, it was issuing permits at the rate of 1,000 dwelling units per calendar quarter. It then had more than 3,600 "permit-ready" lots in the city, an additional 1,000 lots approved for single-family development, and thousands of additional units approved through early stages of the development review process. In contrast, the city had enough sewer and water capacity to serve about 2,600 additional dwelling units (Westminster, City of 1978b, charts 78C(1) through 78C(4) and Report B, p. 13; see, generally, Chapter 4). By the early 1980s, capacity available in Westminster's infrastructure systems exceeded development demand, and the city has had no difficulty in accommodating growth since that time. Thus, the growth management system initially restored the balance between service capacities and demands and then maintained it during and after the peak years of building (see, generally, James Duncan and Associates and Kelly 1991a; Snyder 1982).

In Livermore, growth management began as a citizen initiative to limit new development to the amount that did not create demand exceeding the capacities of the schools and the sewer and water systems. Greenberg found that the Livermore program, like the one in Westminster, served its purpose. "All approved residential projects were thoroughly reviewed, and the availability of infrastructure was assured in advance. By 1980, water supply, wastewater treatment and overcrowding in schools ceased to be major civic concerns" (1986, p. 409).

Montgomery County provides a different example. As the description in Chapter 4 indicates, Montgomery County is one managed-growth community where development pressures continued at a high level in the 1980s. When the county first established a growth management system in 1974, sewers were the critical limitation on development both there and throughout the Washington metropolitan region (Montgomery County Planning Board 1974). Seventeen years later, relative capacities had changed. Although the availability of sewer service remained one of the criteria in the growth management program, the critical link had become traffic (Montgomery County Planning Board 1990b; Montgomery County Planning Department Staff 1987). Traffic has become such a concern that the county uses it in two levels of development regulation. First, the general traffic loads of each of seventeen policy areas of the county play a role in establishing the "staging ceilings," or growth capacities of each of those areas. Second, the county requires that larger projects provide site-specific traffic impact analyses through a local area transportation review process and that the developers then mitigate any unacceptable impacts (Montgomery County Planning Board 1990a).

Other types of programs may not be as effective at ensuring a balance between the capacity of public facilities and the demands placed on them. Boulder's determination that it would accept population growth of 2 percent each year and Petaluma's decision that it would permit 500 new dwelling units each year (plus a number of exemptions in each community) clearly bore no particular relationship to the capacities of public facilities. The programs reflected that fact in their terms, because both limited their controls to residential development. Clearly commercial and industrial uses also consume water and generate sewage. It is noteworthy in this context that the federal district court considering the Petaluma program found that the city had adequate capacities in both its sewer and water systems to absorb development beyond that permitted by the system in its early years.[1] It is similarly noteworthy that Boulder lost a lawsuit with a developer when it refused to provide service to that developer when city-controlled lines ran near the development site and had available capacity (see discussion of both cases in Chapter 4).[2]

However, these different types of programs differ not only in effect but also in purpose. Snyder contrasted the "basic motivation" of Boulder, "To limit growth in terms of both rate and magnitude," and Westminster, "To insure that the city maintains the service and fiscal capacity necessary to accommodate growth" (1982, p. 259). Dubbink, in his study of growth management programs in San Juan Capistrano, concluded that technical capacity issues were not the basis for the program there. He commented:

My impression was that the technical findings of the [staff] report had long been eclipsed by the hours of public hearings associated with setting San Juan's yearly growth quota. This seemed to be an essentially political event where the unrest of the protectionists was balanced against the unrest of those with land to develop and the costs of extending services was balanced against the cost of litigation for withholding them (1983, p. 129).

Perhaps the most dramatic illustration of the lack of relationship between some growth management programs and the availability of public facilities came from Ramapo, New York. Its initial point system allocated development "points" to a project based on the relative availability of sewer service, access, park and school sites, fire protection, and drainage. The Ramapo program was a phased growth system tied to an eighteen-year capital budget. Under the program and the capital budget, the community presumably provided for the complete eighteen-year buildout of the town limits. However, when the regional sewer district failed to construct the sewer improvements as scheduled, "the Town Council decided to automatically award the maximum number of points (five) to special permit requests since that time" (Hammer, Siler, George Associates 1977, p. 11).

One could argue, of course, that Ramapo officials were simply trying to be fair to developers by not penalizing them for the fact that a regional entity had fallen behind in its own commitment. On the other hand, if the town had been serious about ensuring the availability of public facilities, there was no excuse for essentially exempting a significant number of projects from the sewer criterion of the point system.

The conclusion of this section is not complicated; it is, in fact, as the introduction to the chapter suggests, a common-sense result. Growth management programs that directly regulate the adequacy of public facilities succeed in ensuring the availability of public facilities as new development takes place. Other types of growth management systems do not ensure that availability.

Certainly a program that slows the growth rate or limits the geographic area within which growth may take place may reduce the likelihood and the extent of any service problems, but that is quite different from ensuring that services are available as development takes place. Livermore imposed an adequate public facilities requirement early in its growth management history, although it later replaced that requirement with a residential rate-of-growth program. The city of Westminster and Montgomery County have always based their growth management programs in part on the adequacy of public facilities. A Florida law passed in 1985 and phased into effect over the next several years requires that all local governments ensure the "concurrent" availability of adequate public facilities before approving new development (see discussion in Chapter 6). The 1990 state growth management law in Washington ties land development approvals to the availability of transportation facilities, but the state Growth Strategies Commission recommended, "The Act should be revised to link land use planning and development approvals with other public facilities such as parks, schools, sewers, stormwater drainage, fire protection, and water supply and distribution" (Washington State Growth Strategies Commission 1990, p. 13).

In short, if one of the goals of a community in adopting a growth management program is to ensure the adequacy of public facilities, it should include adequate public facility requirements in its program.

A Different Issue of Timing

Just having an adequate public facilities requirement on the books is not quite enough to ensure the availability of public facilities. Many projects are not built when the community initially approves them. It is important to include such projects in the growth management equation.

Westminster did not intentionally overcommit its sewer and water capacities by 400 percent Its city officials were not unconscious of its capacity limitations. A sudden acceleration in building permit applications early in 1977 surprised public officials there. Many of those applications were not for new projects. They were for revivals of projects that the city had approved years earlier but developers had apparently abandoned. Of four lawsuits brought against the city's growth management program, three were brought by foreclosing lenders who wanted to revive dormant projects. Westminster, like most communities, then had no system for tracking developments that had received various stages of approval but had not been built.

Although the situation in Westminster in 1977 may have been extreme, it was not unique. Old, unbuilt subdivisions dot the countryside around most major metropolitan areas. Site plans for shopping centers and apartment houses that were never built sit fading in planning offices. Scattered vacant lots in an urban area may not seem significant individually, but their total can be quite significant. In a vital economy, buildings will gradually occupy most of the subdivided lots. While many unbuilt projects may remain permanently dormant, some may be revived. This is more likely to occur in a booming economy and in a context in which an old project approval may offer the developer the possibility of relief from more rigorous requirements under current rules.

Controlling the problem of unbuilt projects is not particularly difficult if a community is conscious of the issue. One key element in such a process is a provision for various approvals to lapse if they are not used within a specified period. For example, Westminster's city code provides that a preliminary plan lapses if a final plan application is not submitted within one year, and that the final plan lapses if a subdivision plat or building permit application is not submitted within one year after its approval.[3] A 1991 New Hampshire law permits local governments under certain circumstances to revoke approved subdivisions. Among those circumstances is the failure of the developer to conduct sufficient construction to vest development rights during a specified time.[4]

These procedures do not totally address the issue, however. One question is how far the project can get in the system before the adequate public facilities review affects it. Both the city of Westminster and Montgomery County consider adequate public facilities availability at all stages of development review. In contrast, Boulder, Livermore, and Petaluma do not implement their housing permit review processes until the subdivision stage (James Duncan and Associates and Kelly 1991a). Thus, a project in one of those communities could presumably obtain zoning and other preliminary planning approvals with no assurance that the community would permit actual building of the project. That not only creates additional risk for the developer, it creates the risk of the city granting some form of approval to a project that it may not be able, or willing, to serve. Although the legal significance of this kind of action varies from state to state, it represents poor public policy anywhere.

In most states, local governments cannot provide for the lapse or reversion of zoning approvals. It is also very difficult in most states to vacate a final subdivision plat without the consent of the property owners. Many growth management communities overcome that difficulty by requiring a separate development permit that controls the issuance of an actual building permit. Westminster requires the issuance of a "service commitment" before it will approve a final (site) plan, but that service commitment then serves as the basis for the issuance of subdivision approvals and building permits as well.

The city of Westminster and Montgomery County essentially "encumber" the capacity to serve a project for a limited time during which the development approval permits construction in the project. If the developer does not build the project within that time, the approval lapses, the encumbered capacity reverts to the system, and the developer must get back into line. The developer may still be able to build the project when the developer wants to do so, but the developer runs the risk of delay due to future capacity problems if the project is not built during the initial approval period when capacity is reserved for it.

This discussion may seem somewhat esoteric. However, in the boom-and-bust real estate markets of high-growth communities, it is not unusual for a community to continue to approve development projects right up to the peak of a real estate market. When the market turns down, many developers abandon those projects. Whether the community then forgets those project approvals or, like Montgomery County and the city of Westminster, tracks them will determine the success or failure of an adequate public facilities program when the market again revives.

FISCAL IMPACTS OF GROWTH
AND GROWTH MANAGEMENT

Growth generally increases both revenues and expenses for local governments. Snyder found that, between 1970 and 1979, as Westminster's growth accelerated revenues grew more quickly (707 percent) than expenses (462 percent). However, a dramatic increase in capital expenditures absorbed the difference (1982, p. 234). One of the reasons for the concern about the fiscal impacts of growth is that growth is not always profitable (Breen, Costa, and Hendon 1986; Coe 1983; Gonzalez and Mehay 1987; Mehay 1981; Burchell and Listokin 1978). On the other hand, a statewide study in Colorado found that growth counties were better off by all fiscal measures than nongrowth counties (Lucas 1974). In the Colorado study, per capita expenditures were generally lower in the growth counties (Lucas 1974, pp. 18–27). A New Jersey study found that residential development generally created a fiscal surplus when school costs and revenues were removed from the equation (State of New Jersey County and Municipal Government Study Commission 1974, pp. 10–12).

Although methods of fiscal impact analysis such as those described in the studies just cited examine both costs and revenues, the emphasis of the examination here is on the expenditure side. There are several reasons for that, but one basic one. An $80,000 house with a typical family that can afford such a home should yield the same amount of revenue to the local government in 1999 whether it is built in 1993 or 1997 and whether it is built on the west side, on the east side, or in some other part of town. That will not always be true. For example, the nearest shopping for the house on the west side may lie within the community and generate sales tax for that community while the nearest shopping for the east side location may be in another community that will thus receive the sales tax from new residents there. Addressing such issues goes somewhat beyond the scope of most growth management programs, which deal with timing and location issues on a fairly gross basis. It also overcomplicates the task presented here.

Thus, the examination here proceeds largely on the assumption of stable per-unit revenues with an examination of potential cost savings from alternative development patterns. Note also that rate-of-growth and growth phasing programs may delay construction of a particular house or other building. Such delays will affect both revenues and expenditures and are thus disregarded in this analysis.

The landmark study on the relationship between growth and the fiscal impacts of development is *The Costs of Sprawl* (Real Estate Research Corporation 1974). It compared the capital and operating costs of communities of 10,000 units and neighborhoods of 1,000 units with six different development patterns:

I. **Planned Mix.** Housing mix 20 percent single-family conventional, 20 percent single-family clustered; 20 percent townhouses; 20 percent walk-up apartments; 20 percent high-rise apartments. "Neighborhoods are contiguous and large areas of open space preserved."

II. **Combination Mix.** Housing mix the same as for I. Assumes development pattern is 50 percent planned (same as I) and 50 percent sprawl.

III. **Sprawl Mix.** Housing mix the same as I. Sprawl, leapfrog development pattern.

IV. **Low-density planned.** Housing mix is 75 percent single-family clustered, 25 percent single-family conventional. Lower densities than I.

V. **Low-density sprawl.** Housing mix is 25 percent single-family clustered and 75 percent conventional single-family.

VI. **High-density planned.** Housing mix is 10 percent single-family clustered, 20 percent townhouse, 30 percent walk-up apartments, 40 percent high-rise. High densities with lots of open space (p. 90).

The study found significant differences in capital and operating costs. Table 9.1 shows summary figures from the findings.

The differences between Type VI (high-density planned) and Type V (low-density sprawl) are, of course, quite significant. The high-density project incurs only 68 percent of the capital costs of traditional low-density sprawl and 89 percent of the comparable operating costs.

However, that often-cited comparison is deceptive. The two represented radically different lifestyles. Type VI assumed that 40 percent of the residents would inhabit 900-square-foot high-rise apartments, whereas Type V assumed that all residents would inhabit 1,600-square-foot single-family residences. The study tacitly acknowledged that the same people would not inhabit both projects, because it projected the average occupancy for the high-rise units at 2.8 persons and average occupancy for the detached units at 3.5 (1974, p. 37).

Table 9.1
Public Service Costs for Different Patterns of Development

Development Type	Capital Costs	Operating Costs*
I. Planned mix	$124,870	$19,373
II. Combination mix	$130,459	$19,516
III. Sprawl mix	$135,556	$19,652
IV. Low-density planned	$145,823	$20,672
V. Low-density sprawl	$164,620	$21,109
VI. High-density planned	$109,948	$18,731

Sources: Real Estate Research Corporation, 1974, *The Costs of Sprawl: Environmental and Economic Costs of Alternative Residential Development Patterns at the Urban Fringe;* capital costs are from sub-total on Table 44, page 97; operating and maintenance costs are from Table 45, page 98; this table by author from cited data.

However, the figures used here (and in the original report) project the expenses for all housing types based on an assumed constant population; otherwise, the costs for the higher-density projects, with fewer children, would be dramatically lower because of the reduction in school-related costs.

The cost difference between the two types of projects that consist entirely of single-family dwelling units (Types IV, low-density planned, and V, low-density sprawl) is small, with a 3 percent savings in capital costs and a 2 percent savings in operating costs. The reason for the differences in the two comparisons is quite straightforward. Virtually all the public capital cost savings of the high-density project over the sprawling one result from the need to construct fewer linear feet of roads and the utility lines that lie under them. The clustering of single-family dwellings similarly generates most of the saving between those two types of projects, but the saving is much smaller because each house is still on its own lot; some of the lots are simply narrower and thus require fewer feet of street. The authors acknowledged the significance of these differences. "Thus, while planning results in cost savings, density is a much more influential cost determinant. Clearly, the greatest cost advantages occur when higher density planned developments are contrasted with low density sprawl" (Real Estate Research Corporation 1974, p. 21).

Real Estate Research Corporation, a reputable Chicago-based consulting firm, prepared *The Costs of Sprawl* under contract to the Council on Environmental Quality, the Department of Housing and Urban Development, and the Environmental Protection Agency. Although the study relied on projections, entirely hypothetical data, the figures used above were all objectively determinable at the time. The data cited here were entirely reliable and remain reliable, if deflated, for analytical purposes. The important question is not whether they are accurate. The important question is, "What do they mean?" A careful analysis indicates that simply planning better for the same types of housing results in some saving, but it is very small. The real savings come from persuading people to move from single-family houses to high-rise apartments or from attracting a different demographic group that will. That is not a realistic policy option for most local governments, although the regional government in Portland has implemented such a program.

In a 1984 comparison of "planned development" or "unplanned development" on a 7,500 acre site in Houston, Peiser found that the planned development approach yielded savings of approximately 1.6 percent in construction of utilities. The primary cost difference in Peiser's comparison resulted from the assumption that the unplanned development would require multiple-package water and sewer plants. Peiser's comparison of road construction costs in the two is not useful for purposes of this chapter because he made different assumptions about who would pay for different roads in the two models and then calculated the costs only for those to be constructed by the principal developer. Peiser's comparison held the dwelling unit mix and population constant, thus making the two types of projects reasonably competitive in the market.

The Costs of Sprawl was the subject of two contemporaneous critiques, one a review by Alan Altshuler and the other a longer article specifically labeled a "critique." Altshuler challenged many of the assumptions of the report, mostly those relating to its analysis of energy consumption, air pollution, and other items beyond the scope of the analysis here. However, one of his grounds for dissent does affect the fiscal analysis. He argued, "The key question, it appears, is whether density per se affects the demand level for community service. The authors of *The Costs of Sprawl* explicitly assumed that it did not. Numerous other analyses, however, have judged that the residents of high density communities do seem to require and/or demand more expensive packages of community services than those who live at low densities" (1977, p. 208). Altshuler cited examples ranging from the likelihood that suburban residents might be willing to live without sidewalks to the greater need and political demand for police and fire services when people live at higher densities. Altshuler argued that if the study were "calibrated against the experience of real communities," the result might be quite different (1977, p. 208). Muller had previously cited a study from Fairfax County, Virginia, that supported an argument like that made by Altshuler (1975, p. 5).

Windsor (1979) challenged *The Cost of Sprawl*'s conclusions on similar grounds and others. He was particularly critical of the variations in floor areas of the different dwelling units and the resulting population differences. He also noted that the report failed to account for what would happen to the unused land saved through the higher density project and that any use of that land would also have fiscal implications.

Windsor recalculated some of the figures from *The Costs of Sprawl.* Although in general he found smaller cost differences among housing types than did the original report, he actually found a greater saving in infrastructure costs when comparing the low-density planned and low-density sprawl development patterns; he computed a saving of about 11 percent for the planned development. He found a far smaller saving than did the original, however, for infrastructure in the high-density planned development; there he computed a saving of approximately 20 percent (1979, Table 6, p. 288).

One issue that neither Windsor nor Altshuler addressed is the revenue side. Although this chapter makes no attempt to examine differences in revenues that may result from alternative development *locations, The Costs of Sprawl* examined alternative development *types.* The smaller apartment units in the study would clearly generate lower property taxes than the larger and more expensive single-family houses. As the study acknowledged, they would contain fewer residents, which would thus reduce sales tax revenues. Further, the lower cost might attract residents with lower incomes than those who would inhabit the single-family dwellings. Thus, reduced revenues would clearly offset, at least in part, the reduced costs of the "most efficient" development type in the study. That would presumably not be true of the same cost, same size, single-family dwelling units in the planned and sprawl projects. Thus, the 3 percent capital cost and 1 percent operating cost savings of the planned project should pass through to the bottom line.

Frank (1989) synthesized data from nine major studies involving the costs of infrastructure and different development patterns and adjusted the data from all of them to 1987 dollars. He noted that the principal variables in the equations are the costs of streets, sewers, water systems, storm drainage, and schools (p. 39). Because the

Table 9.2
Capital Costs of Streets and Utilities for Different Development Types per Dwelling Unit

Development Type	Streets	Utilities	Total
Single-family 1 unit per acre	$12,308	$19,789	$32,097
Single-family 3 units per acre	$7,083	$11,388	$18,461
Single-family cluster 5 units per acre	$7,526	$8,843	$16,369
Townouses 10 units per acre	$6,785	$6,019	$12,804
Mixed 12 units per acre*	$6,229	$6,865	$13,184
Multi-family 15 units per acre	$5,297	$3,384	$8,691
Multi-family 30 units per acre	$3,773	$3,096	$6,869

Source: James E. Frank, 1989, *The Costs of Alternative Development Patterns: A Review of the Literature;* selected data extracted by author from Table 8, page 40 in the original.
*Mix of 20 percent of single-family clustered, single-family conventional, townhouses, garden apartments, and high-rise apartments (comparable to "planned mix" in *The Costs of Sprawl*).

capital cost of schools varies primarily with the number of pupils, that factor is disregarded here. However, Frank found the potential for enormous saving in streets and utilities. Table 9.2 summarizes part of his data.

Note that the differences shown in Table 9.2 just represented the differences based on the pattern of development. Frank noted that most of these cost differences were assessed to developers in the form of subdivision improvement requirements and ultimately passed on to the buyer, who gained the enjoyment of a larger lot (1989, pp. 41–42). That assertion is undoubtedly valid, as the requirement that developers pay all on-site subdivision costs was almost

Table 9.3
Capital Costs for Different Development Patterns in Leapfrog and Remote Locations per Dwelling Unit

| | | Distance** | |
Development type	Leapfrog	5 miles	10 miles
Single-family 1 unit per acre	No Data	$7,300	$14,600
Single-family 3 units per acre	$3,297	$7,300	$14,600
Single-family cluster 5 units per acre	No Data	$7,300	$14,600
Townhouses 10 units per acre	$5,019	$6,875	$13,750
Mixed 12 units per acre*	$3,870	$6,875	$9,400
Multi-family 15 units per acre	$5,019	$6,875	$13,750
Multi-family 30 units per acre	$5,019	$5,840	$11,680

Source: James E. Frank, 1989, *The Costs of Alternative Development Patterns: A Review of the Literature;* selected data extracted by author from Table 8, page 40 in the original.
*Mix of 20 percent of single-family clustered, single-family conventional, town-houses, garden apartments, and high-rise apartments (comparable to "planned mix" in *The Costs of Sprawl*).
**Distance to employment, sewage plant, water plant, receiving body of water.*

universal in the early 1990s. However, it disregarded the significance of the operating costs the local government absorbs. Seventy-five feet of street costs more to maintain than sixty feet of street.

Table 9.3 gives additional figures from the Frank report. He computed these additional costs based on the *location* of development, costs he said are generally not fully passed through to the developer and are thus subsidized by the community (1989, pp. 41–42).

Frank's figures were dramatic. However, it is risky to accept them at their apparent face value. Some of the additional cost for leapfrog and remote locations clearly paid for infrastructure extended through undeveloped land to reach those leapfrog and remote locations. Peiser would argue that the leapfrog and distance figures are simply short-term cash-flow figures and that over the long run infill development would use that infrastructure to produce a reallocation of the cost over a much larger number of units and a resulting reduction in the per-unit cost (see discussion in Chapter 7). Frank acknowledged similar economic arguments in his conclusion, in which he discussed who should bear the cost of excess capacity: whether it should be allocated evenly among ultimate users, acknowledging that some of them will not pay their share for many years, or be allocated fully to present users. However, he did not apply that economic logic to the figures given in this table (1989, p. 44).

In 1989, a team of consulting firms, led by James Duncan and Associates of Austin, Texas, conducted a major fiscal impact study for the Florida Governor's Task Force on Urban Growth Patterns (James Duncan and Associates et al. 1989a). It is the only major study based on actual case studies of developed areas. The Duncan team made no attempt to examine internal development costs which, as this chapter has suggested and as that study noted, "have been widely studied and shown to be strongly related to density, as well as typically borne by developers and passed on to consumers" (p. 4). The study also controlled for location and thus did not test the factors that Frank assigned for developments located at a long distance from existing development, although the study did cite Frank's work on that type of cost.

The Florida study findings confirmed the substantial cost savings from contiguous development patterns. The study examined eight case study areas and assigned them to five categories:

- **Scattered:** A pattern of urban growth which is generally characterized by low density development that has prematurely located ("leapfrogged") past vacant land into relatively undeveloped areas. Other factors usually characterizing this urban form are extended distances to urban employment centers and central public facilities, minimal nonresidential support services and lower levels of services. . . .

- **Contiguous:** A pattern of urban growth which is generally characterized by moderate density development and is located adjacent to or near established urban areas. Other factors usually characterizing this urban development form are mixed land uses, proximity to nonresidential support services and satisfactory levels of public services. . . .

- **Linear:** A pattern of urban growth which is generally characterized by relatively low densities and intensities of mixed use development extending outward from established urban areas along one or more major transportation corridors. Other factors usually characterizing this urban development form are decreasing land use intensities along the corridors and heavy dependence upon vehicular access. . . .

- **Satellite:** A pattern of urban growth which is generally characterized by moderate to high intensity mixed use development that occurs primarily within discrete outlying suburban or exurban areas. Other factors usually characterizing this urban development form are a cultural and economic relationship to, but a physical separation from, established major urban centers. . . .
- **Compact:** A pattern of urban growth which is generally characterized by higher intensity development that occurs within an established urban area. Other factors characterizing this urban development pattern include more vertical development, redevelopment of underutilized parcels and undercapacity public facilities. . . . (James Duncan and Associates et al. 1989a, p. 8).

The Duncan team's Florida findings regarding capital costs are presented in Table 9.4. Table 9.5 presents the net fiscal impacts of different development patterns, reflecting annual tax revenues and

Table 9.4
Capital Costs for Different Types of Existing Development

Area	Urban Form	Unit Cost
Downtown Orlando	Compact	$9,208
Southpoint	Contiguous	$10,560
Countryside	Contiguous	$12,707
Tampa Palms	Satellite	$14,816
Cantonment	Scattered	$15,102
University	Linear	$16,628
Kendall	Linear	$16,628
Wellington	Scattered	$23,639
AVERAGE		$14,773

Source: James Duncan and Associates, Van Horn-Grey Associates, Ivey, Bennett, Harris and Walls, Inc., and Wade-Trim, Inc., 1989, *The Search for Efficient Development Patterns*, Figure 2.2, page 15.

Table 9.5
Fiscal Impacts of Different Types of Existing Development

Area	Urban Form	Unit Cost*	Unit Revenue*
Downtown Orlando	Compact	$12,788	$9,323
Southpoint	Contiguous	$2,785	$2,755
Countryside	Contiguous	$8.146	$7,502
Tampa Palms	Satellite	$843	$795
Cantonment	Scattered	$1,216	$758
University	Linear	$3,445	$2,413
Kendall	Linear	$5,903	$4,386
Wellington	Scattered	$5,110	$3,800
AVERAGE		$4,929	$3,966

Source: James Duncan and Associates, Van Horn-Grey Associates, Ivey, Bennett, Harris and Walls, Inc., and Wade-Trim, Inc., 1989, *The Search for Efficient Development Patterns*, Figure 2.6, page 20.
*Excluding education, which was included in the original.

operating costs. This table excludes the education component of the original. Education varies significantly with demographic patterns, and attempting to compare operating costs for different development patterns without supporting demographic data is not a meaningful exercise for purposes of this book. One thing is immediately clear from Table 9.5. In contemporary Florida, growth does not bring in adequate revenues to pay the operating costs. In downtown Orlando and Southpoint, including education brightens the net fiscal picture, bringing downtown Orlando nearly to a breakeven point and actually showing a surplus of revenues over costs for Southpoint. Both areas clearly reflect lower per-unit occupancies, presumably because of an older population with fewer children. Although such populations often demand increased municipal services such as buses, they typically produce a net fiscal gain for schools.

It is revealing that the compact development of downtown Orlando became one of the least efficient when education was removed. The results of the other patterns were more predictable. The scattered and linear forms of development were the least efficient, and the contiguous form the most. The net fiscal impact differences were significant. Note that it is not possible to compare the cost side from one community to another because there is little comparability among the unit types, values, and other factors that affect costs. Thus, this study is not comparable to the others cited but stands on its own as an analysis of net fiscal impact.

Landis performed a paired-community comparison of communities that manage growth and those that do not. All the communities were in California, and the paired communities were near each other. He found that "the various growth control communities slightly outperformed their respective pro-growth counterparts. That is, revenue growth outpaced expenditure growth by a greater margin in the slow-growth cities than in the pro-growth cities" (1991, p. 30). Landis did not attribute great significance to his findings. He suggested that

Overall, it appears that growth-control communities have been better able to manage spending than their pro-growth counterparts while not suffering undue revenue declines. This does not necessarily mean that growth control is good for city budgets, however. What is more likely is that city finances are in better shape in those communities with traditions of good government, good management, good planning, and higher levels of citizen involvement, exactly the types of communities most likely to try to control growth (p. 36).

The Governor's Commission on Growth in the Chesapeake Bay Region (Maryland Study Commission 1991b) applied James Duncan and Associates' cost figures to two alternative statewide growth scenarios. Again excluding education costs, under the "trend" growth scenario of continuing sprawl, the commission projected capital infrastructure costs for roads and utilities totaling $9,191 per single-family unit, but under a more compact and contiguous scenario, projected $4,104 per unit (p. 78, exh. 19). When the commission aggregated all costs for all development (not just residential) statewide, the fiscal impact figures were particularly interesting. They showed a reduction of capital costs from $7,701,686 under "trend" development to $6,519,701 under "vision" development, a 15 percent saving. However, the revenue side showed a reduction of less than 1 percent from $5,311,370 for "trend" development to $5,272,394 for "vision" development (p. 108, Fig. 1; the differences between the development types are explained briefly near the end of Chapter 7).

MARGINAL VERSUS AVERAGE COSTS

The Maryland study noted candidly that much of the cost saving under "vision" growth resulted from "targeting much of the projected growth to previously developed and/or adjacent growth areas" (1991, p. 109). In other words, the Maryland planners proposed to limit *marginal* costs by using existing capital plant to the maximum extent practicable. Savings on short-run costs may be only short-run savings, deferring the need for a community to extend its interceptor sewer line or freeway. On the other hand, in a typical community, the practice of overdesigning facilities extending in several directions while growth may go in only one often results in significant excess capacity. Insofar as a "vision growth" pattern or other adequate public facilities requirement takes advantage of capital plant capacities that might otherwise be wasted, marginal cost savings can result in long-term savings and significantly reduce long-term average costs.

Frank (1989) analyzed this issue differently. He referred to the marginal or incremental costs actually incurred (such as the cost of extending a new sewer line to the site) as "precipitated" costs. He contrasted those with "inherited" costs, which are the average cost factors for facilities with excess capacity that is used by the new development.

In purely economic terms, with perfect foresight and perfect planning so that all capacity is ultimately used, it should make little difference whether costs are precipitated or inherited. In the operation of a particular local government, it can make the difference between building a new school for several million dollars or just adding a few students (and some new tax revenues) to a school that already exists. A school is a particularly dramatic example to many people because the handful of new students who suddenly push an existing school past capacity generates an enormous (and highly visible) marginal cost per student to the district that must build a new school. However, a new development that requires a major expansion of the sewer plant or the water treatment plant may have an even greater precipitated cost effect on a particular local government at a particular time.

Average cost information is important over the long run, but marginal (precipitated) cost information is critical over the short run. Whether the marginal cost involves buying a police car for a small town or a new sewer plant for a large one, a community that approves a development that pushes it past the threshold at which that expenditure becomes necessary must be certain that it has a way to pay the cost.

TIME AND FISCAL IMPACTS

Careful fiscal impact studies discount future costs and revenues using a reasonable rate of return and thus compute the present value of a future stream of income or costs. They also discount future capital expenditures, recognizing that a dollar spent next year is cheaper in today's money than one spent today because of the interest income. Thus, they attempt to account for the effects of time on the computations. Most such studies disregard inflation and project both costs and revenues in present dollars. There are three reasons for that approach. First, inflation is notoriously difficult to predict. Second, inflation presumably affects both costs and revenues. Third, the comparisons conducted in fiscal impacts make more sense if presented in "constant," or uninflated, dollars.

However, there are two other aspects to the issue of time and fiscal impacts. One is lead-time. Although state laws on the subject vary enormously, in most cases revenues from new development will lag behind costs. A new house is typically assessed during the first year after construction is complete, resulting in a tax bill the following January 1. In the meantime, residents may have occupied the house for eighteen months or more, certainly for at least twelve. Residents new to an area begin using services the day they move into the house, and yet their first income tax bill to the state will not come due until sometime in the following spring. Commercial development included in the fiscal impact analysis of a mixed-use project may not be built until one of the later years of the project.

The State of Colorado commissioned a detailed study of the lag involved in tax revenues, based on projected development in the oil shale region. The study found that revenues would lag behind cost "needs" for nearly seven years in a tri-county area, although revenues would then exceed costs over the long run ("Tax lead time study" 1974, pp. 1–13). Much of the deficiency was attributable to capital costs that might be financed through bonds or through developer (or, in this case, industry) exactions. The point is not that the lag-time problem is insurmountable but that it must be addressed. Obviously, the lag-time issue in suburban development is most severe for noncontiguous development that generates the need for major offsite capital expenditures that that community cannot fully exact from the developer. Certainly a thorough fiscal impact analysis accounts for such factors. However, most of the fiscal impact literature focuses on average costs, figures that will be entirely valid after a few years but do not recognize the lead time problem (see, for example, Burchell 1990).

There is still another aspect of time that the fiscal impact literature does not address at all. Time brings market risks. Virtually all fiscal impact projections are based on full buildout of the project analyzed. Those are in turn based on the developer's projections, which are usually the same optimistic projections that the developer gave to the bank that financed the project. The chance that they will be wrong is great, and time increases that risk significantly.

The worst-case circumstance occurs when the developer installs most of the public facilities but completes few of the tax-generating houses and commercial buildings before the economy turns sour and halts the project. The local government then finds itself with virtually the full operating costs (and, for noncontiguous development, some measure of offsite capital costs) and only a fraction of the projected revenues. Because school costs vary with the number of pupils, the problem is not as great with schools as with other facilities. However, with roads, sewer lines, water lines, and drainage facilities, the maintenance costs are nearly as great whether a few families use them or they operate at capacity. If the developer completes absolutely *no* private (taxable) buildings, the community may have the option of simply abandoning the public facilities to the elements, but that is not a likely scenario.

Westminster provides a useful illustration. In the early 1970s, the city aggressively annexed land. Acknowledging willingly the need to serve the new territory, the city then borrowed heavily to construct the major trunk water lines and interceptor sewer lines necessary to serve the city's expansion to the north and west. It was an early user of this type of exaction. The city thus counted on large fees from developers, to be paid at the time of sewer or water connection in addition to traditional tap fees, which basically reimbursed the city for the costs of inspecting new connections, or "taps." Then the real estate market turned down in 1973. By the time the city faced the growth crunch in 1977, the city confronted two conflicting problems. Although it had serious limitations on its capacity to serve new development, it needed the revenue from sewer and water connection fees from such development to meet existing bonded debt (see, generally, Kelly 1982; Westminster, City of 1978b). The Westminster story has a reasonably happy ending in its successful implementation of a growth management program, but the story could have ended differently. Had growth not revived, the city would have faced a continued fiscal crisis caused by its commitment to service facilities that essentially facilitated the leapfrogging of growth far into its new territory.

The figures can be staggering. In some Colorado special districts where developers completed most of the public facilities but few of the taxable private improvements tax bills for individual homeowners jumped from $500 to $10,000 per year ("Colorado's special district woes" 1991; Mehle 1991). A number of such districts in Colorado have filed for bankruptcy, thus leaving bondholders with substantial losses (Mehle 1991). The problem would not appear so dramatic if the project had simply been included within the financial operations of a municipal government, so that the negative fiscal impact would be averaged out over the gross operations of the community. However, that would just mask the numbers, not change them.

Peiser's argument that sprawl is efficient over the long run because it ultimately encourages more intensive use of the omitted parcels (Peiser 1989; discussed in some depth in Chapter 7) must be considered in this context. If a community permits discontinuous (leapfrog) development based on Peiser's argument and the infill occurs rapidly, then Peiser's argument can hold and the community may be in good fiscal shape. However, if the same community approves leapfrog development based on Peiser's advice and the economy then turns sour for several years or, worse yet, the largest employer in town pulls out or lays off a few thousand workers, then the community will be left with an inefficient and fiscally costly pattern of development for many years.

GROWTH PHASING AND EXACTIONS

Landis identified another potential concern for growth managing communities, although his data neither supported nor denied his hypothesis. "By slowing the pace of development, growth controls limit the financial leverage cities have over developers. In particular, developers may be less willing to build or finance large capital projects for cities unless they can be assured of a long-term development entitlement, the types of assurances yearly growth caps make impossible" (1991, p. 33). He went on to suggest that the result would be that growth-managing communities would have to pay a larger proportion of the costs of new infrastructure than pro-growth communities.

His assertion, although undocumented, is worth considering because it is so logical. Note that there are two separate issues inherent in this hypothesis. One is the short-term issue of cash flow. If a community cannot exact a major public improvement from a developer, the community may have to advance the cost of that improvement. However, Landis suggested that this is not just a short-term cost-shifting from the developer back to the community but a long-term one. If a particular community can advance the costs of improvements and then recover most or all of the costs through impact fees, there will be only a short-term shift. However, if Landis' hypothesis is fully correct, communities that establish some types of growth management systems may find themselves paying a larger share of the costs of growth than they have in the recent past.

Peiser's issue is of concern only for communities with competitive rate-of-growth programs or highly restrictive phased growth programs. These both create uncertainty for a developer. Such programs typically require annual applications for development approvals, leaving the developer with no assurance of being able to complete the kind of long-term, large-scale project that justifies advancing the cost of a major capital improvement (on this issue, see generally Peiser 1984). Other types of growth management programs do not create any greater uncertainty than other land use controls. With an urban growth boundary, a developer knows that a proposed project is either inside or outside the boundary. A responsible developer (and the developer's banker) should know whether a proposed project has "adequate public facilities." Those types of programs simply do not create the uncertainty that a competitive program does.

CONCLUSION

Growth management clearly affects the fiscal position of a local government. Any program that encourages or requires growth to occur closer to existing development and existing facilities will reduce costs to some extent without affecting revenues. Over the long run in a steadily growing community, the savings will not be very significant. However, in a particular year when new development takes place in a remote or underserved location, the fiscal impacts can be significant. Further, if economic forces change and the growth rate slows (or even halts) shortly after that development occurs, the community may suffer for many years. Growth phasing programs, adequate public facilities requirements, and urban growth boundaries all tend to encourage development in more efficient *locations*, although adequate public facilities requirements are the most effective in doing so. Growth management programs can also encourage more efficient *patterns* of development, but the cost savings from doing so do not appear to be significant.

NOTES

1. *Construction Industry Association of Sonoma County* v. *City of Petaluma*, 375 F. Supp. 574 (1974).
2. *Robinson* v. *Boulder*, 547 P.2d 228 (Colo. 1976).
3. Code of Westminster, Title 11, Chaps 4 and 5.
4. N. H. 1991 New Laws, H.B. No. 434, p. 781.

10

Growth Management and the Diversity of Housing Opportunities

All land use controls affect the cost and availability of housing in some way. As part of the larger system, a growth management program may either mitigate or aggravate the problems that have led a number of study commissions to determine that there is a serious problem in the cost and availability of housing in the United States (see, generally, Task Force on Housing Costs 1978; *Reducing the Development Costs of Housing* 1979; Council on Development Choices for the 80's 1980; Loke 1982; Advisory Commission on Regulatory Barriers to Affordable Housing 1991). It is important to understand how growth management programs relate to this larger system.

GOVERNMENT REGULATION AND HOUSING COSTS

Government regulation affects housing costs in many different ways (Advisory Commission on Regulatory Barriers to Affordable Housing 1991 and other sources cited in the preceding paragraph). Most or all of those fall in one of the following seven categories:

- **Quality Improvements.** Government frequently establishes regulations to improve the quality of housing. Smoke detectors, substantial insulation, and "egress windows" in bedrooms are all requirements that most communities impose on new housing today that few communities imposed thirty years ago. These are "quality improvements" in the sense that the consumer who pays more for the house with such a feature also gets something more. Whether all the quality improvements are items the consumer needs or wants is a topic that goes far beyond the scope of this chapter (but see, for example, Downs 1991a, pp. 1107–1114).

- **Cost shifting.** "Make growth pay its own way" is a rallying cry of growth-control advocates in many communities. Today, through impact fees, requirements for land dedication, and negotiated deals, communities require developers to pay for improvements that the community at large once financed from general revenues, bonded debt, or intergovernmental aid programs. New parks, fire stations, and arterial (major) roads all fall in this category. Economists debate the extent to which these costs are passed on to consumers (see, for example, Downing and McCaleb 1987; Singell and Lillydahl 1990). If they are passed on, they clearly represent a form of cost shifting from the public sector to the consumer. The consumer who buys a new house today is unlikely to get any better-quality access to parks or fire stations than a consumer who bought a comparable house thirty years ago; it just costs more because of the cost shift.

- **Overspecification.** Sometimes government simply imposes unreasonable requirements. Without entering the endless debate over what is "reasonable," it is noteworthy that most building codes continued to prohibit flexible electrical cable and PVC (plastic) pipe for a decade or more after they had been thoroughly tested and approved by federal agencies. Both are cost saving because of their ease of installation and reduced labor cost. Most local governments have now acknowledged their safety by permitting them in residential installations today. Thus, they provide an easy example of overspecification that increased housing costs for a number of years (see, generally, Seidel 1978, Chap. 5, pp. 71–100). Clearly there are other unreasonable requirements still on the books in many communities.

- **Regulatory overhead.** Time is money, or so most business people think. There is evidence for their position. A developer who suffers project delays from government red tape pays interest on borrowed money or loses interest on capital while the land and other capital investments languish pending regulatory approval. If approvals take longer than is necessary for a thorough review, the system imposes unnecessary regulatory overhead on development projects.

- **Market impacts.** The law of supply and demand dictates that prices will rise in the face of steady demand and a restricted supply. Some regulatory systems restrict the land supply while others restrict the housing supply. Either type of program will affect the cost of housing through market impacts.

- **Stifling innovation.** It is remarkable that over the last century, during which technology has changed totally the way humans communicate and travel, there has been little if any innovation in housing technology. Over the last century, humans have witnessed the invention of flight and its implementation as a primary method of long-range transportation, the development of radio and the implementation of sophisticated audio and video communication systems over the air, and the invention of many labor-saving devices using high technology. Despite a number of proposals for technological innovation (for some interesting examples, see Jandl 1991), during that time the way that humans construct housing, particularly in the United States, has changed little. Because the homebuilding market in particular and the construction market in general are highly competitive markets that, economists would argue, should be both efficient and innovative, one suspects that the lack of innovation can be traced to other factors. Highly prescriptive building codes look like a good target.

- **Exclusionary effects.** By protecting single-family neighborhoods, many communities limit or preclude the construction of townhouses, apartments, and other forms of housing that clearly cost less than single-family detached homes and that provide important housing alternatives for significant numbers of housing consumers (see, generally, Babcock and Bosselman 1973; Fishman 1978).

Many of the issues suggested in this list go far beyond the scope of this book. Nevertheless, it seems useful to have a conceptual framework against which to review the impacts of growth management programs to housing costs.

How Growth Management Programs Relate to These Categories

Of the seven categories listed above, three are most pertinent to growth management: regulatory overhead, market impacts, and exclusionary barriers. Quality improvements are typically building-code issues, as the examples used above suggest. Some land use controls, such as requirements for street trees or sod in the front yard, may possibly amount to quality improvements, but such controls are usually separate from growth management programs.

Chapter 4 suggests briefly that increased cost-shifting through the imposition of exactions has paralleled the evolution of growth management in the United States. Those concerned about the impacts of growth are often the ones who seek to "make growth pay its own way" through exactions. However, the issues of cost-shifting and exactions are separate—a community can choose to manage growth without shifting development costs, and many communities that shift development costs have not adopted any sort of growth management program. Thus, the complex issues related to cost-shifting and exactions remain for consideration in other works (see sources cited in Chapter 9).

Overspecification affects requirements for both housing and public improvements. Many communities require that every street be wide enough for their widest fire trucks to turn around, regardless of whether the fire department will ever need large trucks on a particular street (has anyone ever seen a hook and ladder truck on a cul-de-sac?), and regardless of whether the truck may have a reverse gear to use in leaving a fire. Thus, although this issue relates to land use controls, like cost-shifting, it is quite separate from the adoption of growth management programs.

Stifling innovation appears to be largely a building-code issue. To the extent that zoning requires single-family detached houses in too many neighborhoods and thus precludes the development of more townhouses and apartments, it may stifle creative design. However, this issue is not the same as the issue of technological innovation that might revolutionize the production of housing.

The rest of this chapter thus addresses the remaining issues—in particular, the market impacts of some growth management systems.

THE EFFECTS OF REGULATORY OVERHEAD

"Not in My Back Yard" Removing Barriers to Affordable Housing, prepared by the Advisory Commission on Regulatory Barriers to Affordable Housing, was the 1991 product of a federal study commission on housing costs (see citations to earlier but similar studies in the first paragraph of this chapter). Because Secretary Jack Kemp of the Department of Housing and Urban Development appointed the commission, the study is often called, and is called here, the Kemp Commission Report. The report was a conceptual one. Although it provided anecdotal evidence of particular impacts, it made no attempt to quantify the impacts of regulatory barriers on the market. It did list the ways in which regulatory barriers affect the market.

That commission noted in 1991 that "burdensome and uncoordinated approval and permitting systems" were a significant barrier to affordable housing in many jurisdictions (p. 2–12). It cited the problem of multiple and potentially conflicting reviews by separate jurisdictions, a problem addressed fifteen years earlier in a report published by the Urban Land Institute (Bosselman, Feurer, and Siemon 1976). It also addressed the issue of procedural delays. In a side note to a chapter, it gave two anecdotal examples: a housing development on Staten Island, New York for which it took two developers more than twelve years to get approvals and permits from twenty-eight government agencies, and a project for which a developer who was clearly once both optimistic and rich had spent $95 million for "carrying costs and regulatory costs" over a sixteen-year period of seeking permits, without constructing anything (p. 2–13).

There are three excellent earlier studies of the delay issue. All are somewhat dated, making the numbers they contain of little interest. However, the principles are applicable today, and the Kemp report certainly provided evidence that the problem continues.

A 1978 study by Rice University found that the average processing time for a typical development had increased by five months over the previous decade, from eight months to thirteen months (Rice Center for Community Design + Research 1978). The study determined that the additional five-month delay cost the individual housing buyer a minimum of $560 to $840. That amount was between 1 percent and 1.5 percent of the cost of an average house in Houston at that time (p. 97; average house price from p. 3). The principal element in the increase was interest on capital invested in the project, although overhead and inflation each played a role.

A study by the Center for Urban Policy Research (CUPR) of projects in several states reached similar conclusions at about the same time (Seidel 1978). The survey of homebuilders included in that study found that the average processing time for a project had increased from five months in 1970 to more than thirteen months in 1975 (Seidel 1978). The authors computed the average carrying cost at $38 per month for a quarter-acre lot, implying a lot-cost increase of $404 from the eight-month increase in processing time (p. 321). Those findings were remarkably consistent with the findings of the Rice study in Houston. It is interesting that the delay costs were somewhat higher in Houston, which long prided itself on its limited regulation and which had yet to adopt zoning, as of mid-1992.

As both the CUPR and Rice studies noted, builders generally try to maintain a consistent ratio between house price and lot cost and consequently are likely to increase the price of the house placed on a lot by a multiple of 4 or 5 times the increase in cost of the lot.

On the basis of nine case studies in Colorado, a team associated with Bickert, Browne & Coddington reached similar conclusions in another study (Lincoln, Coddington, and Penberthy 1976). The team found somewhat shorter processing times there (six and seven months were typical), but those also represented significant increases. Those numbers were probably misleading, because it does not appear that the Colorado study team included all steps in the development review process in its calculations. It nevertheless found regulation-induced cost increases of $1,500 to $2,000 per dwelling unit over the 1970–1975 study period. Arvada, the only case study breaking out delay costs as a separate item, showed delay costs (presumably resulting only from the increased processing time) amounting to about $245 per lot (Lincoln, Coddington, and Penberthy 1976). That was a little more than 0.75 percent of the price of a "modest house" used as a benchmark in the study.

Analysis

Delay costs, a major irritant to builders, are frequently cited in surveys such as those described above. At less than 1 percent of the price of a house, delay cost is probably not significant in the issue of affordable housing. On an $80,000 house with interest at 9 percent, an increase of 1 percent, or $800, would increase monthly payments by about $7, if fully financed. If, as some studies suggest, builders actually increase the cost or price of the house by a multiple of the lot cost, the implication could be a cost increase of $3,000 to $4,000 and an increase in payments of $30 or so per month, obviously more significant numbers. On the other hand, no one gains from such a delay, and it is thus difficult to justify any cost increase resulting from it.

With quality increases, the consumer presumably gets a better house. With cost-shifting, a local government saves some amount of money as a tradeoff to the increased cost imposed on the consumer. In those cases, there are at least two sides to the cost–benefit analysis. There is no economic or other basis for a similar argument regarding delay costs when the delay exceeds the reasonable processing time necessary for a thorough project review.

Do growth management programs result in unnecessary delay? Many of them are administered as additional steps in the development-review process, each additional step adding incrementally to the review process (James Duncan and Associates and Kelly 1991a). It is noteworthy that both Boulder and Petaluma took steps in the mid-1980s to reduce the complexity of their review processes by eliminating the qualitative review of each project and substituting a first-come, first-served system of allocating permits in years when demand exceeds supply (Gawf 1985; Petaluma, City of 1991; discussed in James Duncan and Associates and Kelly 1991a, pp. 27, 39).

A community can minimize delay costs by integrating the growth management review with the rest of the development process so that there is no extra step. The establishment of an urban growth boundary does not imply any changes in the regulatory process and thus should not affect the processing time or costs of development. With an adequate public facilities requirement, it is easy to add the public facilities standards to existing steps of development review, thus eliminating the need for any additional step in the review process.

For a growth phasing system or rate-of-growth system, the problem is more difficult. Montgomery County integrates its development-phasing review with the first stage of subdivision review, which is procedurally efficient.[1] However, uncertainty is another major concern of developers (Advisory Commission on Regulatory Barriers to Affordable Housing 1991), who may prefer a system in which they can obtain the "go/no-go" decision on growth phasing before investing in the substantial engineering costs involved in a preliminary subdivision plat. One approach to that is simply to place the coordination of the reviews at the developer's option. Under such an approach, a developer may choose to expedite the process by including the application for a growth management allocation with the first application otherwise required, taking the risk that the denial of one may moot the other. Alternatively, the developer has the choice of reducing the risk by making the first round of applications in two stages.

MARKET IMPACTS OF GROWTH MANAGEMENT PROGRAMS

Clearly growth management programs have significant potential to affect both the land and housing markets. The Kemp Commission listed "growth controls" at the top of the list of suburban regulatory barriers to affordable housing (Advisory Commission on Regulatory Barriers to Affordable Housing 1991, Chap. 2, pp. 1–4). The law of supply and demand dictates that when supply is constrained in the face of constant demand, price will increase. Rate-of-growth programs may constrict housing supply. Phased growth, adequate public facilities, and urban growth boundary programs will affect the supply of developable land over the short run.

It is important to understand clearly the principles at work before examining some numbers related to them. First, as it is impossible to remind the reader too often, most communities that adopt growth management programs are part of larger metropolitan areas. Thus, a Ramapo, a Livermore, or a Petaluma does not control enough of the market for its actions to affect prices of land significantly, at least in theory. However, these communities were high-growth communities when they adopted their programs because location, amenities, or other factors caused them to attract growth. Those factors may bring a premium to land in such communities, even if there is a significant supply of competing land in the area.

A community may adopt a growth management program that does not significantly affect supply, even if the community intended that it do so. For example, applications for building permits in both Boulder and Petaluma fell far short of the numbers that the two cities were willing to issue during most of the 1980s and early 1990s. The number of dwelling units built in Petaluma fell far short of the number allowed by the plan (see Chapter 4). Because of annexations and program exemptions, the rate of increase in the number of dwelling units in Boulder far exceeded the 2 percent per year permitted by the plan. That number increased from 21,632 in 1970 to 32,131 in 1990 (Bureau of the Census 1991a). In Boulder, the actual population growth rate in the 1980s was only 1 percent per year. See discussion in Chapter 4. A community might adopt an urban growth boundary that extends out so far from the city that it would have little if any impact on the land market. Under those circumstances, the actions of the cities should not, in principle, have much of an effect on price, because there is no apparent effect on practicable supply.

The very existence of the restrictions, however, may create a form of psychological shortage rather like the reactions of consumers several years ago when the rumor of a toilet paper shortage spread through the country. Although the facts later demonstrated that there was no shortage, one can easily imagine the short-term reaction of the average consumer. More than a century and a half ago in *Extraordinary Popular Delusions and the Madness of Crowds*, Charles Mackay (1841) documented how the psychological effects of apparent scarcities created wild speculations in markets. The book remains in print and on the assignment lists at business schools. Thus, just as perceived scarcity once created inordinate value for tulip bulbs, the mere perception of a shortage of land (or housing) caused by a growth management program may affect the price of land and housing beyond the market effects an economist might expect.

An economist would anticipate the greatest effects of growth management programs on land prices to occur in areas where there is a measurable, relatively short-range limitation on the supply of land or housing. In a study using 1970s data from California, Elliott (1981) confirmed that hypothesis. He found that growth management programs had a far greater effect on housing prices in a county where most communities had adopted relatively stringent growth controls. The effects of a single growth management program in a county were far less significant. On the basis of a literature review, Lillydahl and Singell concluded,

Where growth control measures are ubiquitous and where controls may grant monopoly power to builders, average housing prices may be as much as 35 to 40 percent higher than similar communities without growth control. In cities located in metropolitan areas where growth controls are largely absent, growth controls may have little or no effect on housing prices, but they increase building activity in surrounding communities. Most growth control communities exist between these two extremes, with typical price effects between 10 and 20 percent (1987, p. 71).

Similarly, after a comprehensive review of the literature, Fischel concluded that "land use controls, especially overall growth control programs, are important constraints on the land market. This in turn affects housing values, especially in suburban and exurban communities" (1990, p. 53). In citing Fischel's work, it is important to note that Fischel is an economist who clearly believes that the free market works better than most government regulations. He has been as critical of zoning as he is of growth management programs (Fischel 1985). Regardless of whether one agrees with Fischel's view of government regulation, his economic analysis is straightforward and generally consistent with that of other researchers in the field.

Economists from the University of California–Davis criticized many of the published studies on the price effects of urban growth management systems in an important 1986 article (Schwartz, Zorn, and Hansen 1986). Subjects of their criticism included several studies cited here. Their basic argument, however, was not that the studies were wrong. They simply regretted the inability of researchers to conduct a growth management analysis in a laboratory where they could constrain the number of variables. To prove their point, they tested the apparent price effects of the growth management system in Davis, California, using some of the methods from the published studies. Their analyses showed significantly different levels of impact on price, depending on the research method; but all confirmed that growth controls increase housing prices. The authors concluded that the careful researcher ought to use multiple methods to test the effects of a particular growth management system (pp. 232–233).

Schwartz and his colleagues made a good scientific argument but a poor public policy one. It is rarely possible to have a complete set of data to make a public policy decision (see, for example, Braybrooke and Lindblom 1963). Public officials still must make decisions. When existing studies provide consistent conclusions, as they do on this subject, that is useful information. It is useful for public officials who must make decisions about growth management programs and for others in society who are interested in those decisions. Because of the possible inconsistencies resulting from different methods and different assumptions, it would be risky to rely very heavily on the particular numbers (or percentages) reflected in the studies cited here.

In a generalized study involving 30 metropolitan areas, Black and Hoben (1985) examined the causes of the differences in price increases for land among those metropolitan areas. Over the study period, 1975–1980, the price of a standard residential lot increased by as little as 31 percent in one area and as much as 176 percent, or five times as much, in another. The authors found that a four-factor model explained 80 percent of the differences. An index of regulatory restriction was the only supply factor in the model; the other three all affected demand. Not surprisingly, the high-priced, high-increase market was one already cited repeatedly in this book as a growth managing community, San Jose (pp. 30–31). Also among the communities with the highest rate of increase were Boulder and Portland. The Black and Hoben study is widely cited, probably because it illustrated clearly the fundamental principles of supply and demand as applied to the land market.

Case Studies

In 1977, Gruen Gruen+Associates, a consulting firm well regarded for its work in the economics side of planning, joined with the Urban Land Institute to perform two major case studies of housing cost increases induced by regulations. One of the case studies focused on San Jose, California (its growth management program is described in Chapter 4). San Jose adopted a three-tiered urban growth boundary in 1970 and later simplified it to two tiers. According to the study, the lines in the tiers were relatively rigid. Demand was relatively inelastic because of the lack of comparable, constraint-free land in other communities in the area (Urban Land Institute Research Division and Gruen Gruen+Associates 1977, p. 20).

The study covered the period 1967–1976. The consultants did not need to rely on regression analyses. With access to primary data, the developers' books, they compared the actual cost and price increases affecting a particular model of house offered over that period. The study found that the sales price of Builder A's homes increased by 80.2 percent over the study period while that of Builder B's home increased by 121.3 percent. Of those increases, some were clearly inflationary and unrelated to local policies. However, the study found that 32 percent of Builder A's price increase and 43.4 percent of Builder B's were attributable to "public policy costs," or the impacts of various taxes and regulations. Builder A's land price increased by 29.5 percent, Builder B's by 168.9 percent. The story behind those figures is also the story behind the difference in the overall price increases. In building houses in 1976, Builder A used land acquired in 1972, thus avoiding a significant portion of the cost impact of the urban growth boundary. Builder B clearly felt the brunt of that. Table 10.1 presents selected figures from the study, adjusted to 1976 dollars. It is interesting to note that Builder B reduced the portion of the price attributable to land cost, presumably by restraining the extent of price increase that otherwise might have been taken.

Using totally different methods, Knaap tested the effects of the Portland urban growth boundary on land prices (1982; also reported in Knaap 1985). Knaap analyzed "every 'arms-length' residential land transaction recorded in fiscal year 1980" (1982, p. 20) in a defined portion of the Portland area. Among the fifteen variables included in the regression analysis, besides the critical one related to the ur-

Table 10.1
Price Effects of Urban Growth Boundary in San Jose, California

Item	Builder A			Builder B		
	1967	1976	Change	1968	1976	Change
Sales price	$42,440	$44,950	+5.9%	$37,847	$49,250	+30.1%
Land cost	$5,432	$4,151	-23.9%	$3,778	$5,973	+58.1%
Land cost as percentage of house price	12.7%	9.3%	N.A.	10.0%	12.1%	N.A.

Sources: Urban Land Institute, Research Division, and Gruen Gruen + Associates, 1977, *Effects of Regulation on Housing Costs: Two Case Studies,* Tables 5 and 6, pages 17 and 18; third row of this table developed by author from data in the original.

ban growth boundary, were variables for zoning, access, and location in relation to a sewer line. Knaap tested both the effects of the principal urban growth boundary and of the intermediate growth boundary. Although he found inconsistent results in testing the intermediate growth boundary, he found that "land values were approximately 50 percent lower outside the urban growth boundary in Washington County and 60 percent lower outside the urban growth boundary in Clackamas County" (p. 44). Chapter 7 explains the differences between the effects of the two types of boundaries. The state exerts significant control over the urban growth boundary, making it difficult to change. Local governments, through the regional council that governs the growth management program, can change the intermediate growth boundary. Thus, the outer urban growth boundary is a long-term constraint whereas the intermediate boundary is, at most, a short-term constraint and may amount to little constraint at all.

Landis (1986) found that the woes of San Jose builders and house buyers continued well past the date of the Gruen study. He examined growth management programs in Fresno, Sacramento, and San Jose, noting some significant differences among the programs and the markets, although he noted that the "growth management systems of San Jose, Fresno, and Sacramento County differed not in intent or broad purpose, but in degree, timing, and style of implementation" (p. 130). According to Landis, county officials in Sacramento were 'flexible' in implementing a growth phasing system and constantly made new land available as it appeared to be needed, at one time providing enough land subject to current development to accommodate an additional 100,000 residents. The focus of the Sacramento system was on the availability of public facilities. Fresno adopted a variable fee system, through which the city held developers financially accountable for decisions to develop in relatively remote locations. San Jose maintained its urban growth boundary program.

Landis also found significant differences among the three housing markets. He characterized Sacramento as a "competitive market" in economic terms, in which there were few if any barriers to entry by new players. He found San Jose to be a "contestable" market, in which new players can enter the market, subject to paying significant entry costs. Among the entry costs cited by Landis are high land costs and substantial impact and other public fees imposed on development. He cited Fresno as a "noncontestable" or "closed market," resulting primarily from a dual land market in which existing players controlled most of the land at the urban fringe that could most easily be developed under the local growth management system (pp. 16–18). Landis then compared developer costs, profits and housing prices in the three markets, using 1980 figures. Table 10.2 presents part of his findings.

Although Landis did not have access to the builders' books, as Gruen+Gruen did for their study, he interviewed a number of builders in each of the communities and thus appeared to have a solid basis for his comparison. It is important to understand that he made no attempt to compare the types of units in the three markets or to compare other factors that influenced the market. Thus, the $129,000 mean price in San Jose may (or may not) buy a substantially different home than $83,000 in Sacramento. However, the significant difference in mean prices is clearly attributable to more than coincidence. The fact that the combination of land cost, profit, and overhead ranges from 28 percent in Sacramento (the competitive market) to to 38.6 percent in San Jose tells part of the story. Note that the low land cost and high profit in Fresno compared to the high land cost and lower profit in San Jose are direct functions of one another. The long-time developers in Fresno profit handsomely from their low-cost,

Table 10.2
Housing Prices, Land Costs, and Builder Profits in Three California Communities

Item	Fresno	Sacramento	San Jose
Mean 1980 sales price, single-family unit	$99,300	$83,000	$129,000
Development and building costs	$66,100	$56,800	$80,150
Profit and overhead	$28,200	$14,700	$29,850
Raw land cost	$5,000	$8,500	$20,000
Profit and overhead as percentage of mean house price	28.4	17.8	23.1
Land cost as percentage of mean house price	5.0	10.2	15.5

Sources: John D. Landis, 1986, "Land Regulation and the Price of New Housing," *Journal of the American Planning Association* 52:9–21, Table 4 at page 19; percentages in fifth and sixth rows of this table developed by author from data in the original.

long-held land, while developers in San Jose must dip into future profits to pay one of the market's "entry costs," high land acquisition costs. Developers in both markets, however, profit substantially more than those in the highly competitive Sacramento market.

Gleeson (1979) tested the effects of a different type of growth management program on land prices in and around a Minneapolis suburb. The Brooklyn Park program combined an adequate public facilities requirement with a public policy decision not to extend public services into agricultural areas. Knaap criticized Gleeson's study as a study of the price differences of urban and nonurban land (1982). The criticism was valid, but that in no way detracts from the value of Gleeson's study. Using a practical system of planning, Brooklyn Park determined what land should be urban and then made it that way. It did so through a combination of planned infrastructure investment in some areas and significant development restrictions in others. Thus, rather than establishing an arbitrary urban growth boundary, it reinforced and guided normal market forces with public investment and regulation. Gleeson's findings were interesting but hardly surprising. He found significant differences between the prices of farmland that was not currently developable under Brooklyn Park policies and urban land that was developable. He then disaggregated the factors in his analysis and assigned a dollar value to various factors, including access, availability of storm sewer, availability of trunk water line and lateral (local) water line, and availability of sanitary sewer trunk and lateral lines (Gleeson 1979, Table 3, p. 359). Predictably, each of those items contributed a portion of the land value; some were, of course, negative factors. Because trunk water and sewer lines were generally available in the developable area, they did not influence land values within the urban area; however the availability of those trunk lines did affect the values of land in farm areas. Studies cited earlier in this book indicate that the factors tested by Gleeson generally affect land developability and thus land values (see discussion in Chapter 5).

There was also some residual difference in values between land in the urban area and the farm area in Gleeson's study. That difference could not be explained by anything except the general categorization of urban or rural. That categorization amounted to a type of urban growth boundary (pp. 359–360). That residual difference is somewhat surprising, because Brooklyn Park appears to be too small to have a significant impact on the housing market of the Twin Cities region (Knaap 1982). Without comparing Gleeson's findings to land values for the entire region, it is impossible to know why the program in Brooklyn Park appears to have had that effect.

A team of economists from the University of California-Davis compared Petaluma to nearby Santa Rosa to determine the "effect of growth control on the price of moderate-priced housing" (Schwartz, Hansen, and Green 1984). Table 10.3 presents some of their findings.

They interpreted the data summarized in Table 10.3 as follows. "These data provide strong evidence of the shift in Petaluma's housing away from the low end of the market after growth control. The data for floor area document the disappearance of the small house from Petaluma" (p. 112). The authors attributed the elimination of the small house to the competitive aspects of the growth management program (that aspect of the program was later abandoned; see history in Chapter 3) and to the governing body's public statements that it

Table 10.3
Percentage of Houses by Price Range, Petaluma and Santa Rosa, California

	Petaluma		Santa Rosa	
Sale Price	1970	1976	1970	1976
Less than $25,000	9.1	0.0	26.2	10.7
$25,001 - $35,000	90.8	74.7	52.3	63.4
More than $35,000	0.1	25.3	21.5	25.9

Source: Seymour I. Schwartz, David E. Hansen, and Richard Green, 1984, "The Effect of Growth Control on the Production of Moderate-Priced Housing," *Land Economics,* 60:110–114, Table 1, at page 112.

wanted "high quality" projects (Schwartz, Hansen, and Green 1984, p. 112). To keep their data in perspective, however, it is important to note that Petaluma was a more expensive community even before it adopted its growth management program (see Table 10.3). Whether growth management was thus a symptom of other factors tending to make development and housing both more expensive in the community or simply the cause of some of the later price increases is not clear. The correlation is clear, but, as with any correlation, that does not explain the cause. The alternative scenario, that the adoption of growth management is more a symptom than a cause, is analogous to Landis's suggestion that the relatively healthy fiscal condition of growth managing communities might be explained by the fact that they are better governed communities rather than by the fiscal impacts of growth management (Landis 1991).

Niebanck (1989) used a different method to compare housing prices in Santa Cruz County, which has had growth controls, and in nearby jurisdictions which have not. Niebanck compared sales of specific houses in Santa Cruz County with sales of comparable houses in the other jurisdictions. He concluded, "It is safe to say that, after 10 years of growth control, the prices of owner-occupied houses, across the board, are at least 10 percent higher than they would have been in the absence of controls" (p. 115).

In a study quite different from his 1986 one, Landis (1991) provided a conceptual context in which to consider the effects of growth controls in California communities in particular. In a working paper, *Do*

Growth Controls Work?, he compared the rate of increase in median house prices in selected pairs of communities; each pair included one community that managed growth and one or more that did not. He found that "median single-family home prices did not rise any faster or to higher levels in the seven case-study communities than in their counterpart pro-growth cities" (p. 21). He acknowledged that there may be a number of reasons why these results seem to contradict the law of supply and demand. Among explanations he suggested were that

the controls, as implemented, may not really be all that effective. Second, there may be adequate spill-over opportunities in other nearby communities, so that growth displaced from one city can easily and costlessly be accommodated in nearby or adjacent communities. . . . The price effects of localized growth controls may be quite small in relation to other, region-wide forces which are acting to raise or depress housing prices (p. 24).

He also noted that there may be other forms of growth limits in the control communities. Landis did not acknowledge the problems inherent in using median housing sale prices. Such a comparison, used in several of the studies because the figures are usually readily available, compares the sales of whatever houses happen to be sold in particular communities at particular times. Whether those houses are at the high end, at the low end, or in fact representative of the middle of the market depends on many factors that such a comparison does not reflect.

However, the next section of the same report provided a better explanation of Landis's results. He projected housing need for selected metropolitan counties in California, using 1980 as a base. His apparent intent was to compare counties where there were strong growth controls with those where there were not. What he found was that "throughout California, but especially in the state's coastal markets, housing supply failed to keep pace with housing demand. . . . The problem of insufficient housing production was (and still is) systemic throughout California, and not limited to cities and counties that have enacted formal growth controls" (p. 28). Fischel independently and without reference to any of Landis's work, took this argument one step further. He argued that "the disparity between the growth of California's housing values in the 1970s and that of housing values in the rest of the United States was caused by growth controls" (Fischel 1991, p. 1145).

Fischel identified California's coastal zone program and stringent environmental regulations as some of the state regulatory programs with exclusionary effects Fischel argued in depth and Landis essentially implied that California has adopted a statewide package of growth-limiting land use and environmental regulations. Thus, comparisons of communities within California probably understate the nature of the problem. In the later study, Landis concluded that

Compared to such regional shortfalls, the growth-limiting effects of local growth-controls programs are but a drop in the bucket. These findings should not be viewed as an exoneration of local growth-control programs, however. To the extent that such programs contribute to regional housing shortfalls, they directly contribute to rising housing prices and declining affordability (1991, p. 28).

Pollakowski and Wachter (1990) conducted a study in Montgomery County, Maryland, comparing changes in housing prices among different planning areas of the county on the basis of the relative restrictiveness of each area. The Montgomery County system, being relatively rare in providing different sets of controls in different planning areas, may thus be one of few for which such a study could be conducted. Although Pollakowski and Wachter used aggregate market data, they created a housing index and then tested their model for a "standard-quality house" rather than for mean or median house prices. Using those methods, they, like all the other researches cited here, found a strong correlation between restrictive land-use controls and increases in housing prices.

Beaton (1991) examined the effect of the Pinelands growth management program on land and housing prices in South Jersey. He found a substantial increase in the prices of houses within the protected areas of the Pinelands, probably reflecting amenity value. He also found increases in land prices, including the prices of those lands most restricted under the New Jersey program. He speculated that over the long run some of those values may drop. However, the conclusions regarding the housing prices unequivocally showed the costs of restrictive growth control in the market.

A 1991 study of the implementation of a housing choice policy in conjunction with Portland's urban growth boundary concluded that, "the Portland region's 'pro-housing' policies have helped to manage regional growth while promoting affordable housing" (Ketcham and Siegel 1991, p. 68). However, the conclusion was based on a significant increase in the proportion of multifamily units in the new housing stock and an increase in the number of single-family houses on small lots. The study's findings may have some meaning for housing costs if the single-family houses built on the smaller lots are comparable in size and quality to those formerly built on larger lots and if the houses on the smaller lots are in fact less expensive. If builders have simply built smaller houses on smaller lots, the Portland program has only shifted the housing supply. The Portland study indicated that the houses on the smaller lots (5,000 to 7,001 square feet) were about 12 percent cheaper than houses on medium lots (7,001 to 9,000 square feet) and about half the price of houses on large lots (over 9,001 square feet) (Table 5, p. 44). However, the authors acknowledged that the price differences reflect changes in the house cost by builders to maintain a house price-to-lot cost ratio of 4 to 1 or more. The house on the smaller lot is cheaper, but it is probably smaller (some of the houses on 5,000 square-foot lots are undoubtedly townhouses) and may be of lesser quality. Thus, the increase in the number of cheaper houses on smaller lots, like the increase in the proportion of apartments, illustrates a regulatory shift in the supply side of the market, not a real reduction in the cost of delivering a particular housing product.

The Costs of Sprawl illustrated clearly how a community could reduce average housing costs by shifting from a mix of single-family houses in unplanned development patterns to a high-density mix including a large number of apartments and townhouses (development types are described above). However, such a regulatory shift in the housing supply with no adjustment in demand may simply lead to further increases in prices of the most desirable types of housing and to higher levels of frustration in the market among those who do not obtain their preferred form of housing. Thus, the Portland study leads logically to the next section of this chapter, which discusses how growth management affects housing opportunities and choices.

Analysis

Any growth management program that significantly restricts the supply of housing or the supply of land on which developers can build housing is likely to affect the price of housing in the community. A rate-of-growth system that establishes a rate below market demand most clearly illustrates such a system. An urban growth boundary that reserves too little land for urban development may have that effect. A phased-growth system that restricts land supply below market demand may have a similar effect.

An adequate public facilities program, in contrast, appears simply to limit the ability of a developer or outlying landowner to profit from leapfrog development. Studies cited in Chapter 5 that showed significant price differences for land located near public facilities, as well as the Gleeson study and others cited in this chapter, illustrate that builders will pay more for land with services than for land without them In Gleeson's study, which involved an adequate public facilities requirement, the value differences were substantial. Only if a community stops expanding its critical infrastructure systems will an adequate public facilities requirement unduly constrain the land market.

GROWTH MANAGEMENT AND DIVERSITY OF HOUSING OPPORTUNITIES

The problem of exclusion is in part a matter of economics. Given enough money, most families could overcome the most exclusionary of local land use control systems, but some systems simply limit the total number of housing opportunities or the type of opportunities available in a particular community. Although the market will allocate the available units among competing users, there may simply not be enough units to satisfy the reasonable demand, and the allocation may or may not be consistent with public policy goals.

There appear to be two quite different exclusionary trends occurring in growth management communities. The effect of growth management in some appears to be the elimination of the lower end of the housing market, with continued vitality of the single-family house on a larger lot. In others, it is the single-family house on a large lot that the community is driving away. These alternative scenarios have different demographic and public policy implications.

In Petaluma (see discussion concerning Table 10.3, and Schwartz, Hansen, and Green 1984) and Davis, growth management appears to have erased the low end of the housing market. As shown in Table 10.3, Petaluma housing costs increased significantly more than those in Santa Rosa, a nearby and somewhat comparable community. Economists who found the difference attributed much of it to the elimination of lower cost houses (Schwartz, Hansen, and Green 1984). The University of California–Davis study of that community (Schwartz, Zorn, and Hansen 1986) found that not only the price but the quality of older housing in the community increased after the adoption of growth controls. Fischel (1990) interpreted data from the study as showing that "older housing in Davis was filtering up rather than down" (p. 31). The cost increases in other communities, discussed in the previous section of this chapter, suggest comparable results. A thorough literature review by Lillydahl and Singell (1987) found similar results from a number of studies. They concluded that while growth management efforts "may have helped maintain the desired community character, housing prices have increased and in many cases the availability of low- or moderate-priced housing has declined substantially or even disappeared" (p. 73).

Where the effect of a growth management program is to preserve opportunities for single-family houses on large lots while precluding or limiting the construction of apartments, townhouses, and other affordable alternatives, that growth management program is similar in its effect to various schemes of exclusionary zoning. Courts in New Jersey, Pennsylvania, Virginia, New Hampshire, and elsewhere have struck down exclusionary zoning schemes under which very large lot sizes, prohibitions on apartments, excess improvement requirements, and undue development delays, among other techniques, limited the availability of housing for the lower end of the market (see, generally, Babcock and Bosselman 1973; Downs 1973; Elickson 1977; Dowall 1984; Niebanck 1989). Regardless of the good intentions behind a growth management program, its effects may run up against bans on exclusionary zoning. Part of the New Jersey remedy is the requirement that each community absorb a "fair share" of a region's growth (see discussion of principles in Franklin, Falk, and Levin 1974; Fishman 1978; Blaesser et al. 1991). As figures discussed later in this section show, a major effect of some growth management programs, at least over the short run, has been to reduce the share of the region's growth that the growth managing city accommodates. That is also typically the apparent intention of rate-of-growth programs and some growth phasing and urban growth boundary programs.

The Portland study illustrated a very different trend. Of new housing units approved from 1985 through 1989, some 54 percent were multifamily, only 46 percent single family (Ketcham and Siegel 1991, pp. 24–25). That was a radical shift in the housing supply in a metropolitan region where 66.4 percent of 489,470 housing units counted in the 1990 census were single-family units (Bureau of the Census 1991a). Only 13,036 of the single-family units, or 2.7 percent of the total, were attached (townhouse) units. Even in Portland itself, more than 64 percent of the housing units were single family, of which only 1.8 percent were attached units, meaning that more than 62 percent of the city's housing stock has consisted of single-family detached units.

The changes in housing mix significantly assisted Portland in meeting its housing goal, because the study found that 77 percent of households could afford two-bedroom apartments, while only 25 percent could afford to purchase new houses on small lots with a 5 percent down payment. The percentage who could afford to purchase increased to 31 percent with an increase in down payment to 20 percent of the price. An increased down payment reduces monthly payments, thus increasing the portion who can "afford" such units according to ordinary income-ratio lending criteria. As a practical matter, down payments are often more difficult for families to find than slight increases in monthly payments, so that aspect of the study is questionable.

Boulder, which also has adopted goals to improve the availability

Table 10.4
Boulder Housing Mix, 1970–90 (in Percentages)

Unit Type	1970	1980	1990
Single-family detached			41.7
		50.8	
Townhouse	58.1		6.8
Mobile home		2.4	3.2
Duplex, triplex, fourplex	12.1	10.7	10.1
Multi-family, 5 or more units	29.9	36.0	38.2

Sources: Raw data from Bureau of the Census, 1991, *Census of Population and Housing: Summary Population and Housing Characteristics,* Part 7, Table 8; Bureau of the Census, 1983, *Census of Population and Housing, Census Tracts, No. 138, Denver-Boulder Standard Metropolitan Statistical Area,* Table H-7; Bureau of the Census, 1972, *Census of Population and Housing, Census Tracts, Denver, Colorado, Standard Metropolitan Statistical Area,* Table H-2; all percentage computations by author.

of affordable housing, has also changed its housing mix over the last decade, as can be seen from Table 10.4. Miller (1986) documented the change in the mix, but not the resulting demographic change described later.

Downs has argued that exclusion of multifamily housing through restrictive zoning is one of the most serious obstacles to the development of affordable housing in this country (Downs 1991a, p. 1101). A program such as that undertaken in Portland responds directly to that criticism. If the effect of the change is to provide increased housing opportunities for those who otherwise might lack them, an action for which Downs argued in *Opening up the Suburbs* (1973), clearly the region will benefit. If the effect of the change is to force families accustomed to (or hoping to become accustomed to) living in single-family houses to move into apartments, the benefits are less clear and the social costs are significant.

The Costs of Sprawl illustrated how a community could reduce housing costs, energy costs, and municipal costs by encouraging more compact forms of development containing smaller dwelling units (Real Estate Research Corporation 1974). Much of the criticism of the report has centered on the apparently unrealistic assumption that people who would otherwise live in single-family detached units would willingly live in the high-rise, high-density model that optimized benefits in that early 1970s study (critiques are discussed in Chapter 9). As the following discussion of the effects of the Boulder program shows, implementing such a program in a single community in a larger region may simply force people to live in other communities. However, where a state or regional entity implements a region-wide program that significantly changes the housing mix, as in Portland, there seems to be nowhere else for people to go. Thus, if the region maintains the program over the long run, area residents will presumably have no choice except to adjust their housing desires to what the market will supply.

How this shift in the housing supply will affect the Portland region and its residents over the long run is not clear. The effects of the shift in Boulder are much clearer. A 1992 City of Boulder newsletter, *Research Perspectives*, carried this headline, "Growth masks out-migration of young families; in-migration of established families" ("Growth masks out-migration" 1992, p. 1). The city's analysis of census and other data show substantial net out-migration for age cohorts 0–4, 5–9, 17–24, 45–54, and 55–64. There was a small out-migration for the 65–74 age group and substantial in-migration among senior citizens (75–84, 85+) and college-age students (17–24). The Boulder location of the main campus of the University of Colorado explains the latter figure. The only other young age group that showed net in-migration was the 10–16 age group. In contrast, Boulder County outside the city showed net in-migration in all age groups except 17–24, which had substantial out-migration, and 55–64, which showed out-migration of 1 percent (all data from "Growth masks out-migration" 1992, Tables 2, 3, and 4, pp. 2–3). Miller (1986) commented cheerfully that "the construction and sale of less expensive attached houses in Boulder . . . mitigated the effect of the price increase of detached homes on the housing market overall," although he tempered his enthusiasm for his own findings somewhat in this comment: "Of course, while Boulder homebuyers paid less, they also received less" (p. 325).

Boulder's own research report explained some of the trends:

The profile of net out-migration among younger children and net in-migration among older children may be explained by families with young children leaving the city to find more affordable housing in the rest of the county . . . . As parents age and earn more, because both parents can work more easily when their children are older and because older parents tend to earn more

Table 10.5
Persons per Household, Boulder and Surrounding Communities, 1970–90

Place	1970	1980	1990
Boulder	2.84	2.40	2.18
Lafayette	3.03	2.62	2.69
Longmont	3.04	2.75	2.61
Louisville	2.99	2.59	2.68
Boulder County	3.04	2.63	2.45
Colorado	3.08	2.65	2.51

Sources: Bureau of the Census, 1991, *Census of Population and Housing: Summary Population and Housing Characteristics*, Part 7, Table 5; Bureau of the Census, 1981, *Census of the Population: Characteristics of the Population, Chapter A, Number of Inhabitants*, Part 7, Table 14; and Bureau of the Census, 1972, *Census of Population, Vol. 1, Characteristics of the Population*, Part 7, Tables 10, 16 (state), and 32 (Louisville only).

than younger parents, they can better afford housing in the city of Boulder ("Growth masks out-migration" 1992, p. 3).

That is probably a correct demographic analysis, but it ignores the impact of the legislated shift in the housing market.

A discussion at a governing body meeting in Boulder early in 1992 illustrated the issue better in human terms:

Boulder City Councilman Bob Greenlee says his daughter and her husband can't afford to live in Boulder; they are trying to buy a house in Louisville. Representatives of the Fire and Police Departments said it's hard for their employees to feel committed to their work, because their homes are elsewhere. . . .

But Deputy Mayor Matthew Applebaum responded, "There are lots of townhouses and condominiums and apartments available in the city. They *choose* to go to Louisville or Lafayette or Broomfield and live in a house with a garage and a big yard. I like living in a house myself; it would be hard to go back to an apartment, but there is a choice" ("Housing cost, elitism come" 1992).

The exchange was reminiscent of the title of an early critique of the Ramapo program, *Controlling Urban Growth—But for Whom?*

Table 10.6
Percentage of Population under 18, Boulder and Surrounding Communities, 1970–90

Place	1970	1980	1990
Boulder	27.5	17.4	15.1
Lafayette	36.0	28.2	31.6
Longmont	37.3	30.7	28.5
Louisville	34.1	26.6	30.7
Boulder County	23.4	24.9	23.0
Colorado	35.2	28.0	26.1

Sources: Raw data from Bureau of the Census, 1991, *Census of Population and Housing: Summary Population and Housing Characteristics,* Part 7, Table 1; Bureau of the Census, 1981, *Census of the Population: Characteristics of the Population, Chapter B, General Population Characteristics,* Part 7, Table 14; and Bureau of the Census, 1972, *Census of Population, Vol. 1, Characteristics of the Population,* Part 7, Tables 16, and 32 (Louisville only); some computations by author.

(Franklin 1973). Other census data, not used by the city in its own analysis, confirms the trend of families moving away from Boulder and into surrounding communities.

Tables 10.5 and 10.6 clearly show that family size has shrunk more rapidly in Boulder than in the rest of Boulder County and that much of that shrinkage can be traced to the reduction in the number of families with children. It is all arguably attributable to the shift in the housing market achieved by Boulder. Those demographic changes are entirely consistent with the city's own analysis, quoted earlier, and with the anecdotal exchange at the Boulder council meeting. Figure 10.1 shows the locations of Boulder and the surrounding communities to which the Boulder growth management program appears to have diverted many families with children. These are not adjacent suburbs but distinct communities, creating a pattern of leapfrog development (beyond the greenbelt, also shown in Figure 10.1) and leaving those who move there and work in Boulder with locally significant commuting times.

Figure 10.1
Boulder Region, Showing Greenbelt and Surrounding Communities

Sources: Map adapted by Jerzy Lewicki from Boulder, City of 1991, "Boulder Open Space, Parks and Trails Map" (Zia Maps); and Boulder County, 1991, "Boulder County Road Map" (Boulder County).

Not all growth management programs appear to have had such a significant effect on housing opportunities for families. Tables 10.7 and 10.8 show that the percentage of persons under 18 in Petaluma and Livermore both fell much more quickly than the percentage in the county after the initial adoption of the growth management programs in those communities. However, unlike Boulder, both communities have stayed above the county means in the percentage of persons under the age of 18, suggesting that they remain significant factors in the family home market.

The same types of programs that affect housing cost are, by definition, likely to limit the opportunities for affordable housing in a community. However, the effects of growth management programs in different communities show two different types of exclusion. Some programs, such as the one in Petaluma, tend to reinforce patterns of

Table 10.7
Percentage of Population under 18, Petaluma and Area, 1970–90

Place	1970	1980	1990
Petaluma	37.6	29.3	25.8
Santa Rosa	30.2	24.8	23.8
Sonoma County	33.2	30.4	24.7
California	33.4	27.0	26.1

Sources: Raw data from Bureau of the Census, 1991, *Census of Population and Housing: Summary Population and Housing Characteristics,* Part 6, Table 1; Bureau of the Census, 1982, *Census of the Population: Characteristics of the Population, Chapter B, General Characteristics of the Population,* Part 6, Table 14; and Bureau of the Census, 1972, *Census of Population, Vol. 1, Characteristics of the Population,* Part 6, Table 16; some computations by author.

Table 10.8
Percentage of Population under 18, Livermore and Alameda County, 1970–90

Place	1970	1980	1990
Livermore	41.2	33.0	27.2
Alameda County	31.2	25.1	23.7
California	33.4	27.0	26.1

Sources: Raw data from Bureau of the Census, 1991, *Census of Population and Housing: Summary Population and Housing Characteristics,* Part 6, Table 1; Bureau of the Census, 1982, *Census of the Population: Characteristics of the Population, Chapter B, General Characteristics of the Population,* Part 6, Table 14; and Bureau of the Census, 1972, *Census of Population, Vol. 1, Characteristics of the Population,* Part 6, Table 16; some computations by author.

exclusionary zoning, protecting opportunities for single-family houses on larger lots but increasing overall cost in the housing market, thus adversely affecting those seeking more affordable housing. In contrast, the Boulder program appears to have made the traditional single-family house for a family with children under 18 relatively scarce in the community, a scarcity reflected in significantly reduced household size and significant reductions in the percentage of the population under 18. The regional program in Portland expressly attempts to reduce the portion of the market consisting of single-family detached houses and to increase the portion of multifamily units. The two programs have quite different social implications.

CONCLUSION

Many growth management programs have clearly affected both housing costs and housing opportunities. While the costs related to unnecessary delay are both relatively small and relatively easy to limit or to eliminate, the other impacts are more complex. Programs that constrain the housing or land market clearly increase housing costs and change the mix of housing opportunities available in the community.

Dowall (1982) suggested a complex scheme of managing the land market as a cure. Under his proposal, local planners would ensure that as growth controls limited opportunities in one submarket in the community, other public actions would open comparable opportunities in other submarkets. He used a hypothetical community with a demand for 600 housing units over the next year to explain his model. One defect with the model was that he proposed that the community guarantee a surplus of only 100 units above projected demand—essentially a fourteen-month market. With the wild vagaries of the real estate market in many communities, that entire supply could be consumed in a few months. One relevant example comes from Westminster, which issued more building permits in the first quarter of 1977 than it had issued in the entire previous year (Westminster, City of 1978b). Even if the supply were indeed adequate for a year, the relative scarcity of the immediately developable lots would surely result in a windfall to the owners of those properties and an increase in housing prices (see, generally, Fischel 1985). The Portland approach, in which the urban growth boundary contains an initial twenty-year supply of developable land, seems more rational. Nevertheless, there is merit to Dowall's monitoring system. Regardless of the actual total supply, it is worth ensuring that reductions in one area are offset by increases in others.

It is important to remember that although any growth management program can increase delay costs of new housing by adding more steps to the process, only some types of programs tend to increase costs by constricting land or housing supply. A simpler approach than Dowall's land-monitoring system seems to be to minimize the use of those techniques that have the greatest impact on the market. The next chapter addresses that subject in more depth and in a broader context.

NOTE

1. Section 50-35, Montgomery County Code (1991).

11

Is Growth Management
a Good Idea?

This question is more complex than it might appear. The answer depends on a community's goals and the constituency with which it is concerned. The answer depends also on the planning and governmental structure for the growth management program and on the type of growth management program being considered.

From the perspective of the community involved, to manage growth is generally a good idea, particularly if the alternative is *not* to manage growth. However, managing growth effectively is much more complex than just adopting some sort of point system that allows X hundred dwelling units per year or that permits only developments that earn more than Y points on an arbitrary scale and denies approval to all others. Further, if by "managing" growth a particular community means "limiting" growth—either directly or indirectly—that is not a particularly good idea, at least from a state or regional perspective. The successful effort of one community to limit its growth rate while the region of which it is a part continues to grow simply shifts regional growth to other communities.

Montgomery County has managed growth for nearly two decades. It has done so through a comprehensive program involving development rights purchases, planned and managed capital investments, and sophisticated adequate public facilities requirements. All those pieces relate to each other and to the county's annual growth policy, which provides the planning basis for the programs. The Montgomery County program has served it well.

Montgomery County recognized from the beginning that it should absorb growth to the extent of its current ability to do so. Westminster absorbed large population increases with its growth management system in effect, using the program simply to keep a balance between the community's actual capacities and the demands placed on them. Like Montgomery County, it continued to accept rapid growth as its region grew rapidly.

In contrast, Petaluma and Boulder have attempted to limit, rather than manage, growth and in so doing have clearly contributed to a shifting of growth within the region. Further, the burden of that shift has not been evenly spread across the socioeconomic spectrum. Boulder has clearly diverted a disproportionate number of families with children to nearby communities. Davis's program has effectively increased costs at the bottom end of the housing market in a "trickle-up effect" through which houses that were once "lower cost" have become affordable only to those with higher incomes.

Even under their growth management programs, both Westminster and Montgomery County accepted an increased rate of growth over the short term in order to meet regional demand. In contrast, Ramapo, Boulder, Petaluma, and many of the other communities used as examples in this book attempted to limit growth in a way that was not necessarily related to the community's ability to absorb growth.

The adoption of such programs typically represents an overreaction to a short-term trend. The two-year growth rate of 10 percent per year that led to the adoption of the Petaluma program has never been approached again. Although some might attribute the reduction in growth rate to the success of the Petaluma growth management program, Santa Rosa, a nearby community often compared to Petaluma in this book and elsewhere, and Sonoma County, which contains them both, have grown at rates very comparable to the reduced, post-1972 growth rate of Petaluma. Neither Santa Rosa nor the county had a growth management program during that time (see Table 11.1). Although Boulder was successful in holding its 1980s growth rate to half of its stated goal of 2 percent per year, the average growth rate of all of Boulder County in the 1980s also fell below the city's target rate, although no growth management program was in effect in most of the county (see Table 11.2). The rapid population growth of Rockland County, New York, essentially stopped in the 1980s, despite the fact that Ramapo repealed its famous program early in that decade. These communities adopted growth-limiting programs during temporary growth surges that have gradually waned.

Petaluma's controlled growth rate has been only slightly below that

Table 11.1
Growth in Petaluma, Santa Rosa, and Sonoma County

Place	Population			Percentage Increase	
	1970	1980	1990	1970-1980	1980-1990
Petaluma	24,870	33,834	43,184	36.0	27.6
Santa Rosa	50,006	83,320	113,313	66.6	36.0
Sonoma County	204,885	299,681	388,222	46.3	29.5
California	19,957,715	23,667,902	29,760,021	18.5	25.7

Sources: Raw data from Bureau of the Census, 1991, *Census of Population and Housing: Summary Population and Housing Characteristics,* Part 6, Table 16; Bureau of the Census, 1982, *Census of the Population: Characteristics of the Population,* Chapter A, *Number of Inhabitants,* Part 6, Table 4; and Bureau of the Census, 1972, *Census of Population,* Vol. 1, *Characteristics of the Population,* Part 6, Tables 7 (cities), 9 (state), and 10 (county); percentage computations by author.

of the county, which has no growth management system. Boulder has been more successful than Petaluma in diverting development to nearby small communities which have thus endured extremely high rates of growth. However, the overall growth rate in Boulder County over the 1980s was less than the rate of 2 percent per year that Boulder residents once determined to be acceptable. Boulder's actual growth rate has fallen far below its maximum of 2 percent per year. Clearly both the psychological effects of the program on the market and other aspects of the program have contributed to the development shift to other communities.

In short, just adopting a relatively simplistic program does not amount to managing growth. Many growth management programs fit the adage that for every complex problem there is a solution that is fast, easy, and wrong. Nevertheless, there are some types of growth management programs that make sense for most communities and some that make sense for some communities or in particular circumstances. The following discussion reviews those.

Table 11.2
Growth in Boulder and Boulder County

	Population			Percentage Increase	
	1970	1980	1990	1970-1980	1980-1990
Boulder	66,870	76,685	83,312	14.7	8.6
Lafayette	3,498	8,985	14,548	156.9	61.9
Longmont	23,209	42,942	51,555	85.0	20.1
Louisville	2,409	5,593	13,361	132.2	138.9
Boulder County	131,899	189,625	225,339	43.8	18.8
Colorado	2,207,765	2,889,964	3,294,394	30.9	12.3

Sources: Raw data from Bureau of the Census, 1991, *Census of Population and Housing: Summary Population and Housing Characteristics*, Part 7, Tables 15 (county) and 16 (cities); Bureau of the Census, 1981, *Census of the Population: Characteristics of the Population*, Chapter A, *Number of Inhabitants*, Part 7, Tables 4 (county and state) and 5 (cities); and Bureau of the Census, 1972, *Census of Population*, Vol. 1, *Characteristics of the Population*, Part 7, Table 10; percentage computations by author.

PROGRAMS THAT ARE GOOD IDEAS

Planning for growth is always a good idea. Planning for growth on a regional basis, rather than a local one, is always a good idea. Identifying priority areas for growth and for preservation is an important part of local planning. Carefully managing infrastructure investments—particularly those for arterial roadways, interceptor sewer lines, and major water lines—to reinforce desired patterns of growth is a good idea for any community under any circumstance. Ideally a community should coordinate that process with providers of other facilities—for example, the local school board and the state transportation department.

Growth does follow sewers and highways. That is not just useful information; it is also the basis for a critical technique in managing growth. By building a highway and a sewer line through a wetlands area, a community can virtually ensure either its development or major litigation over refusal to permit that development. By building the highway and the sewer line elsewhere, the community may not guarantee the preservation of the wetlands, but it can make such preservation much more likely. Most communities have some sort of plans for future growth. Too few use those plans to influence their investments in infrastructure. All communities should base infrastructure investment plans on their comprehensive plans for growth. Those plans should tell the community where to build new highways and sewer and water lines. Perhaps more important, those plans should indicate where *not* to build new infrastructure. By using infrastructure "growth shapers" as part of a growth management package, a community can significantly influence its future urban form.

Using annexation policy as part of a growth management program is always a good idea in states where municipalities can expand their boundaries through annexation. A community in such a state should actively annex and plan to serve only that territory that fits its general expansion plans. There may be occasional exceptions when it is important to a community to control a particular location, such as the only interstate highway interchange serving the area. However, the simple desire to "control" large areas of land does not justify annexation beyond the reasonable growth needs of the community. The most important aspect for a community to remember about annexation as it relates to growth management is that annexation power—particularly the power to refuse to annex—is one of the more effective devices in the growth management toolbox. Annexation increases the likelihood of development. A refusal to annex limits the likelihood of development, although that limitation is less effective in areas where other municipalities or other entities of government are attractive alternative service providers.

Adopting adequate public facilities standards is always a good idea. Economically, adequate public facilities requirements appear to reinforce market patterns that naturally establish higher values for property with public services than for property without them. Although establishing an adequate public facilities requirement in a community that did not previously have such a requirement may cause a short-term increase in the cash price of a house, it is simply shifting the cost from a social benefit to a cash benefit. If there were no such requirement, new residents (or old ones) would pay the cost of that lack in a reduced quality of life. That reduced quality of life might be measured in greater distances from fewer parks, in over-crowded classrooms, or in longer-than-normal traffic delays. Living under those conditions is clearly a cost. Further, it is a cost that most communities are unwilling to tolerate over the long run. Thus, it is likely that a community will eventually pay such a cost by building facilities, thus converting the cost to cash.

Whether adequate public facilities requirements reduce sprawl depends entirely on where public facilities are available. If a com-munity has extended major public services several miles out of town to serve an airport or an industrial park, adequate public facilities all along that route may thus encourage a form of linear sprawl. In many metropolitan areas, the availability of public services from nearby communities may limit the influence of one community's policy on regional urban development. However, Brooklyn Park, Minnesota, has demonstrated that even within a major metropolitan area a community can use a combination of adequate public facilities standards and careful planning of infrastructure extensions to shape urban form.

Developers often argue that the standard established for "ade-quacy" of facilities in a community may be excessive. A community may require streets to be thirty-five feet wide, when studies suggest that twenty-six would be adequate. A community may require eight acres of park land for every 1,000 projected residents in new areas, although it has survived for years with only five in the rest of the community. Obviously the increased requirements increase costs. There is considerable merit in the Florida approach, under which a community must spend its own money to bring existing facilities up to the same standards that the community requires in new develop-ments. That brings a healthy sense of balance to the decision-making process, because few communities have sufficient surplus funds in the 1990s to build oversized facilities with their own money.

It is important that a community that establishes adequate public facilities requirements continue to expand its infrastructure network as its population grows. If a community requires that all new devel-opment have access to infrastructure and at the same time stops building infrastructure, it will effectively stop growth at the level that its present capacity can serve. If used in that way, an adequate public facilities requirement can become a tool of exclusion. How-ever, that would represent an abuse of the technique, not a logical consequence of its normal implementation.

PROGRAMS THAT MAY BE GOOD IDEAS

A regional urban growth boundary is probably a good idea where there is an institutional framework to implement it. Such a framework clearly exists in Hawaii, and it appears to exist around the metropolitan areas in Oregon. The key to making a regional urban growth boundary work is some sort of regional planning. In Hawaii, the planning is actually statewide. In Oregon, there is state-mandated regional planning.

Neither the Oregon system nor the Hawaii one have totally resolved the issue of the permanency of the boundaries. There appears to be an excessive number of individual changes to the boundaries in Hawaii. That creates the appearance of a highly political system, whether it actually is or not. On the other hand, the net change in the total urbanized area is quite small. Metropolitan Portland has established a far more rigid demarcation as the outer boundary of the region. However, it is probably too rigid. In the unlikely event that the region's growth projections are accurate (few long-range planning projections are), the region will run out of land before the target year because of "underzoning" (zoning for less than planned development) and "underbuilding" (building at a lower intensity than the maximum allowed by zoning). Ideally, there would have been no underzoning or underbuilding. However, for planners to expect that all land would develop at exactly the planned levels seems naive. The land shortage resulting from the undercalculation of actual land needs may result both in excessive market prices for scarce land in later years of the program and in an eventual physical shortage of land for housing and other uses. Presumably state, regional, and local officials will cooperate to ensure that such a scenario does not play out. However, there is no mechanism in place to ensure that it does not. A more flexible boundary would serve the region better. On the other hand, as the Knaap study (1985) demonstrated, if the boundary is too flexible, no one will take it seriously and it will accomplish little.

The Oregon experience also illustrates the difficulty of establishing long-term boundaries. Despite the long-time commitment to the protection of the environment in Oregon, planners in the Portland region apparently included steep slopes and other sensitive lands in their computation of the development capacity within the boundaries. Clearly such lands should have been omitted. One can second-guess the work of the planners who made the calculations. On the other hand, perfect planning and perfect foresight are unlikely to exist; and where they do, the political process may reject them. Thus, a different planning process would probably have avoided that planning error but created others. A system of regional planning must provide a modest amount of flexibility both to address defects in the original process and, more important, to respond to changing demographic trends. It must, however, be sufficiently permanent to be taken seriously. That is a delicate but perhaps not impossible balance to achieve.

The minimum density requirement used in the Portland region seems like a logical corollary of growth management. To the extent that one of the goals of growth management is to reduce sprawl and to ensure the efficient use of land, requiring that land that is developed be optimally developed makes a good deal of sense. With an urban growth boundary based on projected densities of population some sort of requirement to ensure that development actually occurs at such densities is essential; traditional zoning will not do that because the zoning system is designed to ensure that development take place at not more than the planned densities. Both theoretical work and practical experience suggest that it is still possible to provide a complete range of housing types at the average minimum densities prescribed in the Portland region, which are in the range of eight dwelling units per acre. In other words, if Portland had simply established minimum densities rather than targets for specific types of smaller dwelling units, the market would have been capable of providing a full range of housing types while achieving the density goal.

If planners and public officials in a region want to make development more compact, they should consider such a minimum density requirement. There is no evidence that other types of growth management programs make development more compact. As Table 11.3 shows, Boulder's density has actually declined over two decades, while the density in Petaluma and Livermore decreased in the 1980s. In contrast, pro-growth Santa Rosa, often used as a comparison community for Petaluma, has consistently and significantly increased its density, which is now 33 percent higher than that of Petaluma. The reason that density has fallen in some growing communities is that the communities have annexed territory, reflected in increases in land area. Although there are good reasons for annexation (see Chapter 5), it is surprising for a community that is presumably trying to limit growth to engage in annexations that far exceed the land necessary to continue to absorb development at current rates and densities.

In addition to saving land through more efficient use of land that is developed, minimum density requirements produce fiscal benefits. Fiscal impact studies show clearly that it is cheaper to serve development at higher densities. Those savings alone may not be great enough to justify such a program, but they are a nice additional benefit of a minimum density standard.

Table 11.3
Area and Density Changes in Selected Communities (Densities in Persons per Square Mile; Area in Square Miles)

Place	1970		1980		1990	
	Area	Density	Area	Density	Area	Density
Boulder	13.0	5143	19.5	3933	22.6	3687
Livermore	11.9	3168	13.2	3663	19.6	2895
Petaluma	7.5	3316	9.2	3678	12.3	3511
Longmont	7.9	2938	9.8	4382	13.1	3935
Santa Rosa	19.9	2513	26.6	3132	33.7	4773

Sources: Bureau of the Census, 1991, *Census of Population and Housing: Summary Population and Housing Characteristics*, Parts 6 (Livermore, Petaluma, and Santa Rosa) and 7 (Boulder and Longmont), Table 16 in each; Bureau of the Census, 1983, *City and County Data Book*, Table C; Bureau of the Census, 1972, *City and County Data Book*, Tables 6 (Boulder, Livermore, and Santa Rosa) and B-2 (Petaluma and Longmont).

A minimum density program will work best with some form of regional planning. In Portland, the urban growth boundary represents a major element of the regional plan. Consumers have no convenient alternative locations that are not subject to the rules. To mandate greater density in a single community within a metropolitan area than the one the market suggests consumers want may simply drive growth from that community to others nearby. Thus, to be effective, such a requirement probably should be mandated throughout the region in which growth is likely to occur. However, because the evidence cited in Chapter 7 suggests that it is possible to provide a full range of housing types even at relatively high densities, this effect may not occur. There is no experience from which to draw a conclusion about the effects of a minimum density program in a single community.

Buying land to preserve it is generally a good idea. Boulder's greenbelt will be green long after the growth management programs in many other communities have been forgotten. Land acquisition is expensive, but the expense is really a long-term investment. In Boulder's case, the land amounts to a local growth boundary, which, as the next section suggests, is probably not a good idea. Although it creates a greenbelt, a popular idea in planning, it has also created leapfrog sprawl, an extremely unpopular idea in planning. Thus, there can be too much of a good thing or unintended negative consequences of a perfectly logical act. Nevertheless, most public land acquisition programs do not have such negative consequences. All communities concerned about their urban form, about preserving environmentally sensitive lands, and about managing growth in general should seriously consider land acquisition as one of the tools to use.

PROGRAMS THAT ARE DIFFICULT TO JUSTIFY

For rate-of-growth programs, most phased growth programs, and local growth-boundary programs, the only possible justifications are self-serving rationalizations of the communities adopting them. Clearly such programs are likely to shift growth from one community to another. Viewed from a regional planning perspective, the population shift typically increases commuting costs and shifts the burdens of growth to communities that may or may not be able to bear them. In the case of Boulder, the shift has been to much smaller surrounding communities, some of which have had phenomenal percentage growth rates directly related to Boulder's effort to slow its own. Such leapfrog development is viewed by some as more pernicious than simple suburban sprawl. Depending on where it occurs, it may consume additional prime farmland or other land that should be preserved. When a boundary is regional, such issues can be considered. However, a local government adopting such a boundary has little reason to consider more than its own needs and, perhaps, the impact on land immediately adjacent to it.

Over the long run, the leapfrog suburbs are likely to lead to demand for additional connecting highways for commuting and to other public expenditures. This dispersion of growth makes it more difficult to share such community-wide facilities as libraries and hospitals. On a pure cost–benefit basis, it appears that the net increase in costs to the region far exceeds any cost savings to the community adopting the program, and cost savings are often one of the major arguments for the adoption of such a program.

Viewed from a social perspective, these same programs limit housing choices. While most exclusionary zoning techniques over the years have tended to exclude apartments and townhouses, single-family housing suitable in price and size for families with young children appears to be most affected by the Boulder and Portland programs. Portland expressly limits the proportion of such houses. Boulder does not appear to discriminate against that dwelling type specifically, but the demographic patterns indicate that the people who typically live in such houses are moving to surrounding communities. Clearly such economic impacts fall most heavily on those with the fewest economic choices. Although growth managing communities are not typically places likely to house many of the poor, those with market-limiting programs limit the opportunities available to those who may not be "poor" for census purposes but who clearly have less economic flexibility and fewer choices than others.

Montgomery County planners were farsighted indeed in recognizing nearly two decades ago the appropriate role of growth management. Its *First Annual Growth Policy Report* stated in part:

In this report, the Board does not recommend a specific limit on the total number of people the County might ultimately house or the number that should be "admitted" each year. The County is not sovereign; people have a right to move; and we are persuaded that such population "caps" are both unwise and of dubious constitutionality (Montgomery County Planning Board 1974, p. 6).

From a local perspective, an urban growth boundary may serve its real purposes. If what Boulder wanted was a firm urban edge and a community surrounded by a greenbelt, it got exactly what it sought. If what it wanted was to stop sprawl, it simply traded leapfrog sprawl for the continuous sprawl that it precluded. That may or may not be a good trade in design terms, but it is a bad trade in fiscal terms. Although Boulder may save money by not serving the leapfrog development, some combination of governmental entities will incur increased costs over the long run to establish and expand free-standing infrastructure systems or long line extensions from Boulder. Either of those alternatives is more expensive than simply serving additional development adjacent to an existing community, as the evidence cited in Chapter 9 clearly shows.

Rate-of-growth programs and phased growth programs are typically presented as methods of balancing the capacities of and demands on public facilities. That is a somewhat specious defense of the programs. It is most unlikely that the capacity of all public services in a particular community would expand at the rate necessary to absorb an additional 500 dwelling units or 2 percent population increase each year. The real purpose of establishing such limits appears to be to control a rate of growth that is "too fast." In the case of Petaluma, where the actual growth rate exceeded 10 percent per year for a short time, such concerns are understandable. Should Boulder or Petaluma be permitted to limit its participation in regional growth? From a regional or statewide perspective it is difficult to answer that question affirmatively. From a local perspective, it is also easy to understand the development of support among citizens for limiting growth, even if the only result is to shift the problem to other communities. This reflects the self-serving nature of many growth management programs.

Communities often implement phased growth systems as an additional stage in the development review process, thus increasing development costs attributable to regulatory overhead. As the experience with San Jose and other communities indicates, a growth phasing system may adversely affect housing costs by distorting the land market (see generally Chapter 10). A phased growth program need not have that effect if it provides for large enough "phases," but some programs have had that effect.

A comprehensive program such as that of Westminster or Montgomery County certainly contains growth phasing elements that affect the rate of growth. However, those programs are based squarely on the actual capacities of public facilities. Thus, once Westminster overcame its short-term capacity problems, it absorbed growth demand at a far faster rate than nearby Boulder, which had adopted its rate-limiting program. Over the medium run, the market caused a slowing of growth in Westminster, also. Because some industries may move into town and others close down, mortgage rates fluctuate and consumer confidence rises and falls, demand for housing and other elements of growth is not constant or steady. To the extent that a community attempts to level the market through such a program it also distorts the market. Some might argue that it is "only" the market and thus not a concern. However, that market represents people's needs and desires for housing. It is those needs and desires that become more expensive to fulfill or take longer to fulfill or may go unfulfilled. The market is simply a collection of individual players—in this particular market those players are people, many of them representing families and children and others whose causes may seem socially more worthy than the "market" as an abstract economic concept. Although Westminster and Montgomery County are classified here as "comprehensive" programs, they are comprehensive programs clearly based on the capacities of public facilities and they fall squarely under the finding that adequate public facilities standards do a great deal of good and little if any harm to anyone.

A PROGRAM ON WHICH TO RESERVE JUDGMENT

It is difficult to reach a conclusion on the Portland policy of mandating a housing mix quite different from the one traditionally found in the market. An adequate policy analysis of the impact of creating a supply shift in the entire housing stock will require a good deal more data than are available now. The published data indicating that the program has held housing costs down and made housing more affordable are misleading for the same reason that many of the comparisons in *The Costs of Sprawl* were misleading—they attempt to compare two entirely different types of housing. New housing in Portland includes a far greater percentage of apartments, townhouses, and condominiums than the market produced before adoption of the program. Such units are generally less costly than single-family detached houses. Thus, comparing current "average" costs of a dwelling unit with previous "average" costs is meaningless. None of the Portland studies do what Niebanck did in California, which was to analyze the price trends of a particular type of dwelling. Without these data, it is impossible to know the real effects of the Portland program on housing costs.

To the extent that the Portland program ensures the availability of more apartments and other smaller dwelling units, it will create great social benefits by expanding the diversity and quantity of housing available to the low end of the housing market. To the extent that it goes beyond that and requires that apartments supplant some single-family units in the housing supply, it will have significant social impacts. Whether those impacts will be positive, negative, or neutral is difficult to evaluate without additional data. Perhaps people who wanted to live in single-family houses will be perfectly content living in apartments or condominiums as they see more of their neighbors doing so. However, it is not clear that forcing people with the economic means to afford "the American dream" to live in less than a single-family house will create a net social benefit. It clearly will create resentment among some of them. It is conceivable that it will have the same sort of effect as the Boulder program and that some people will actually move outside the Portland region and endure long commutes in order to live in single-family houses. Only time and a good deal of additional research will tell.

Whether such a requirement is a good idea is a different question. It is important to remember that the Portland program not only mandated higher densities but also required that those densities be achieved with a different housing mix. The goal in Portland centered on increasing the statistical affordability of housing in the region by

Figure 11.1
Evaluative Checklist of Growth Management Programs

ISSUE/TECHNIQUE	Adequate Public Facilities	Phased Growth	Urban Growth Boundaries
PUBLIC SERVICES			
Optimize fiscal impacts of growth	++	+	+
Balance public service capacities and demands	+++	+	+
Limit growth in traffic congestion	++	+	-
URBAN FORM			
Define urban edge		+	++
Limit continuous sprawl		+	++
Limit discontinuous (leapfrog) development	++	++	-
Make development more compact	+	+	+
COMMUNITY CHARACTER			
Stop growth			
Maintain semirural character			
Establish greenbelt			+

Rate of Growth	Minimum Density	Capital Investment	Annexation	Land Acquisition
	++	++	++	
+	+	+++	++	
		+++		
		+	+	+++
		+	+	
		++	+	
	+++	+	+	
			+	+++

continued

Figure 11.1 (continued)

ISSUE/TECHNIQUE	Adequate Public Facilities	Phased Growth	Urban Growth Boundaries
ENVIRONMENTAL			
Preserve sensitive lands within urban area			
Preserve sensitive lands near urban area	+		++
Preserve open space	+		+
HOUSING			
Promote affordable housing		--	---
Promote diverse housing opportunities		-	--

Note: + symbols indicate relative benefits of program for specific purpose; − symbols indicate costs (negative impacts) of program.

changing the mix to include more lower-priced products. If the goal of a community is simply to increase the compactness of development without unnecessarily disturbing the housing mix, the community could impose a maximum density requirement without the housing-type targets used in Portland. If a community wants to conserve land—that is to reduce the total amount of land a given amount of growth will consume—such a technique will work well.

RELATIONSHIP OF PROGRAMS TO ISSUES

Figure 11.1 provides a summary of how well each technique addresses the major issues that lead communities to consider adopting growth management programs and how each affects other, typical community goals.

Rate of Growth	Minimum Density	Capital Investment	Annexation	Land Acquisition
				+++
		++	++	+++
				+++

--	+			

CONCLUSION

Is growth management a good idea? Yes, if it is based on good planning and a solid understanding of the costs and benefits of different growth management techniques. The strongest message of this book is the need for effective regional planning in our nation's metropolitan areas. Such regional planning must originate with the state, as it has in Hawaii and Oregon.

What is the message, though, for local governments in states without such regional planning? Should they attempt to manage growth? Yes. However, in most cases they will significantly improve the local, regional, and social cost–benefit ratio by using a combination of tools rather than one of the relatively simplistic growth management programs. By including adequate public facilities standards in its local controls, a local government encourages development to occur near existing infrastructure. By planning where to locate its infrastructure—extending it voluntarily into areas where it wishes to target development and avoiding extensions (even those that would more than pay for themselves) into areas where it does not want growth—a community can strengthen the importance of its adequate public facilities standards.

A community should annex selectively, accepting eagerly those lands where it wants future urbanization and avoiding those lands where it does not. Through zoning and subdivision controls within its boundaries (and, in some states, even beyond those boundaries) a community can encourage appropriate land uses and a quality of development suitable for the circumstances. A community may want to consider reducing the impact of new development on the land supply by including minimum density requirements, as well as maximums, in its zoning ordinances. Some communities may want to follow the examples of those that have dedicated revenue sources to large-scale acquisition of lands to be preserved. Most communities should occasionally use strategic land acquisitions to help to manage urban form and to protect lands or topographic features of particular local significance.

Through this combination of modern and traditional techniques, a community can exert powerful control over the shape of its future growth. Implementing such a system requires a combination of political will and management skill. Managing such a system is more complex than administering one of the simpler growth management programs. Using a complicated package of tools that the average citizen may not fully understand will probably not provide as much press as adopting a program to limit new growth to an annual rate of 2 percent or 500 dwelling units. On the other hand, the evidence demonstrates clearly that such a program works and that it does so without the negative impacts on housing opportunities and regional sprawl that characterize several types of growth management programs.

Bibliography

Abberger, Will. 1991. "Growth management through land acquisition." In *Balanced growth: a planning guide for local government,* edited by John M. DeGrove, pp. 66–70. Washington: International City Management Association.

Abe, Mary Morgan. 1977. "Urban growth management: trends, issues and responsibilities." Ph.D. diss., Claremont Graduate School.

Advisory Commission on Regulatory Barriers to Affordable Housing. 1991. *"Not in my back yard": removing barriers to affordable housing.* Washington: U.S. Department of Housing and Urban Development.

Advisory Committee on City Planning and Zoning. 1928. *A standard city planning enabling act.* Washington: U.S. Department of Commerce.

Advisory Committee on Zoning. 1926. *A standard state zoning enabling act under which municipalities may adopt zoning regulations.* Rev. ed. Washington: U.S. Department of Commerce.

Alexander, Ernest R., K. David Reed, and Peter Murphy. 1988. *Density measures and their relation to urban form.* Madison: Center for Architecture and Urban Planning Research, University of Wisconsin.

Alonso, William. 1964. *Location and land use: toward a general theory of land rent.* Cambridge: Harvard University Press.

Altshuler, Alan. 1977. "Review of *the costs of sprawl." Journal of the American Institute of Planners* 43: 207–209.

American Institute of Planners, Research Office. 1976. *Survey of state land use activity.* Washington: U.S. Department of Housing and Urban Development.

American Law Institute. 1975. *A model land development code.* Washington: American Law Institute (with commentary by Alison Dunham, Chief Reporter).

Audirac, Ivonne, Anne H. Shermyen, and Marc T. Smith. 1990. "Ideal urban form and visions of the good life: Florida's growth management dilemma." *Journal of the American Planning Association* 56: 470–482.

Babcock, Richard F., ed. 1987. "Symposium: exactions: a controversial new source for municipal funds." *Law and Contemporary Problems* 50: 1–194.

——. 1966. *The zoning game.* 1975 trade paperback ed. Madison: University of Wisconsin Press.

Babcock, Richard F., and Fred P. Bosselman. 1973. *Exclusionary zoning: land use regulation and housing in the 1970's.* New York: Praeger Publishers. Published in cooperation with the American Planning Association.

Babcock, Richard F., and Charles L. Siemon. 1985. *The zoning game revisited.* Boston: Oelgeschlager, Gunn & Hain. Published in association with Lincoln Institute of Land Policy.

Baerwald, Thomas J. 1981. "The site selection process of suburban residential builders." *Urban Geography* 2: 339–357.

Bain, Henry. 1969. "The Organization of Growth." In *The new city,* edited by Donald Canty, pp. 135–143. New York: Praeger.

Bair, Fred H., Jr. 1979. *Planning cities,* edited by Virginia Curtis. Chicago: Planners Press.

Banta, John S. 1989. "Environmental protection and growth management." In *Understanding growth management: critical issues and a research agenda,* edited by David J. Brower, David R. Godschalk, and Douglas R. Porter, 134–156. Washington: Urban Land Institute.

Barnett, Jonathan. 1988. "Urban design." In *The practice of local government planning.* 2nd ed., edited by Frank So and Judith Getzels, 175–197. Washington: International City Management Association.

Barra, Tomas de la. 1989. *Integrated land use and transport modelling: decision chains and hierarchies.* Cambridge Urban and Architectural Series, edited by Leslie Martin and Lionel March, 12. Cambridge: Cambridge University Press.

Bassett, Edward M. 1936. *Zoning: the laws, administration and court decisions during the first twenty years.* New York: Russell Sage Foundation.

Beaton, W. Patrick. 1991. "The impact of regional land-use controls on property values: the case of the New Jersey Pinelands." *Land Economics* 67: 173–194.

Binkley, Clark, Bert Collins, Lois Kanter, Michael Alford, Michael Shapiro, and Richard Tabors. 1975. *Interceptor sewers and urban sprawl.* Lexington: Lexington Books.

Black, J. Thomas, and James E. Hoben. 1985. "Land price inflation and affordable housing." *Urban Geography* 6: 27–47.

Blaesser, Brian W., Susan Connor, Eric Damian Kelly, Stuart Meck, John M. Payne, James M. Rubenstein, Charles Tucker, and Norman Williams Jr. 1991. "Advocating affordable housing in New Hampshire: the *Amicus Brief* of the American Planning Association in *Wayne Birtton* v. *Town of Chester." Washington University Journal of Urban and Contemporary Law* 40: 3–48.

Boggs, H. Glenn, and Robert C. Apgar. 1991. "Concurrency and growth management: a lawyer's primer." *Journal of Land Use & Environmental Law* 7: 1–27.

Bosselman, Fred, and David Callies. 1971. *The quiet revolution in land use control.* Washington: Council on Environmental Quality.

Bosselman, Fred, Duane A. Feurer, and Charles L. Siemon. 1976. *The permit explosion: coordination of the proliferation.* Management & Control of Growth, 4. Washington: Urban Land Institute.

Boulder, City of. 1991. Boulder open space, parks and trails map. Zia Maps.

Boulder, City of, Open Space Department. 1992a. Boulder's open space: then and now.

——. 1992b. Some facts about Boulder's open space.

Boulder County. 1991. Boulder County road map.

Brand, Daniel. 1991. "Research needs for analyzing the impacts of transportation options on urban form and the environment." In *Transportation, urban form and the environment,* p. 196. Transportation Research Board Special Report, 231. Washington: Transportation Research Board.

Braybrooke, David, and Charles E. Lindblom. 1963. *A strategy of decision: policy evaluation as a social process.* Free Press Trade Paperback 1970 ed. New York: The Macmillan Company.

Breen, Eleanor, Frank Costa, and William S. Hendon. 1986. "Annexation: an economic analysis: whether a small village or town should annex adjacent land is a cost/revenue problem." *American Journal of Economics and Sociology* 45 (2): 159–172.

Brower, David J., David R. Godschalk, and Douglas R. Porter, eds. 1989. *Understanding growth management: critical issues and a research agenda.* Washington: The Urban Land Institute.

Brower, David J., David W. Owens, Ronald Rosenberg, Ira Botvinick, and Michael Mandel. 1976. *Urban growth management through development timing.* New York: Praeger Publishers.

Burchell, Robert W. 1990. "Fiscal impact analysis: state of the art and state of the practice." In *Financing growth: who benefits? who pays? and how much?* edited by Susan G. Robinson, pp. 71–90. Washington: Government Finance Research Center.

Burchell, Robert W., and David Listokin. 1978. *The fiscal impact handbook: estimating local costs and revenues of land development.* New Brunswick, N.J.: Center for Urban Policy Research.

Bureau of the Census. 1991a. *1990 census of population and housing: summary population and housing characteristics.* Washington: U.S. Department of Commerce.

——. 1991b. *State and metropolitan data book.* 4th ed. Washington: U.S. Department of Commerce.

——. 1988. *County and city data book.* Washington: U.S. Department of Commerce. A Statistical Abstract Supplement.

——. 1987. *Government Organization.* 1987 Census of Governments, 1. Washington: U.S. Department of Commerce.

——. 1983. *1980 census of population.* Washington: U.S. Department of Commerce.

——. 1982. *Census of population and housing: summary characteristics for* governmental units and standard metropolitan statistical areas. Washington: U.S. Department of Commerce.

——. 1972a. *1970 census: characteristics of the population.* Washington: U.S. Department of Commerce.

——. 1972b. *County and city data book.* Washington: U.S. Department of Commerce. A Statistical Abstract Supplement.

——. 1962. *County and city data book.* Washington: U.S. Department of Commerce.

——. 1952. *1950 census: characteristics of the population.* Washington: U.S. Department of Commerce.

Burrows, Lawrence B. 1978. *Growth management: issues, techniques and policy implications.* New Brunswick, N.J.: Center for Urban Policy Research.

Callies, David L. 1992. "Dealing with scarcity: land use and planning." In *Politics and public policy in Hawaii,* edited by Zachary A. Smith and Richard C. Pratt, pp. 130–145. Albany: State University of New York Press.

——. 1984. *Regulating paradise: land use controls in Hawaii.* Honolulu: University of Hawaii Press.

——. 1980. "The Supreme Court is wrong about zoning by popular vote." In *Management & control of growth: updating the law,* vol. 5, edited by Frank Schnidman and Jane Silverman, pp. 81–83. Washington: Urban Land Institute.

Callies, David L., Nancy C. Neuffer, and Carlito P. Caliboso. 1991. "Ballot box zoning: initiative, referendum and the law." *Washington University Journal of Urban and Contemporary Law* 39: 53–98.

Canty, Donald, ed. 1969. *The new city: a report of the national committee on urban growth policy.* New York: Frederick A. Praeger.

Carson, John M., Goldie W. Rivkin, and Malcolm D. Rivkin. 1973. *Community growth and water resources policy.* New York: Praeger Publishers.

Caves, Roger W. 1992. *Land use planning: the ballot box revolution.* Sage Library of Social Research, 187. Newbury Park: Sage Publications.

Cervero, Robert. 1991. "Congestion relief: the land use alternative." *Journal of Planning Education and Research* 10: 119–129.

——. 1989. "Jobs–housing balancing and regional mobility." *Journal of the American Planning Association* 55: 136–150.

Chapin, F. Stuart, Jr. 1963. "Taking stock of techniques for shaping urban growth." *Journal of the American Institute of Planners* 29: 76–86.

Chinitz, Benjamin. 1990. "Growth management: good for the town, bad for the nation?" *Journal of the American Planning Association* 56: 3–8.

Clancy, Joseph. 1986. "Montgomery County's development hurdles." In *Growth management: keeping on target?* edited by Douglas R. Porter, pp. 95–98. Washington: Urban Land Institute.

Clawson, Marion. 1971. *Suburban land conversion in the United States: an economic and governmental process.* Baltimore: Johns Hopkins University Press. A Resources for the Future Book.

Cobb, Charles E., Jr. 1986. "A developer's view of Boca Raton." In *Growth management: keeping on target?* edited by Douglas R. Porter, pp. 53–56. Washington: Urban Land Institute.

Coe, Charles K. 1983. "Costs and benefits of municipal annexation." *State and Local Government Review* 15: 44–47.

"Colorado's special district woes." 1991. *Public investment* (June): 2–3.

Commission on Population Growth and the American Future. 1972. *Population and the American future*. Washington: The Commission. Final report.

Cooper, George, and Gavan Daws. 1990. *Land and power in Hawaii*. Honolulu: University of Hawaii Press.

Cooper, Sandra. 1986. "Growth control evolves in Boulder." In *Growth management: keeping on target?* edited by Douglas R. Porter, pp. 35–44. Washington: Urban Land Institute.

Council of State Governments. 1976. *State growth management*. Washington: U.S. Department of Housing and Urban Development.

Council on Development Choices for the 80's. 1980. *Development choices for the 80's: interim report*. Washington: U.S. Department of Housing and Urban Development.

Cronin, Thomas E. 1980. "The pros and cons of popular initiatives." In *Management & control of growth: updating the law*, edited by Frank Schnidman and Jane Silverman, 5: 69–71. Washington: Urban Land Institute.

Curtin, Daniel J., Jr., and Thomas C. Wood. 1989. *Ballot box planning, growth control*. San Francisco: McCutchen, Doyle, Brown & Enersen. Prepared for the Ninth Annual Zoning Institute of the American Institute of Certified Planners.

Danish, Paul D. 1986. "Boulder's self examination." In *Growth management: keeping on target?* edited by Douglas R. Porter, pp. 25–30. Washington: Urban Land Institute.

Davies, H. W. E., D. Edwards, A. J. Hooper, and J. V. Punter. 1989. *Planning control in Western Europe*. London: Her Majesty's Stationery Office.

Deakin, Elizabeth A. 1991. "Jobs, housing and transportation: theory and evidence." In *Transportation, urban form and the environment: proceedings of a conference*, pp. 25–42. Special Report Series, 231. Washington: Transportation Research Board.

DeGrove, John M., ed. 1991. *Balanced growth: a planning guide for local government*. Practical Management Series, edited by Barbara H. Moore. Washington: International City Management Association.

——. 1989. "Growth management and governance." In *Understanding growth management: critical issues and a research agenda*, edited by David J. Brower, David R. Godschalk, and Douglas R. Porter, pp. 22–42. Washington: Urban Land Institute.

——. 1984. *Land, growth & politics*. Chicago: Planners Press.

deHaven-Smith, Lance. 1991. *Controlling Florida's development*. Wakefield, N.H.: Hollowbrook Publishing.

Dowall, David E. 1984. *The suburban squeeze: land conversion and regulation in the San Francisco Bay area*. Berkeley: University of California Press.

——. 1980. "An examination of population-growth-managing communities." *Policy Studies Journal* 9: 414–426.

Downing, Paul B., and Thomas S. McCaleb. 1987. "The economics of development exactions." In *Development exactions*, edited by James E. Frank and Robert M. Rhodes, pp. 42–58. Chicago: Planners Press.

Downs, Anthony. 1991a. "The Advisory Commission on Regulatory Barriers to Affordable Housing: its behavior and accomplishments." *Housing Policy Debate* 2: 1095–1137.

——. 1991b. "Obstacles in the future of U.S. cities." *Journal of the American Planning Association* 51: 13–15.

——. 1988. "The real problem with suburban anti-growth policies." *The Brookings Review,* 6 (2): 23–29.

——. 1973. *Opening up the suburbs: an urban strategy for America.* New Haven: Yale University Press.

Dubbink, David. 1984. "I'll have my town medium rural, please." *Journal of the American Planning Association* 50: 406–418.

——. 1983. "Cosmopolitan villages: growth management planning and the vision of small town society." Ph.D. diss., University of California, Los Angeles.

Ducker, Richard. 1988. "Land subdivision regulation." In *The practice of local government planning.* 2nd ed., edited by Frank S. So and Judith Getzels, pp. 198–250. Washington: International City Management Association.

ECO Northwest, Inc. 1986. "Growth management study of Boca Raton." In *Growth management: keeping on target?* edited by Douglas R. Porter, pp. 57–60. Washington: Urban Land Institute.

Elickson, Robert C. 1977. "Suburban growth controls: an economic and legal analysis." *Yale Law Journal* 86: 385–511.

Elliott, Michael. 1981. "The impact of growth control regulations on housing prices in California." *Journal of the American Real Estate and Urban Economics Association* 9: 115–133.

Environmental Impact Center, Incorporated. 1975. *Secondary impacts of transportation and wastewater investments: research results.* Washington: Council on Environmental Quality. Natl. Tech. Info. Svc. No. PB-246 085.

Fagin, Henry. 1955. "Regulating the timing of urban development." *Law and Contemporary Problems* 20 (2): 298–304.

Finkler, Earl. 1973. *Nongrowth: a review of the literature.* Planning Advisory Service, 289. Chicago: American Society of Planning Officials.

——. 1972. *Nongrowth as a planning alternative: a preliminary examination of an emerging issue.* Planning Advisory Service, 283. Chicago: American Society of Planning Officials.

Finkler, Earl, and David L. Peterson. 1974. *Nongrowth planning strategies: the developing power of towns, cities and regions.* New York: Praeger Publishers.

Finkler, Earl, William J. Toner, and Frank J. Popper. 1976. *Urban nongrowth: city planning for people.* New York: Praeger.

Fischel, William A. 1991. "Comment on Anthony Downs's 'The Advisory Commission on Regulatory Barriers to Affordable Housing: its behavior and accomplishments.'" *Housing Policy Debate* 2: 1139–1160.

——. 1990. *Do growth controls matter? a review of empirical evidence on the effectiveness and efficiency of local government land use regulation.* Cambridge: Lincoln Institute for Land Policy.

——. 1985. *The economics of zoning laws: a property rights approach to*

American land use controls. Baltimore: The Johns Hopkins Press.

Fishman, Richard P. 1978. *Housing for all under law: new directions in housing. land use and planning law.* Cambridge: Ballinger Publishing Company. A Report of the American Bar Association Advisory Commission on Housing and Urban Growth.

Fleischmann, Arnold. 1986. "The politics of annexation: a preliminary assessment of competing paradigms." *Social Science Quarterly* 67: 128–142.

Florida Department of Community Affairs. 1991. "Techniques for discouraging sprawl." In *Balanced growth: a planning guide for local government,* edited by John M. DeGrove, pp. 36–41. Washington: International City Management Association. Originally published by Department of Community Affairs as Technical Memo 4, No. 4 (1989).

Forkenbrock, David J., Thomas F. Pogue, Norman S. J. Foster, and David J. Finnegan. 1990. *Road investment to foster local economic development.* Ames, Ia.: Midwest Transportation Center.

Frank, James E. 1989. *The costs of alternative development patterns: a review of the literature.* Washington: Urban Land Institute.

Frank, James E., and Robert M. Rhodes, eds. 1987. *Development exactions.* Chicago: Planners Press.

Franklin, Herbert M. 1973. *Controlling urban growth—but for whom?* Washington: The Potomac Institute.

Franklin, Herbert M., David Falk, and Arthur J. Levin. 1974. *In-zoning: a guide for policy-makers on inclusionary land use programs.* Washington: The Potomac Institute.

Freilich, Robert H. 1975. "Development timing, moratoria, and controlling growth: preliminary report." In *Management & control of growth,* edited by Randall W. Scott, David J. Brower, and Dallas D. Miner, 2: 361–396. Washington: Urban Land Institute.

Freilich, Robert H., and Peter S. Levi. 1975. *Model subdivision regulations.* Chicago: American Society of Planning Officials.

Fuguitt, Glenn V., Paul R. Voss, and J. C. Doherty. 1979. *Growth and change in rural America.* The Management and Control of Growth Series, 7. Washington: Urban Land Institute.

Fuguitt, Glenn V., and James J. Zuiches. 1975. "Residential preferences and population distribution." *Demography* 12: 491–504.

Fulton, William. 1991. "The second revolution in land use planning." In *Balanced growth: a planning guide for local government,* edited by John M. DeGrove, pp. 116–124. Washington: International City Management Association.

Galloway, Thomas D., and John D. Landis. 1986. "How cities expand: does state law make a difference?" *Growth and change* 17 (October): 25–45.

Gawf, Ed. 1985. Memorandum to James W. Piper, city manager, and members of city council. Boulder, Colorado, January 15, 1985.

Gilmore, John S., and Mary K. Duff. 1975. *Boom town growth management: a case study of Rock Springs, Green River, Wyoming.* Boulder: Westview Press.

Gleeson, Michael E. 1979. "Effects of an urban growth management system on land values." *Land Economics* 55: 350–365.

Gleeson, Michael E., Ian Traquair Ball, Stephen P. Chinn, Robert C. Einsweiler,

Robert H. Freilich, and Patrick Meagher. 1975. *Urban growth management systems.* Planning Advisory Service, 309, 310. Chicago: American
Society of Planning Officials.

Glickfeld, Madelyn, and Ned Levine. 1992. *Regional growth . . . local reaction:
the enactment and effects of local growth control and management
measures in California.* Cambridge: Lincoln Institute of Land Policy.

Godschalk, David R., and David J. Brower. 1989. "A coordinated growth
management research strategy." In *Understanding growth management:
critical issues and a research agenda,* edited by David J. Brower, David
R. Godschalk, and Douglas R. Porter, pp. 159–179. Washington: Urban
Land Institute.

Godschalk, David R., David J. Brower, Larry D. McBennett, and Barbara A.
Vestal. 1977. *Constitutional issues of growth management.* Chicago:
The ASPO Press.

Goldberg, Michael A., and Daniel D. Ulinder. 1976. "Residential developer
behavior 1975: additional empirical findings." *Land Economics* 52:
363–370.

Gonzalez, Rodolfo A., and Stephen L. Mehay. 1987. "Municipal annexation
and local monopoly power." *Public Choice* 57: 245–255.

Governor's Commission on Growth in the Chesapeake Bay Region. 1991a.
Protecting the future: a vision for Maryland. Baltimore: Maryland Office
of Planning.

——. 1991b. *Fiscal Studies.* Baltimore: Maryland Office of Planning.

Governor's Commission on Vermont's Future. 1988. *Report of the governor's
commission on Vermont's future: guidelines for growth.* Montpelier:
State of Vermont.

Gray, Frank B. 1975. "The city of Petaluma: residential development control."
In *Management & control of growth,* edited by Randall W. Scott, David
J. Brower, and Dallas D. Miner, 2: 149–159. Washington: Urban Land
Institute.

Greenberg, Douglas Andrew. 1986. "Growth and conflict at the suburban
fringe: the case of the Livermore-Amador Valley." Ph.D. diss., University
of California, Berkeley.

Greenberg, Michael R. 1974. "A commentary on the sewer moratorium as a
piecemeal remedy for controlling development." In *Growth controls,*
edited by James W. Hughes, pp. 189–195. New Brunswick, N.J.: Center
for Urban Policy Research.

"Growth masks out-migration of young families; in-migration of established
families." 1992. *Research Perspectives* NA, 21 (Winter): 1–4. A publication of the City of Boulder Research Department.

Hamblen, Matt. 1991. "Montgomery County at the crossroads." *Planning* 57
(6): 7–12.

Hammer, Siler, George Associates. 1977. *Impact on Ramapo fiscal and eco-
nomic conditions of the town's growth control ordinance.* Washington:
Hammer, Siler, George Associates. Unpublished; prepared for National
Association of Homebuilders; cited copy hand-labeled "draft."

Hanson, Mark E. 1992. "Automobile subsidies and land use: estimates and
policy responses." *Journal of the American Planning Association* 58:
60–71.

Hanson, Mark E., and Harvey M. Jacobs. 1989. "Private sewage system impacts in Wisconsin: implications for planning and policy." *Journal of the American Planning Association* 55: 169–180.

Healy, Robert G. 1976. *Land use and the states*. Baltimore: The Johns Hopkins Press. A Resources for the Future Book.

Healy, Robert G., and John S. Rosenberg. 1979. *Land use and the states*. 2d ed. Baltimore: The Johns Hopkins Press. A Resources for the Future Book.

Heeter, David. 1969. *Toward a more effective land-use guidance system: a summary and analysis of five major reports*. Planning Advisory Service, 250. Chicago: American Society of Planning Officials.

Hendler, Bruce. 1977. *Caring for the land: environmental principles for site design and review*. Chicago: American Society of Planning Officials.

Hepner, George F. 1983. "An analysis of residential developer location factors in a fast growth urban region." *Urban Geography* 4: 355–363.

Hilton Head, Town of. 1986. "Executive summary: comprehensive plan for the Town of Hilton Head Island." In *Growth management: keeping on target?* edited by Douglas R. Porter, pp. 123–128. Washington: Urban Land Institute.

Hilton Head Island, Town of. 1985a. *Comprehensive Plan for the Town of Hilton Head Island, South Carolina*. Hilton Head Island, S.C.: Town of Hilton Head Island. Prepared by John Rahenkamp & Associates.

——. 1985b. *Transportation element of the comprehensive plan*. Hilton Head Island, S.C.: Town of Hilton Head Island. Prepared by Wilbur Smith and Associates.

Honolulu, City and County of. 1991. *Development plan status review*. Honolulu: Department of General Planning.

"Housing cost, elitism come under fire." 1992. *Boulder Daily Camera* (2 Feb).

Howard, Ebenezer. 1902. *Garden cities of to-morrow*. 1965 ed. Cambridge: MIT Press. Edited and with a preface by F.J. Osborn; introductory essay by Lewis Mumford; this edition originally published in 1946; original first published in 1898 as *To-morrow: a peaceful path to real reform*, updated by author and published under this title in 1902.

Howe, Deborah A., and William A. Rabiega. 1992. "Beyond strips and centers: the ideal commercial form." *Journal of the American Planning Association* 58: 213–219.

Hughes, James W., ed. 1974. *Growth controls*. New dimensions in urban planning, 1. New Brunswick, N.J.: Center for Urban Policy Research.

Innes, Judith. 1991a. *Group processes and the social construction of growth management: the cases of Florida, Vermont, and New Jersey*. Working Paper, 544. Berkeley: Institute of Urban and Regional Development.

——. 1991b. *Implementing state growth management in the U.S.: strategies for coordination*. Working paper, 542. Berkeley: Institute of Urban and Regional Development.

James Duncan and Associates, and Eric Damian Kelly. 1991a. *Adequate public facilities study*. Austin: James Duncan & Associates. Prepared for Montgomery County, Maryland; separate Technical Appendix.

——. 1991b. *Technical appendix to adequate public facilities study*. Austin: James Duncan and Associates. Supplement to report prepared for Montgomery County, Maryland.

———. 1991c. Montgomery County adequate public facilities study: screening survey results. Unpublished preliminary survey for *Adequate public facilities study.*

James Duncan and Associates, Van Horn—Gray Associates, Inc., Ivey, Bennett, Harris, and Walls, and Wade-Trim, Inc. 1989a. *The search for efficent urban growth patterns: a study of the fiscal impacts of development in Florida.* Contract No. 89LP-16-14-00-22-002. Tallahassee: Florida Department of Community Affairs.

———. 1989b. *The search for efficient urban growth patterns: technical appendices.* Contract No. 89LP-16-14-00-22-002. Tallahassee: Florida Department of Community Affairs.

Jandl, H. Ward. 1991. *Yesterday's houses of tomorrow: innovative American homes, 1850–1950.* Washington: The Preservation Press.

Johnson, Arthur T. 1989. *Intergovernmental influences on local land use decision making.* Washington: National League of Cities.

Johnston, Robert A., Seymour I. Schwartz, and Steve Tracy. 1984. "Growth phasing and resistance to infill development in Sacramento County." *Journal of the American Planning Association* 50: 434–446.

The journey to work: relation between employment and residence. 1951. Planning Advisory Service 26. Chicago: American Society of Planning Officials.

Kaiser, Edward J., Karl Elfers, Sidney Cohn, Peggy A. Reichert, Maynard M. Hufschmidt, and Raymond E. Stanland Jr. 1974. *Promoting environmental quality through urban planning and controls.* Washington: U.S. Environmental Protection Agency. Supt. Docs. No. EP1.23/3:600/5-73-015.

Kasowski, Kevin. 1991. "Oregon: fifteen years of land use planning." In *Balanced growth: a planning guide for local government,* edited by John M. DeGrove, pp. 125–129. Washington: International City Management Association. Originally printed in *Developments* newsletter, Winter 1990.

Kassoff, Eric S. 1991. "Alternative infrastructure financing: development districts pave the way." *Land Use Law & Zoning Digest* 43 (1): 3–6.

Kelly, Eric Damian. 1988. "Zoning." In *The practice of local government planning.* 2d ed., edited by Frank S. So and Judith Getzels, pp. 251–284. Washington: International City Management Association.

———. 1986. "Planning vs. democracy." *Land Use Law & Zoning Digest* 38 (7): 3–6.

———. 1984. "Piping growth, the law, equity and economics of sewer & water connection policies." *Land Use Law & Zoning Digest* 36 (7): 3–7.

———. 1982. "Comment on Westminster growth control cases." *Land Use Law & Zoning Digest* 34 (3): 14–15.

———. 1976. "*Robinson* v. *Boulder,* a balance to *Ramapo* and *Petaluma.*" *Real Estate Law Journal* 5: 170–174.

Kendig, Lane, Susan Connor, Cranston Byrd, and Judy Heyman. 1980. *Performance zoning.* Chicago: Planners Press.

Ketcham, Paul, and Scot Siegel. 1991. *Managing growth to promote affordable housing: revisiting Oregon's goal 10.* Portland: 1000 Friends of Oregon. Study sponsored jointly by 1000 Friends of Oregon and The Home Builders Association of Metropolitan Portland.

Knaap, Gerrit J. 1985. "The price effects of urban growth boundaries in metropolitan Portland, Oregon." *Land Economics* 61: 26–35.

——. 1982. "The price effects of an urban growth boundary: a test for the effects of timing." Ph.D. diss., University of Oregon.

Krasnowiecki, Jan. 1969. "Model land use and development planning code." In *Final report: legislative recommendations,* edited by Maryland planning and zoning law study commission, pp. 53–122. Baltimore: Colony Press.

Landis, John D. 1991. *Do growth controls work? a new assessment.* Working Paper, 547. Berkeley: Institute of Urban and Regional Development.

——. 1986. "Land regulation and the price of new housing." *Journal of the American Planning Association* 52: 9–21.

Land Use Planning Committee, ed. 1971. *Planning and zoning for better resource use.* Ankeny, Ia.: Soil Conservation Society of America.

Leach, James. 1986. "A homebuilder looks at Boulder's growth controls." In *Growth management: keeping on target?* edited by Douglas R. Porter, pp. 31–33. Washington: Urban Land Institute.

LeGates, Richard T., and Sean Nikas. 1989. *Growth control through residential tempo controls in the San Francisco Bay Area.* Working Paper Series, 89-11. San Francisco: San Francisco State University Public Research Institute.

Lewis, Sylvia. 1990. "The town that said no to sprawl." In *Balanced growth: a planning guide for local government,* edited by John M. DeGrove, pp.18–28. Washington: International City Management Association.

Lillydahl, Jane H., and Larry D. Singell. 1987. "The effects of growth management on the housing market: a review of the theoretical and empirical evidence." *Journal of Urban Affairs* 9: 63–77.

Lincoln, James R., Jr., Dean C. Coddington, and John R. Penberthy. 1976. *An analysis of the impact of state and local government intervention on the home building process in Colorado, 1970–1975.* Denver: Bickert, Browne, Coddington & Associates, Inc.

Llewelyn-Davies Carson Ltd. 1978. *Relationship of water supply and urban growth in the Denver region.* Denver: Llewelyn-Davies Carson Ltd. Prepared for the U.S. Army Corps of Engineers.

Loke, Evelina T., ed. 1982. *Homeownership: the American dream adrift.* Chicago: United States League of Savings Associations.

Lucas, Therese E. 1974. *The direct costs of growth: a comparison of changes in local government expenditure in growth and non-growth counties in Colorado.* Denver: Colorado Land Use Commission.

Mackay, Charles. 1841. *Extraordinary popular delusions and the madness of crowds.* Reprint 1932 ed. New York: Farrar, Strauss & Giroux.

Mandelker, Daniel R. 1971. *The zoning dilemma.* Indianapolis: Bobbs-Merrill Company.

Maryland Planning and Zoning Law Study Commission. 1969. *Legislative recommendations: final report.* Baltimore: Colony Press, Inc. Three appendixes include "Appendix c, model land use and development planning code" by Jan Krasnowiecki.

McHarg, Ian L. 1971. *Design with nature.* Paperback ed. Garden City: Doubleday/Natural History Press.

Meadows, Donella H., Dennis L. Meadows, Jorgen Randers, and William W. Behrens III. 1972. *The limits to growth.* New York: Universe Books. Often called "The Club of Rome Report."

Mehay, Stephen L. 1981. "The expenditure effects of municipal annexation." *Public Choice* 36: 53–62.

Mehle, Michael. 1991. "Districts' losses cost investors." *Rocky Mountain News* (30 December): 6, 22.

Meyer, J. R., J. F. Kain, and M. Wohl. 1965. *The urban transportation problem.* 1972 trade paperback ed. Cambridge: Harvard University Press.

Mields, Hugh, Jr. 1973. *Federally assisted new communities: new dimensions in urban development.* ULI Landmark Report. Washington: Urban Land Institute.

Mill, John Stuart. 1859. *On liberty.* 1986 ed. Buffalo: Prometheus Books.

Miller, Thomas I. 1986. "Must growth restrictions eliminate moderate-priced housing?" *Journal of the American Planning Association* 52: 319–325.

Montequin, Francois-August de. 1990. *The planning of Spanish cities in America: characteristics, classification, and main urban features.* The Working Paper Series. Hilliard, Ohio: The Society for American City and Regional Planning History.

Montgomery County Planning Board. 1990a. *FY 91 annual growth policy.* Silver Spring: Maryland–National Capital Park and Planning Commission.

———. 1990b. *FY 92 annual growth policy.* Silver Spring: Maryland–National Capital Park and Planning Commission. Planning board official draft.

———. 1987. *Alternative transportation scenarios and staging ceilings.* Silver Spring: Maryland–National Capital Park and Planning Commission.

———. 1974. *First annual growth policy report: framework for action.* Silver Spring: Maryland–National Capital Park and Planning Commission.

Montgomery County Planning Department Staff. 1987. *Alternative transportation scenarios and staging ceilings: a background report for the fy89 agp.* Silver Spring: Maryland–National Capital Park and Planning Commission.

Moore, Terrence. 1986. "Saving the Pinelands." In *Growth management: keeping on target?* edited by Douglas R. Porter, pp. 131–136. Washington: Urban Land Institute.

Morris, Marya. 1992. "New transportation law benefits planning." *PAS Memo* (February): 1–4.

Muller, Thomas. 1975. *Fiscal impacts of land development; a critique of methods and review of issues.* Washington: The Urban Institute.

Mumphrey, Anthony J., Jr., John Wildgen, and Louise Williams. 1990. *Annexation and incorporation: alternative strategies for municipal development.* New Orleans: University of New Orleans College of Urban & Public Affairs.

Myers, Dowell. 1989. "The ecology of 'quality of life' and urban growth." In *Understanding growth management: critical issues and a research agenda,* edited by David J. Brower, David R. Godschalk, and Douglas R. Porter, pp. 87–104. Washington: Urban Land Institute.

Myers, Phyllis. 1976. "Zoning Hawaii." *Environmental Comment* NA (July): 17–20.

———. 1974. *So goes Vermont.* Washington: The Conservation Foundation.

National agricultural lands study: final report. 1981. Washington: National Agricultural Lands Study.

Nelson, Arthur C., ed. 1988. *Development impact fees.* Chicago: Planners Press.

New Jersey County and Municipal Government Study Commission. 1974. *Housing & suburbs: fiscal & social impact of multifamily development.* Trenton: County and Municipal Government Study Commission.

Newman, Peter, and Jeffrey Kenworthy. 1989. *Cities and automobile dependence.* Brookfield: Gower Technical.

Niebanck, Paul L. 1989. "Growth controls and the production of inequality." In *Understanding growth management: critical issues and a research agenda,* edited by David J. Brower, David R. Godschalk, and Douglas R. Porter, pp. 105–122. Washington: Urban Land Institute.

——. 1986. "Conclusion: the second generation of growth management." In *Growth management: keeping on target?* edited by Douglas R. Porter, pp. 215–216. Washington: Urban Land Institute.

"Note: public utility land use control on the urban fringe." 1978. *Iowa Law Review* 63: 889–923.

Ohls, James C., and David Pines. 1975. "Discontinuous urban development and economic efficiency." *Land Economics* 51: 224–234.

Olson, Gerald W. 1981. *Soils and the environment: a guide to soil surveys and their applications.* New York: Chapman & Hall.

Parker, Jeffrey A. 1991. "Does transportation finance influence urban form?" In *Transportation, urban form and the environment: proceedings of a conference,* pp. 43–62. Special Report Series, 231. Washington: Transportation Research Board.

Parsons, K. C. 1990. "Clarence Stein and the greenbelt towns: settling for less." *Journal of the American Planning Association* 56: 161–183.

Peiser, Richard B. 1989. "Density and urban sprawl." *Land Economics* 65: 193–204.

——. 1984. "Does it pay to plan suburban growth?" *Journal of the American Planning Association* 50: 419–433.

Pelham, Thomas G. 1992. "Adequate public facilities requirements: reflections on Florida's concurrency system for managing growth." *Florida State University Law Review* 19 (4): 973–1052.

Petaluma, City of. 1991. *Residential growth management system user's guide.* Petaluma: City of Petaluma. Original undated; date estimated.

——. 1987. *Residential growth management user's guide.* Petaluma: City of Petaluma.

Peterson, Craig A., and Claire McCarthy. 1977. "Farmland preservation by purchase of development rights: the Long Island experiment." *De Paul Law Review* 26: 447–491.

Pierce, Lawrence W. Chip, and Kenneth L. Rust. 1991. "Government enterprises." In *Local government finance: concepts and practices,* edited by John E. Petersen and Dennis R. Strachota, pp. 391–416. Washington: Government Finance Officers Association.

Pivo, Gary. 1990. "The net of mixed beads: suburban office development in six metropolitan regions." *Journal of the American Planning Association* 56: 457–469.

Pivo, Gary, Robert Small, and Charles R. Wolfe. 1990. "Rural cluster zoning:

survey and guidelines." *Land Use Law & Zoning Digest* 42 (9): 3–10.

Pollakowski, Henry O., and Susan M. Wachter. 1990. "The effects of land-use constraints on housing prices." *Land Economics* 66: 315–324.

Popper, Frank J. 1981. *The politics of land use reform.* Madison: The University of Wisconsin Press.

Porter, Douglas R. 1991. "Regional governance of metropolitan form: the missing link in relating land use and transportation." In *Transportation, urban form and the environment: proceedings of a conference,* pp. 63–80. Special Report Series, 231. Washington: Transportation Research Board.

——. 1989. "Significant research needs in the policy and practice of growth management." In *Understanding growth management: critical issues and a research agenda,* edited by David J. Brower, David R. Godschalk, and Douglas R. Porter, pp. 180–193. Washington: Urban Land Institute.

——. ed. 1986. *Growth management: keeping on target?* Washington: Urban Land Institute.

Rahenkamp, John. 1991. "Boroughing Isn't Boring." *Pennsylvania Planner* 46: 1.

——. 1986. "Coming to grips with growth in Hilton Head, South Carolina." In *Growth management: keeping on target?* edited by Douglas R. Porter, pp. 119–122. Washington: Urban Land Institute.

Rahenkamp Sachs Wells & Associates, and The American Society of Planning Officials. 1977. *Innovative zoning: a digest of the literature.* HUD-PDR-289-2. Washington: U.S. Department of Housing and Urban Development.

Rahenkamp Sachs Wells & Associates, The American Society of Planning Officials, and David Stoloff. 1977. *Innovative zoning: a local official's guidebook.* HUD-PDR-289-1. Washington: U.S. Department of Housing and Urban Development.

Real Estate Research Corporation. 1974. *The costs of sprawl: environmental and economic costs of alternative residential development patterns at the urban fringe.* Washington: Council on Environmental Quality. Supt. of Docs. No. 4111-00021.

Reducing the development costs of housing: actions for state and local governments. 1979. Washington: U.S. Department of Housing and Urban Development. Proceedings of the HUD National Conference on Housing Costs.

Reps, John W. 1969. *Town planning in frontier America.* 1970 Paperback ed. Princeton: Princeton University.

Rice Center for Community Design + Research. 1978. *Technical report: the delay costs of government regulation in the Houston housing market.* Houston: Rice Center for Community Design + Research.

Robinson, Susan G., ed. 1990. *Financing growth: who benefits? who pays? and how much?* Washington: Government Finance Research Center.

Rockland, County of. 1991. Rockland County Planning Department.

Rosenbaum, Nelson. 1976. *Land use and the legislatures: the politics of state innovation.* Washington: Urban Institute.

Rust, Edgar. 1975. *No growth: impacts on metropolitan areas.* Lexington: Lexington Books.

Salvesen, David. 1990. *Wetlands: mitigating and regulating development im-*

pacts. Washington: Urban Land Institute.

Sanborn, William E., and Robert Logan. 1976. "Wyoming: meeting energy impact head on." *Environmental Comment* (July): 13–15.

Sands, C. Dallas, and Michael Libonati. 1981. *Local government law.* Vol. 1. Willamette: Callaghan & Company.

Schiffman, Irving. 1989. *Alternative techniques for managing growth.* Berkeley: Institute of Governmental Studies.

Schnidman, Frank, and Jane Silverman, eds. 1980. *Management & control of growth: updating the law.* Management & Control of Growth, 5. Washington: Urban Land Institute.

Schnidman, Frank, Jane A. Silverman, and Rufus C. Young Jr., eds. 1978. *Management & control of growth: techniques in application.* Management & control of growth, 4. Washington: Urban Land Institute.

Schwartz, Seymour I., David E. Hansen, and Richard Green. 1984. "The effect of growth control on the production of moderate-priced housing." *Land Economics* 60: 110–114.

Schwartz, Seymour I., Peter M. Zorn, and David E. Hansen. 1986. "Research design issues and pitfalls in growth control studies." *Land Economics* 62: 224–233.

Scott, Mel. 1969. *American city planning since 1890.* 1971 Paperback ed. Berkeley: University of California Press.

Scott, Randall W., David J. Brower, and Dallas D. Miner, eds. 1975a. *Management & control of growth: issues, techniques, problems, trends.* Management & control of growth, 1. Washington: Urban Land Institute.

———. 1975b. *Management & control of growth: issues, techniques, problems, trends.* Management & control of growth, 2. Washington: Urban Land Institute.

———. 1975c. *Management & control of growth: issues, techniques, problems, trends.* Management & control of growth, 3. Washington: Urban Land Institute.

Seidel, Stephen R. 1978. *Housing costs & government regulations: confronting the regulatory maze.* New Brunswick, N.J.: Center for Urban Policy Research.

Sengstock, Frank. 1985. *Annexation: a solution to the metropolitan area problem.* Buffalo: William S. Hein & Co. Reprint of 1960 edition published by Legislative Research Center, The University of Michigan Law School, Ann Arbor.

Shelton, David C., and Dick Prouty. 1979. *Nature's building codes: geology and construction in Colorado.* Denver: Colorado Department of Natural Resources.

Singell, Larry D., and Jane H. Lillydahl. 1990. "An empirical examination of the effect of impact fees on the housing market." *Land Economics* 66: 82–92.

Snyder, John M. 1982. "An evaluation of Colorado's attempts to cope with rapid growth." Ph.D. diss., Colorado State University.

So, Frank S., and Judith Getzels, eds. 1988. *The practice of local government planning.* 2d ed. Washington: International City Management Association.

Spengler, Edwin H. 1930. *Land values in New York in relation to transit facil-*

ities. New York: Columbia University Press.

Staff of the U.S. General Accounting Office. 1978. *Land use issues.* Washington: U.S. General Accounting Office.

Stahura, John M., and Harvey H. Marshall. 1982. "The role of annexation in the growth of American suburbs." *Sociological Focus* 15 (1): 15–24.

Stone, Catherine R. 1982. "Prevention of urban sprawl through utility extension control." *The Urban Lawyer* 14: 357–377.

Strong, Ann L. 1991. "Buying farmland development rights: the Chester County program." *Land Use Law & Zoning Digest* 43 (5): 3–7.

———. 1979. *Land banking.* Baltimore: The Johns Hopkins Press.

———. 1977. *Vermont's act 250 and prime farmland.* Philadelphia: Regional Science Research Institute.

———. 1975. *Private property and the public interest: the Brandywine experience.* Baltimore: The Johns Hopkins Press. A Resources for the Future Book.

Tabors, Richard D., Michael H. Shapiro, and Peter P. Rogers. 1976. *Land use and the pipe: planning for sewerage.* Lexington: Lexington Books.

Task Force on Housing Costs. 1978. *Final report of the task force on housing costs.* HUD-1-313(3). Washington: U.S. Dept. of Housing and Urban Development.

Tax lead time study: the Colorado oil shale region. 1974. Denver: Department of Natural Resources.

Teitz, Michael. 1991. "California growth: hard questions, few answers." In *California policy choices,* edited by John J. Kirlin and Donald R. Winkler, 6: 35–74.

Thurow, Charles, William Toner, and Duncan Erley. 1975. *Performance controls for sensitive lands.* Planning Advisory Service, 307 and 308. Chicago: American Society of Planning Officials.

Tiebout, Charles M. 1956. "A pure theory of local expenditures." *The Journal of Political Economy* 64: 416–424.

Transportation Research Board. 1991. *Transportation, urban form and the environment: proceedings of a conference.* Special Report Series, 231. Washington: The author.

"25,000 in St. Petersburg, Florida, to be deported? to Kuwait?" 1974. *Planning* 40 (4): 6.

Ulasewicz, Thomas A. 1986. "Adirondack Park: successful state management." In *Growth management: keeping on target?* edited by Douglas R. Porter, pp. 147–154. Washington: Urban Land Institute.

The urban growth boundary and incorporated cities. 1990. [Portland] Metropolitan Service District.

Urban Land Institute Research Division, and Gruen Gruen + Associates. 1977. *Effects of regulation on housing costs: two case studies.* ULI Research Report, edited by Donald E. Priest. Washington: Urban Land Institute.

Urban Systems Research & Engineering Inc. 1976. *The growth shapers: the land use impacts of infrastructure investments.* Supt. of Docs. No. 041-011-00029-7. Washington: Council on Environmental Quality.

Wakeford, Richard. 1990. *American development control: parallels and para-doxes from an English perspective.* London: Her Majesty's Stationery Office.

Walker, Donald V. H. 1978. "Boulder preserves open space." In *Growth man-agement: techniques in application,* edited by Frank Schnidman, Jane Silverman, and Rufus C. Young Jr., pp. 147–150. Washington: Urban Land Institute.

Warner, Sam B., Jr. 1962. *Streetcar suburbs: the process of growth in Boston, 1870–1900.* Publications of the Joint Center for Urban Studies. Cam-bridge: Harvard University Press and The MIT Press.

Washington State Growth Strategies Commission. 1990. *A growth strategy for Washington State.* Olympia: Department of Community Development.

Westminster, City of. 1978a. *Growth management plan: phase II report.* West-minster, Colo.: City of Westminster.

———. 1978b. *[Untitled working documents on growth management]: reports A, B, C and D.* Westminster: City of Westminster.

Whyte, William H., Jr. 1959. *Securing open space for urban America: con-servation easements.* Technical Bulletin, 36. Washington: Urban Land Institute.

———. 1958. "Urban Sprawl." In *The exploding metropolis.* Anchor Books ed., edited by The Editors of *Fortune,* pp. 114–139. New York: Doubleday and Company.

Williams, Norman, Jr., and John M. Taylor. 1988. *American land planning law.* 1988 rev. ed., 1. Wilmette: Callaghan & Company. Supplemented to 1992.

———. 1985. *American land planning law,* 3A. Wilmette: Callaghan & Company. Supplemented to 1992.

Windsor, Duane. 1979. "A critique of *The Costs of Sprawl." Journal of the American Planning Association* 45: 279–292.

Wingo, Lowdon, Jr. 1961. *Transportation and urban land.* Washington: Re-sources for the Future.

Witt, John W., and Janis Sammartino. 1990. "Facility financing in the 1990's: the second step in urban growth management." *Washington University Journal of Urban and Contemporary Law* 38: 115–155.

Yokley, E. C. 1963. *The law of subdivisions.* Nashville: The Michie Company.

York, Marie L. 1986. "Boca Raton's changing approach." In *Growth manage-ment: keeping on target?* edited by Douglas R. Porter, pp. 45–52. Washington: Urban Land Institute.

LATE BIBLIOGRAPHIC ENTRIES

Note: The following books were published in late 1992, while this book was in preparation. Although they appeared too late to be men-tioned in the text or included in the main bibliography, they are important sources for supplemental information on the topics iden-tified in their respective titles.

DeGrove, John M. With the assistance of Deborah A. Miness. 1992. *The new frontier for land policy: planning and growth management in the states.* Cambridge: Lincoln Institute of Land Policy.

Downs, Anthony. 1992. *Stuck in traffic: coping with peak hour traffic congestion.* Washington: The Brookings Institution.

Easley, V. Gail. 1992. *Staying inside the lines: urban growth boundaries.* Planning Advisory Service, 442. Chicago: American Planning Association.

Index

Note: Page numbers in *italic* indicate maps.

ABOUT THE AUTHOR

ERIC DAMIAN KELLY is Professor and Chair in the Department of Community and Regional Planning at Iowa State University. Prior to joining the University, he consulted and practiced law, specializing in planning and land-use issues. He is a member of the American Planning Association's national *Amicus Curiae* Committee and president elect of the Iowa Chapter of the American Planning Association.